The

Vanishing
Neighbor

The
Vanishing
Neighbor

The Transformation of American Community

MARC J. DUNKELMAN

W. W. NORTON & COMPANY

New York | London

For information about permission to reproduce selections from this book,
write to Permissions, W. W. Norton & Company, Inc.,
500 Fifth Avenue, New York, NY 10110

For information about special discounts for bulk purchases, please contact
W. W. Norton Special Sales at specialsales@wwnorton.com or 800-233-4830

Manufacturing by Courier Westford
Book design by Chris Welch Design
Production manager: Julia Druskin

Library of Congress Cataloging-in-Publication Data

Dunkelman, Marc J.
The vanishing neighbor : the transformation of
American community / Marc J. Dunkelman. — First edition.
pages cm
Includes bibliographical references and index.
ISBN 978-0-393-06396-7 (hardcover)
1. Communities—United States. 2. United States—Social conditions—21st century.
3. United States—Economic conditions—21st century.
4. United States—Civilization—21st century. I. Title.
HN59.2.D84 2014
307.0973—dc23

2014020596

W. W. Norton & Company, Inc.
500 Fifth Avenue, New York, N.Y. 10110
www.wwnorton.com

W. W. Norton & Company Ltd.
Castle House, 75/76 Wells Street, London W1T 3QT

1 2 3 4 5 6 7 8 9 0

For Kathryn

Contents

Part 3: America Explained

Introduction

FROM ONE QUEEN CITY
TO THE NEXT

Beyond wondering whether our new family room would have enough shelving to store all my toys, I wasn't particularly alarmed when Mom and Dad announced in the summer of 1984 that we'd be moving from Cincinnati to Buffalo. At no point was I fazed by the prospect of leaving the only home I'd ever known, let alone the three surviving grandparents who lived nearby. Rather, and maybe in keeping with the tendencies of a kid gearing up for kindergarten, I got swept up by the adventures I imagined we might have awaiting us. Hours of cartoons had ingrained in me the impression that, when it came to big trips, unknown splendors invariably lay ahead.

It wasn't until we'd fully settled into our new home that I began to appreciate just how radically life had changed. Not only were we now four hundred miles away from my favorite ice cream parlor (the Yum Yum Shop in Buffalo didn't have the same flavors as Graeter's, our favorite spot in Cincinnati), but the routines of our daily lives were now much starker in the absence of familiarity. I missed the goldfish crackers my grandparents always had at the ready. I missed the regular visits from family friends and friendly neighbors. And maybe even without noticing explicitly, I missed the chance encounters—my mother bumping into an old high-school friend at the Tri-County Mall—that had peppered our lives in Ohio.

Certainly part of that was nostalgia—no kid wants to give up his favorite flavor of ice cream. But there was something else as well. Lonely moments are inevitable when a family moves. But my sense that something else was missing was made ever more palpable each time we made our annual journey back to Cincinnati for the holidays.

At some point during each visit, my dad's father and brother would whisk a few of us away for a tour of the old neighborhood. We'd begin at Sugar n' Spice, the greasy-spoon diner that had been serving customers since 1941.[1] And then, as I hunkered down in the back of my father's slow-moving Chrysler minivan, the adults up front would begin to reminisce: "That's where Johnny Osher lived—he invented an electric toothbrush and made a fortune selling it to Procter & Gamble." "I always had a crush on the girl who lived down the street—whatever happened to her?" "That poor kid. At five o'clock every evening—even in high school—his mother would call him and his brother in for a bath. It was a riot."

Listening silently to the banter, I imagined then that the sense of community woven into those stories was a function of southern Ohio itself. Even after several years in Buffalo, the contrast was unmistakable. On paper, life in western New York resembled my father's childhood fairly well. I was enrolled in the local elementary school. My parents had made friends around town. I went to Sunday school and played sports on weekday afternoons. But despite it all, our neighbors, unlike my father's, largely remained strangers. When I began delivering the *Buffalo News* during the fall of my fourth-grade year, most of the names on the roster were still unfamiliar. Even after five full years in our new hometown, I wouldn't have been able to recognize the couple living two houses away if we'd bumped into them at our local grocery store.

That disparity turned my nostalgia into longing. If only we could move back to Cincinnati, I imagined, I'd surely be swept into the genteel neighborhood dynamic that had characterized my father's childhood. It wasn't until a couple of decades later, while sitting down for a cup of coffee with Sean Safford, a sociologist who had also grown up in Buffalo, that I realized I'd lost sight of something important. Describing his childhood, Safford explained that when he went home for a visit, his parents rarely went anywhere without bumping into someone his father knew. His father could still name the families who lived in each house on the street where he grew up. His father also liked to regale him with stories of the old neighborhood.

Safford's observation led me to question whether, in all my years pining for Ohio, I'd missed the essential point. Nineteen-fifties-era Cincinnati couldn't be compared in any fair way with 1990s-era Buffalo—quality of ice cream excepted. My parents' Cincinnati lined up fairly well with the Buffalo that had reared Safford's father. Rather, something else had happened to change both cities during the 1960s, '70s, and '80s. I'd been comparing apples to oranges. The real contrast revolved less around *where* each of us had grown up, and more around *when*.[2]

But that begged the question: what had changed over the intervening decades? Certainly the dichotomy couldn't be chalked up to some blithe complaint about social isolation. Far from losing touch, technology had worked to connect Americans like never before. Over the course of a single generation, the cost of a telephone call had fallen dramatically.[3] E-mail had emerged as an entirely new, free, and instantaneous form of communication. And with budget airlines driving the price of air travel down, families living hundreds of miles away could visit one another with much more regularity.

My erstwhile comparisons of Cincinnati and Buffalo seemed to suggest that, amid all the new opportunities to connect, something else had been lost. The sorts of relationships my grandparents had taken for granted while raising their children—between neighbors and colleagues, often across generations—had withered, and others had begun to take their place. Over the course of several decades, the nation's social architecture had been upended. And it wasn't until recently that a more complete picture of that shift has come into clearer view.

Over the last 250 years, the underlying structure of American community has experienced no more than two major transformations. The first coincided with the end of the colonial period. As Brown University historian Gordon Wood outlined in his Pulitzer Prize–winning book *The Radicalism of the American Revolution,* our desire to break away from Britain wasn't driven simply by disgust with the English Crown.[4] The patterns of life prevalent in the "new" world were different from those that characterized life in and around London, and the institutions that the colonies had inherited weren't effective when applied in the new American context. America's patriots wanted to craft a government that was responsive to a very different sort of society. And the tension inherent in that mismatch set the stage for the Revolution.

As Wood illustrated, by the late eighteenth century, much of America—particularly the colonies in New England—had evolved away from the "lord of the manor"–type community prevalent in Britain. The new social architecture centered more on ties that bound together the residents of individual towns and villages. Rather than have a local nobleman keep watch over a district, as in England, the cohort of Americans living nearby took joint responsibility for their collective well-being. Many colonists had moved away from the social architecture depicted later in *Downton Abbey* and toward something more like that portrayed in *Little House on the Prairie.*[5] And because that sort of community wouldn't abide the heavy hand of a monarch—communities working collaboratively were less interested in taking orders from on high—the founding generation designed and embraced an alternative kind of government, reflected in the Constitution, that was more appropriate to colonial American life.

In the centuries that followed, that core community building block—what Alexis de Tocqueville and others before him defined as a "township"—remained the defining feature of American society.[6] Americans moved from farm to factory and from town to city. They withstood the Industrial Revolution. They evolved from a society dependent on slave labor to one focused on innovation. But through all of those changes, the core architecture of "town-shipped" society—where communities of people with different skills and interests, disparate concerns and values, collaborated with their neighbors in the pursuit of the common good—endured.

The township served as the underpinning for both the villages set in late-eighteenth-century New England and small towns dotting the nineteenth-century frontier. It formed the basic architecture of the crowded urban tenements that emerged at the turn of the twentieth century and the first-ring suburbs decades later. In fact, the existence of townships became such a ubiquitous feature of American life that it faded almost entirely from our collective consciousness. Even today, most of us would find it hard to contextualize our lives without assuming that our sense of community was deeply woven into the fabric of our local neighborhood.

More recently, however, that has all begun to change. For the second time in our history—and for the first time since the late 1700s—American community is undergoing a transformation at its very core. That's not simply a melodramatic way of arguing that the "digital revolution" is remaking modern life—though that is certainly a part of the story. Rather, a whole series of changes in our everyday patterns has begun to eat away at the mooring that has long grounded American society. And it's only now that we can glimpse what might emerge in its stead.

———

To date, the upheaval in American community has been as misunderstood as it has been profound. It is central to a whole series of problems we see as separate and unconnected. Our sense today that the American Dream is slipping away—that the legacy of American exceptionalism is newly imperiled—is more intertwined with the structure of American society than we tend to appreciate. The ever-present fear that we may be eclipsed by foreign competition—spliced together with our ongoing frustration that Washington can't get its act together—has distracted us from what's happening on our own front stoops. And it's no mystery why: nearly every "big think" analysis of the nation's place in the world opens with a litany of deflating statistics.

Let's review the stew of discontent that has come to frame America's outlook on the future, starting with the concern that the developing world is poised to overtake us. Anyone who travels across the Pacific returns with vignettes highlighting just how much more advanced Asian infrastructure seems to be. In the time that it took the Chinese to build an entire convention center, *New York Times* columnist Thomas Friedman likes to point out, the Washington subway system was barely able to repair a broken escalator.[7] And the same thing seems to be happening in the world of education: the United States once led the world with an unmatched percentage of young adults with college degrees, but we've since fallen to twelfth; studies now rank us seventy-ninth in terms of elementary school enrollment; and in a key study of fifteen-year-olds around the world, Americans were rated below average in mathematics literacy and merely average in science and reading.[8] Maybe worse still, only 15 percent of college graduates receive their degree in the natural sciences or engineering, which are purported to be the fields that drive economic growth.[9]

None of this has been lost on the broader public. Our apparent inability to keep pace with the rest of the world has undermined our faith in what we assume to be the pillars of American prosperity. Since the 1970s, the percentage of Americans who expressed a "great deal" or "quite a lot" of trust in big business has plummeted from 34 to 19 percent. Faith in banks has fallen from 60 to 23 percent, in public schools, from 58 to 34 percent. Even faith in organized religion has fallen from 68 to 48 percent. Only the military, the police, and small business still capture majority esteem.[10]

Why does the American Age seem to be unwinding? The most common answer is that the future is losing out to the present and past in nearly every facet of our lives. Americans today are more profligate than ever before: before the Great Recession hit, for example, we owed more than a trillion dollars of credit card debt, and the bottom four-fifths of American earners were, on average, spending 110 percent of their incomes each year.[11] Moreover, Washington is overextended and underfunded, evidenced by the fact that a newly retired couple is slated to take out $200,000 more in benefits from Medicare and Social Security than they paid in.[12] And the same endemic indebtedness applies to state government as well: on the hook to cover pensions and health care costs, statehouses currently face a $1 trillion shortfall.[13] As budget hawks are prone to argue, we're too cash-strapped to invest properly in the infrastructure, education, and technology that might drive economic growth.[14]

How do we get out of this mess? No one thinks it'll be easy, but it seems like the first step should be to embrace proper leadership. But that just leads us to what is surely the most troubling chapter of the story: with certain recent exceptions, Capitol Hill is utterly gridlocked. The capital's woeful attempts to trim the federal deficit in 2011 captured the problem in a nutshell. When the two parties couldn't agree on a budget, they chartered a "supercommittee" to forge a solution—but even the supercommittee couldn't agree. Washington's subsequent attempt to force a deal involved a scheme by which Congress would impose brazen cuts unpopular on both sides of the aisle if the parties failed to work out a compromise. But even that didn't work. The so-called sequester, excoriated as bad policy from nearly every point on the political spectrum, was left in place for two whole years.[15]

The takeaway, it seems, is that the institutions tasked with fixing our biggest problems are more severely plagued than the rest of the country. Who could hope to keep pace with China when the folks at the wheel seem incapable of investing in the nation's infrastructure, improving the nation's schools, or balancing the nation's budget? Americans are sick of it. Between early 2010 and late 2012, Congress's public approval rating averaged a dismal 16 percent—falling at one point to a record low of 9 percent.[16] And that likely explains why another poll, taken recently, found that Americans preferred cockroaches and traffic jams to the nation's legislative branch.[17]

So what can we do? The first step, conventional wisdom holds, is to rid Washington of the contemptible influences that have corrupted Capitol Hill. The polarization that has taken hold is being driven, most assume, by ideologues who won't compromise because they're pawns in a dishonest system. The demands of campaign fund-raising have boxed out the interests of ordinary citizens. The filibuster, insiders argue, has paralyzed the Senate.[18] Manipulative redistricting protects incumbents in the House, insulating them from the demands of the ordinary voter.

What's odd about all those diagnoses is that they predate today's dysfunction. Money isn't new to the political equation, even if there's more of it today. Until November 2013, the basic rules governing the filibuster hadn't been changed for more than a generation. Gerrymandering, the process of guaranteeing the results of an election by fixing the boundaries of a congressional district, is such an ancient institution that its namesake, Founding Father Elbridge Gerry, signed the Declaration of Independence.[19] With those more prosaic explanations eliminated, the question remains: what *is* behind Washington's dysfunction? If only we could get the nation's government working again, it seems like we might stand a chance of fixing the rest of it.

In 2007, after several years on Capitol Hill, I took some time to seek out a more convincing explanation for the country's growing despair. Persuaded that the common excuses didn't suffice, I searched through my decade of work in politics. Nothing in my own experience offered a satisfying answer. It was just a merry-go-round of complaints: polarization was driven by money and money by polarization; bad leadership was driving us off the rails and the lousy state of American affairs was driving lousing politics. What I wanted to understand was how the unwinding had begun.

What follows is a record of the intellectual journey that followed. After several years of research, I've concluded that a transformation of American community has come to affect everything from our propensity to innovate to our capacity to care for one another. It has disrupted our social institutions as much as it's thrown a wrench into our politics. Without notice, a quiet revolution over the course of several decades upended the foundation that girded the very pillars—government, businesses, banks, schools—in which the public has lost faith. Its effects, which explain nearly every frustration listed above, run deep and wide.

The key insight is that our national angst has less to do with what politicians, corporate executives, bankers, and other bigwigs are doing (or failing to do) and more to do with subtle changes in the American routine. Adults today tend to prize different kinds of connections than their grandparents: more of our time and attention today is spent on more intimate contacts and the most casual acquaintances. We've abandoned the relationships in between— what I define in a later chapter as "middle-ring" ties. And that shift, made as the result of millions of individual decisions across the whole of society, has quietly spurred the second transformation of American community and left us with the impression that the future is bleak.

The good news is that all is not lost. Once we move beyond the debate over whether our new community architecture is better or worse—what's important is that it's significantly different—we can begin to grapple with our preeminent challenge: addressing the mismatch between the institutions of townshipped society and the realities of contemporary life. Once we understand how the foundations of the American Dream have shifted, we can begin to adjust the way we govern ourselves, drive economic growth, and help those being left behind. What we'll find is that, although many pundits have concluded that the American era is over, the truth is that we're simply in the midst of a painful transition. And as much as we're now enduring a national crisis of confidence, it's not clear yet how things will turn out.

Mine is not a simple thesis. It involves connecting changes in the average American's routine to a broad transformation of American community, and then exploring how that shift has undermined our faith in American exceptionalism. But the argument is grounded in a modest desire: to answer the questions my father used to ask on my visits home to Buffalo. Why is it that so many elements across the wide spectrum of American life seem to be failing? Why haven't we fixed our schools or repaired our financial system? Why is American innovation lagging while our social safety net implodes? Why have Americans lost faith in the institutions that grounded our society throughout the nineteenth and twentieth centuries? And, most excruciating, why hasn't Washington figured out some way to fix it all?

In order to tease apart the constituent parts of the story, I've organized my argument into three parts:

- **Part 1: Rumblings.** The first section looks comprehensively at how the patterns of American life have changed since the end of the Second World War. There's a lot of ground to cover— a whole host of upheavals marks the more than half century that followed America's victory over fascism. Rather than consider each change in isolation, we need to gather some sense of how they've coalesced to transform the routines of our everyday lives. We'll discover that the minirevolutions of the last several decades have had two effects: first, they've broadened our horizons immeasurably; second, they've combined to change how we choose, on average, to invest our time and energy.

- **Part 2: The Missing Rings:** The second section, built on the first, explores how the changes to our daily routines have destabilized what were the basic building blocks of American community. This is the central point: townships, over the course of the last several decades, have been replaced by a new architecture. And that marks the most fundamental change in the structure of American life since the Revolution.

- **Part 3: America Explained:** The final section applies the lessons of the second and explores how that transformation has begun to play out. In the end, we'll find that that the dramatic change in the structure of our communities has disrupted the nation's economic growth, exacerbated the nation's political dysfunction, and undermined our social safety net. But the problem is less that the architecture has changed than that our institutions haven't yet caught up. Our political system still functions as if the old townships prevailed. Our economy still churns as if it were serving a population ensconced in outdated patterns of life. Our social safety net is structured to serve an alien set of demands. The challenge, moving forward, will be to adapt our institutions to the new reality of American community.

In the end, I hope to convince you that changes in the rhythms of ordinary American life—the distinctions I noticed but couldn't articulate as a kid sitting in the backseat of our family minivan—are integral to a complete understanding of why the American Dream seems to be slipping away. The roots of our contemporary problems are much more mundane than most of us imagine. And so to begin that journey of understanding, let's delve into the thinking of the small coterie of scholars who began to sound an alarm decades before the second transformation of American community took full effect.

Part 1

===

Rumblings

1

THE WARNING

In 1945, following a decade and a half of economic tumult and horrific warfare, the United States entered an era of unprecedented peace and prosperity. The GIs lucky enough to return home found a landscape full of opportunity. The economy grew amid an explosion of global demand. Bretton Woods and the Marshall Plan established Washington as a beacon of stability and hope. Even as the Cold War loomed, many sensed that America was finally ready to make good on Woodrow Wilson's decades-old vow to ensure a world "safe for democracy."[1]

Over the years, our impressions of that auspicious age have been refracted through the same lens that inspired the sitcom *Happy Days* and the musical *Grease*. In that fantasy, the 1950s marked the apex of the American Dream. Middle-class families lived well off a single income, suburban life emerged as the comfortable norm, and the promise of the burgeoning baby-boom generation signaled a down payment on the nation's bright future. Indeed, many Americans still hold the 1950s up as a kind of sanctified ideal.

But that collective memory doesn't tell the whole story. In the years that followed, a series of counternarratives emerged to argue that the buttoned-down lifestyle of our popular imagination was anything but idyllic: the ticky-tacky houses that sprang up in suburban Levittowns; the insipidness of a world defined by Wonder Bread; the sense that Americans were perpetually one social miscue away from being ostracized.[2] The truth is that racism was rampant, gender equality a pipe dream, and ethnic tensions on simmer. As Mike Nichols made clear in *The Graduate,* however quaint the 1950s might have been, there was a darker side to the story.[3]

It wasn't just that postwar American life was repressive. As one small coterie of academics observed at the time, an element of cultural McCarthyism threatened then to undermine the American character. In novels like Sloan Wilson's 1955 bestseller, *The Man in the Gray Flannel Suit,* critics suggested that the unfailing determination responsible for propelling previous generations across the frontier and through the Industrial Revolution was being lost.[4] In 1957, Brandeis University's founding president, Abram L. Sachar, complained that "there are many young people today who will not sign a petition for pink raspberry ice cream in the dining hall commons for fear that someday they may have to explain their color predilections to zealous congressional committees."[5] In sum, *conformity* seemed to be undermining the American spirit of ingenuity.

It was largely in an attempt to understand America's listlessness that an editor at *Fortune,* William Whyte, took some time to observe the patterns of life in a newly built neighborhood on the outskirts of downtown Chicago. Park Forest was, in the early postwar period, ingesting a flood of middle-class families looking to escape the crowded tenements closer to the Loop. In watching the new inhabitants, Whyte concluded that the altered routines of 1950s America were laying the groundwork for a new personality type. This nascent class of Americans, he argued, was unusually focused on social cues—they were desperate to win the approval of their neighbors.

Whyte sympathized with the common desire to escape the hectic life of urban neighborhoods. But if a "belief in 'belonging-ness' as the ultimate need of the individual" had emerged as the *sine qua non* of middle-class life, he concluded that a "social" ethic was replacing the Protestant work ethic of old.[6] Whyte feared that those who were subsumed into the genteel circumstances of post-war suburban life—the limp noodles being raised in places like Park Forest—would never develop the grittiness that had empow-ered previous American generations to strike out on their own. In 1956 he wrote *The Organization Man,* a now classic account of his observations, to sound the alarm.

At roughly the same time, a former clerk to Justice Louis Brandeis—a lawyer who, after the Second World War, had decided to abandon the law in favor of a career in the social sciences—emerged with an analogous theory.[7] Writing *The Lonely Crowd,* which would become the best-selling book ever published by a sociologist, Harvard professor David Riesman argued that Americans were undergoing a revolution in their social charac-ter.[8] Whereas previous generations had been defined by "inner directedness"—their behavior was guided by a deeply embedded moral code—younger Americans seemed to be "other-directed." Riesman explained the new norm: "The other-directed person wants to be loved rather than esteemed; he wants not to gull or impress, let alone oppress, others but, in the current phrase, to relate to them; he seeks less a snobbish status in the eyes of others than assurance of being emotionally in tune with them."[9]

In essence, Riesman argued, rather than remaining true to an authentic viewpoint in every circumstance, growing portions of Americans were adjusting their bearings to suit each new social environment.[9] As Charles McGrath, the former editor of the *New York Times Book Review,* summarized the distinction in the year that Riesman died: "inner-directeds are self-motivated and goal-oriented; and other-directeds . . . are slavish conformists who want only to be loved and accepted."[11] The change was likely to have severe implications, Riesman concluded. Like *The Organization Man, The Lonely Crowd* was written to warn Americans of the emerging threat from within.

The concerns Riesman, Whyte, and a small contingent of other academics voiced during that early postwar era were widely discussed throughout the 1950s. Amid the Soviet menace, fear that the United States was losing its edge had a particular resonance. In a global conflict, Americans wanted to project perseverance and grit. But the upheavals of the 1960s pushed that concern to the edges of the nation's consciousness. As students set fire to college campuses and protesters marched against the Vietnam War, obsequiousness seemed the least of America's problems. Far from being too eager to placate authority, the boomers appeared to lack even the least bit of decorum. And as social disorder morphed into a quasi-national panic, concerns about the prevalence of "other-directedness" fell off the radar.

In the decades that followed, and with a handful of important exceptions, books that purported to offer what McGrath, the *New York Times Book Review* editor, called the "big notion"—efforts to salve the confusion emerging from what Malcolm Gladwell has described as the plague of being "information rich and theory poor"—have turned away from the question of community.[12] In many cases, that's because so many grand theses about the direction of American society have been later proven off the mark. As McGrath explained, "no one wanted to risk looking so foolish."[13]

But there was another reason as well: as the postwar period rolled on, academics came increasingly to prize a different sort of scholarship. In lieu of speculating on grand new theories, social scientists focused more frequently on hard data. They veered away from the mushier, more speculative stuff of earlier eras and toward the numerically driven research that was more typical of the harder sciences. *The Lonely Crowd,* for example, contained hardly a single quantitative footnote.

There is something to be said for the new emphasis: it weeds out some of the agenda-driven arguments that might otherwise sneak into the academic literature; conclusions drawn from faulty data crunching can be discredited without a second thought. In other cases, empirically driven scholarship has incubated breathtaking conclusions. Harvard professor Robert Putnam's best-selling book *Bowling Alone,* published in 2000, drew from a vast array of data sources to argue that American community was in decay. Viewed at the time as an intellectual successor to Riesman's wide-ranging interest in broad social relations, *Bowling Alone* managed nevertheless to be a sterling example of the more contemporary academic sensibility.

Moreover, all sorts of interesting conclusions have been gleaned since researchers began to apply data-centered tools to softer disciplines. Just a few years ago, for example, *Freakonomics* applied the tools of statistics to realms traditionally held outside the main of economic studies—and to great effect.[14] More recently, new, sophisticated models and data sets have propelled authors like Nate Silver to international fame, predicting both sporting outcomes and, famously, the outcome of the 2012 presidential election.[15]

But that new emphasis has orphaned some of the questions earlier generations asked. There are, after all, aspects of our lives that elude rigorous data analysis. There's no way to measure numerically how Americans balance the divergent impulses toward inner-directedness and other-directedness, or whether they're more or less driven to conform to the expectations of each varied social environment. We can ask individuals to self-report in opinion polls, and in some cases we can find a proxy—maybe, for example, the frequency with which you call an acquaintance mirrors how much you value the relationship. But it's hard to know how accurate that data really is. How well do you recall how much time you spend, on average, reading e-mails from friends each day? Maybe of more concern, do you call your closest acquaintances, or do you visit them in person instead?

I do not mean to argue that we should abandon the insights that rigorous data collection can offer. Where we can, we ought to exploit every possible regression analysis. But we can't afford to let ourselves be trapped by the limits of quantifiable evidence. As David Riesman and William Whyte demonstrated decades ago, we ought not lose sight of the questions that can't be answered statistically. How, for example, have more recent changes in rhythms of American life changed our collective outlook on the challenges of the day? Amid the explosion of new technologies, new industries, new places to shop, eat, and pray, how has America's social character evolved, if at all? Moreover, if it has, how will that transformation change the trajectory of our history?

In the summer of 2010, basketball superstar LeBron James announced in an ESPN special that he was going to "take [his] talents to South Beach and join the Miami Heat." Many analysts assumed his new team would win the NBA championship the following spring. James's decision—to join superstars Dwyane Wade and Chris Bosh on a roster known later as the "Big Three"— seemed to make Miami's upstart basketball franchise unbeatable. James was, by most estimates, the best player in the world; Wade and Bosh weren't far behind. And so it was hard for many to imagine how any other team could compete with such a remarkable triumvirate.

At the end of the season, however, the Big Three were defeated in their first championship series together by the less-flashy Dallas Mavericks. The loss left many fans scratching their heads: how could the only team in the NBA to have *three* players among the NBA's twenty-five most highly paid lose to a team that could only claim one?[16] The "Dallas Surprise" didn't mean much in the long run—Miami won the league championship in each of the next two seasons. But it did reveal a blindness in American life—one that is the result, in part, of the data-driven focus inside the academy.

Two distinct lenses have emerged to frame our analysis of complex situations: the first, taken from thirty thousand feet, looks from a macro level at statistics in the aggregate. After taking a snapshot of a more expansive picture, we try to glean a broader conclusion. The second lens, alternatively, provides the opposite view, from the micro level out. What does the experience of a single company, or a particular individual, tell us about the bigger picture?

The problem is that the bird's-eye and micro-level views, even when taken in tandem, can get the story wrong. In the case of Lebron James's decision, both lenses fed the conventional wisdom that the Heat were shoo-ins for that first NBA championship. The Big Three's aggregate statistics suggested they were the league's very best. The micro-level analysis tended to hue the same way: James had almost single-handedly made his previous team, the Cleveland Cavaliers, a contender for the NBA crown; in a less barren environment, many assumed he would flourish, propelling his new team in turn.

The macro and micro analyses failed because they neglected the view from the middle. Basketball games are determined neither by a team's statistical profile nor by the talent of any individual player—though each plays an important role. Rather, the dynamic that defines how individual players interact—the substance of their *teamwork*—often plays the determinative role. Do they spread the ball around or does a single player always charge the lane? Do they incorporate all five positions or depend on just a couple of stars? During that first pivotal NBA championship, those sorts of questions decided the series: the team dynamic displayed by the Mavericks was enough to overcome their paper deficit in talent.

That sort of misanalysis isn't limited to the world of sports. The same misapprehension prevents us from accurately interpreting complex situations across the board. When we think about the economy, for example, we're conventionally plied with statistics— potential demographic shifts or changing interest rates—that invariably affect the business cycle. Alternatively, we seek out individual stories—how Steve Jobs managed to lead Apple to the top of the tech heap, for example—and ask how they apply to the broader economy. From these two strategies, we try to develop a more comprehensive understanding of how the economy works. And in some cases that strategy works. But without a sense of what's happening in the middle, we're often left without the whole picture.

Was Apple's success the result of Jobs's legendary understanding of consumer desires or of the fact that Apple's engineers and marketing departments were so thoroughly integrated into the design process? Did the tech boom emerge in America because the Clinton administration got interest rates under control (a macro- level explanation) or because Bill Gates and Andy Grove were better technologists (a micro-level reason), or was there a more complex alchemy at work?

In almost every case, macro- and micro-level explanations play important roles in explaining the reality. Steve Jobs was a genius.[17] Toyota and Honda played it smart when competing with Ford, Chrysler, and General Motors. The economic boom of the 1990s wouldn't have emerged absent President Clinton's economic program or the ingenuity displayed by private entrepreneurs who saw how the Internet would define the future.

Too frequently, however, those conventional lenses spur us to ignore the powerful dynamics that exist beyond the scope of any individual's influence, but beneath any global landscape. We neglect the crucial, hard-to-measure stuff hidden between individual stories and quantifiable statistics. That marks a huge blind spot. As in the case of the Miami Heat's failure to beat the Dallas Mavericks, interpersonal dynamics can play the determining role.

Here's the problem: our failure to understand what's happening in the middle is short-circuiting our ability to glean a clear picture of what's going on in American society writ large. Which perspective we employ to understand a problem too frequently determines which among several potential causes we're inclined to endorse. Using the micro lens, conservatives tend to focus on how defects in the American character explain problems like poverty; their counterparts on the left believe macro-level concerns like our failure to invest in infrastructure or education are at the root of the issue. Both views get crucial elements of the story right. But what they each lack is a sufficient analysis of what's happening in between— how the mundane interactions of everyday life affect the landscape of American opportunity.

What we need is a renewed focus on the role played by interpersonal dynamics. In any given neighborhood, as on any given basketball team, social relationships vary: some groups are woven tightly together, while others are mere collections of strangers; some are divided along racial lines, and others separated by politics; some are insular and isolated while others are worldly but distracted. Understanding the nature of those connections is crucial to getting the big picture right.

There's an obvious reason that social structure is so frequently ignored: it's almost impossible to measure. Basketball analysts are prone to focus on individual and team-wide figures because they are the only indicators that can be compared with true specificity. But anyone who knows the game of roundball well enough will acknowledge that "team chemistry" is just as important as any other factor. The nature of the connections between individual players matters more than whether the shooting guard has a particularly deft jump shot or the starting lineup has a particularly tall frontcourt.

When the same concept is applied to society, team chemistry is known by another term: community. And that's the key insight. To evaluate the plight of the American Dream, we need a better understanding of how Americans connect with one another. What is the essential alchemy of our personal relationships? Who demands our respect and attention? Finally, and maybe most importantly, how have those patterns of community changed?

To answer those questions, we need to engage in an investigation that distinguishes the two factors broadly familiar to anyone who's ever watched a crime drama: *motive* and *opportunity*. The key to uncovering why and how community has changed is found in understanding where those elements intersected in earlier eras—and where they meet today.

Motive: First, we need to get our minds around what people want from their social connections. What sorts of satisfaction do we get from time spent with a spouse, a child, a parent, a friend, or an acquaintance? What is it that we want out of each relationship— support, understanding, humor, gossip, respect, appreciation? Motive is a proxy for what David Riesman and William Whyte focused on in the early postwar period: social character. It's a measure of what drives us to connect.

Opportunity: Second, no matter what we want from our social universe, we need a better sense of how the landscape of opportunity has evolved. Which relationships are individuals capable of maintaining, and which are out of reach? It may be difficult to keep up with your best friend from high school if you decide to attend a college thousands of miles away. If both Mom and Dad are caught up in meetings at the office, a child may form a warmer relationship with a grandparent or nanny.

Fortunately, while we rarely put those two elements together in a single analysis, new evidence can now offer us a better sense of how both have evolved over the last several decades. We are awash, for example, in a sea of new data about how desires have changed. You need do nothing more than listen to a few episodes of the *Charlie Rose Brain Series* or read Nobel laureate Daniel Kahneman's book *Thinking Fast and Slow* to know that our understanding of human motivation has grown by leaps and bounds.[18] Simultaneously, we've been deluged with evidence of how information technology, among other advances, has rewired society, putting people across the world in closer proximity.

But amid all the new data points and theories, we've failed to generate the perspective required to fit the moving pieces together. To understand how the architecture of American community has changed, we need to understand how the intersection of those two elements has shifted. In that pursuit, let's first get about the challenge of deciphering how the landscape of American opportunity has changed, piece by piece, over the last several decades.

2

THE THIRD WAVE

I n one of the great ironies of recent American history, the so-
called gurus behind former House Speaker Newt Gingrich's
conservative governing philosophy were once labor activists
tied, allegedly, to the American Communist Party. Alvin and Heidi
Toffler spent the late 1940s and early 1950s organizing the employees of a window-fan factory in Cleveland.[1] Yet over the ensuing
decades, as Alvin worked his way from the front lines of the labor
movement to *Fortune* magazine, they largely abandoned the union
movement—or, at least, they lost faith in the idea that labor's struggle with management marked the central dilemma of twentieth-
century economics. Instead, the couple began to wonder whether
our conventional understanding of America had overlooked more
remarkable trends. And through that curiosity, they began to col-
laborate in writing books that looked at America's challenges on a
grander scale.[2]

The Tofflers' core insight—a thesis that propelled several of
their books onto best-seller lists through the 1970s and 1980s
and later led the *Financial Times* to label Alvin "the world's most
famous futurologist"—was that at some point during the Eisenhower administration, the United States had begun to transition
away from an explicitly industrial paradigm.[3] For the previous
several generations, the nation's economy had been shifting from

one centered on farming to one fueled by manufacturing. But the Tofflers thought things were moving in yet another direction. And it wasn't just that certain elements of American life were changing on a piecemeal basis; rather, the very foundation of American society was going through a fundamental transformation. The Tofflers began making connections between changes that appeared only tangentially related: the ties that bound families together, the sources of American energy, the power of the mass market. And to understand any individual change, they argued, you needed to understand the broader dynamics.[4]

By the early 1990s, the Tofflers' ideas jumped from the worlds of economics and management squarely into the center of the political debate. As the Cold War subsided, both progressives and conservatives were struggling to redefine their agendas; both were finding that the politics of the industrial age no longer seemed applicable. Accepting the 1992 Democratic presidential nomination, Bill Clinton pledged to move beyond the "brain-dead politics" of left and right.[5] And for the same reason, Newt Gingrich, a hard-charging junior congressman from Georgia with designs on national power, began to draw heavily from the Tofflers' research, inviting them oftentimes to speak to groups of Republican legislators.

In time, the Tofflers' connection to Gingrich would cloud their reputation. Inasmuch as the Speaker was prone to cite them in his effort to reshape conservative politics, his detractors began to associate the couple's ideas with Gingrich's up-and-down political profile. While they had once been compared frequently to management visionaries such as Peter Drucker, the Gingrich connection and a few misguided predictions (they once suggested, for example, that humans would soon establish colonies under the sea) obscured the intellectual contributions that had made them so influential.[6] Indeed, the Tofflers' broad approach to history offers a helpful framework for understanding today's challenges.

The enduring frame that I use throughout the next several

chapters is bound up with the Tofflers' view that the history of human civilization can be divided into three successive "waves" of change.[7] The first upheaval was marked by the ancient advent of agriculture. Armed with the ability to harvest food in much greater quantities, humans abandoned the nomadic existence of hunter-gatherer societies and embraced patterns of life centered in established towns and cities. For centuries, First Wave societies, as the Tofflers labeled them, flourished around the world, their growth and prosperity limited largely by a level of technological sophistication that could only sustain societies of a certain size.

The Second Wave, which, by the Tofflers' estimation, crested in the mid-1950s, was fueled by the advances of the Industrial Revolution. In their view, the effects of humanity's new technological sophistication hadn't been limited to the way humans produced food and widgets. Rather, Second Wave society comprised a set of institutions largely distinct from those that came before: nuclear families, for example, had replaced multigenerational households; corporations had become the standard way to organize a business; big bureaucracies, more rare in earlier eras, had become more typical.[8]

What the Tofflers most wanted was for their readers to appreciate the emergence of the Third Wave.[9] During the 1970s and 1980s, they argued, an entirely new framework had developed, distinct from the rhythms of the nineteenth and early twentieth centuries. Like its predecessors, Third Wave society, which was only beginning to come clear in the 1970s and 80s, engendered its own unique framework.

The issue wasn't just that new technologies like the fax machine were driving the information age, or that changes in the way we interacted were laying the foundation for what Marshall McLuhan had termed, contemporaneously, a "global village."[10] The Tofflers argued that certain distinctions that defined Second Wave society—between home and work, between consumer and

producer, between mass production and specific customization—
were being breached. Elements of life that simply looked like aber-
rations from the norm in Second Wave society, such as life in the
suburbs, a broad aversion to naked bigotry, "no fault" divorces, longer lifespans—the list could go on—actually represented constituent parts of the Third Wave.

Few anticipated how the changes that the Tofflers labeled the
Third Wave would coalesce to upend American community. But, as
we'll see, three broad categories of changes—the technological and
economic revolutions of the last sixty years, the explosion in American mobility, and the evolution of our lives at home—combined to
undermine the basic building blocks of community life. Far from
being disconnected, they're all parts of the same organic whole.
But before we can piece those successive changes together, we first
have to break them down.

No single phrase or book defined the last quarter century more
famously than Thomas Friedman's *The World is Flat*. As the *New
York Times* columnist has long argued, since the fall of the Berlin
Wall in 1989, a new global architecture has emerged, more inter-
dependent and interconnected than anything before.[11] And the
statistics bear that out. Since roughly 1990, the global marketplace
has more than doubled in size, growing to encompass roughly two
billion people. International trade grew by a factor of two, and
then expanded again by a third.[12] And the share of American GDP
driven by exports has more than doubled.[13]

But globalization hasn't been confined to the economic realm:
it has also driven the spread of ideas. Since Freedom House
began compiling statistics in the early 1970s, the percentage of
"free" or "partly free" countries around the world has grown
from just over half to more than three quarters.[14] The combined
effect—empowering people around the globe both financially and

politically—has spread wealth in ways few might have imagined: between 1981 and 2004, the percentage of people around the world living on a dollar a day has dropped from 40 to 18.[15]

At the same time, the digital revolution has spread global access to information to places no one could have dreamed in the early postwar era. In 1990, there was barely more than one computer for every five Americans; by 2005, that same figure was nearing four for every five.[16] Today, 80 percent of American adults are connected to the Internet, and nearly 86 percent use a cell phone.[17] And that doesn't even take into account the effect of "social networking," a technology now employed by a full half of Americans, including 80 percent of those between the ages of eighteen and twenty-nine.[18] As former Google CEO Eric Schmidt recently explained: "In our lifetimes we're going from almost no one being able to communicate to almost everyone being able to communicate. We're also going from almost no one having any kind of information and access to libraries to virtually everyone having access to every piece of information in the world. That is an enormous accomplishment to humanity."[19]

Although we've become focused on the growth of the Internet, the bigger story is how much more data we consume, regardless of the medium. The number of televisions per American household doubled between 1970 and 2008, and the number of telephone calls grew from 425 million in 1985 to more than 13 billion in 2006.[20] Today we devour three times as much information as we did in 1960—despite the fact that newspaper readership has broadly declined.[21] That trend is only expected to grow. Ericsson, the telecommunications manufacturer, estimates that by 2017, global mobile data traffic will have grown twenty-one times over, and mobile broadband subscriptions will grow more than five times over.[22]

The third element of the "flattening" globe has been the explosion of commerce designed to provide a "service" to customers, rather than a manufactured good. Between 1900 and 2006, the percentage of Americans employed in "working" jobs fell from 57 to 24, while service jobs grew from 23 to 45.[23] During even more abbreviated periods, the ratio of manufacturing to service jobs in Chicago flipped from 3:1 to 1:2 and the percentage of "industrial" jobs in Manhattan fell from 40 to 5 percent.[24]

Those changes have largely tracked the decline of the nation's private-sector unions. At its peak in the mid-1950s, organized labor could claim to represent a third of the American workforce; today, unions represent barely more than one of every ten workers.[25] Describing the scene out the window of a train traveling between New York and Washington, NPR's Planet Money correspondent Adam Davidson recently noted in the *New York Times*:

> For most of the 180 or so years of the train line's existence, the end-points of this journey—New York and D.C.—were subordinate to the roaring engines of productivity in between. The real value in America was created in Newark's machine shops and tanneries, Trenton's rubber and metal plants, Chester's shipyards, [and] Baltimore's steel mills. . . . Washington collected the taxes and made the rules. Wall Street got a small commission for turning the nation's savings into industrial investment. But nobody would have ever confused either as America's driving force. . . . This model was flipped inside out as Wall Street and D.C. became the central drivers, not secondary supports, of the nation's economy.[26]

In truth, the United States still manages to produce as much stuff as China—despite the conventional wisdom that American industry is moribund. But because we're so much more productive today—we can generate products so much more efficiently—American manufacturing firms have shed massive numbers of their employees.[27] On mill in Indiana, for example, today produces the same amount of steel it did several decades ago—but with 80 percent fewer workers.[28]

On a macro level, these three big changes—globalization, digitization, and the emergence of the service economy—have rewired the way Americans make a living. That change has, in turn, uprooted the way we've come to map out our careers. The notion that an individual should choose a vocation and then spend the bulk of his or her working life at a single firm was an inherently Second Wave phenomenon. Today, a growing portion of the American workforce has embraced an entirely different set of assumptions.

After the First Wave, during the period when agriculture was still central to our economy, jobs were intermittent and labor was transient. Indeed, for most of human history, workers and artisans had spent their lives roaming from job to job, assuming that when one task was done they would need to seek another. Life in Second Wave society, however, was different: industrial jobs provided for something more secure—a *career*. Employees could expect, in many circumstances, to spend their working lives employed by the same company.[29] In turn, people's livelihoods often came to define their identity. What you *did* became commensurate with who you *were*.

The Third Wave has upended that Second Wave norm. Denizens of the new global, digitized, service-oriented economy may be eager for job security, but few assume they'll spend the bulk of their working years with any one firm (let alone in any one profession). At the same time, we've moved away from "defined benefit" pensions (which reward an individual for staying in one job for a long time) and toward "defined contribution" plans that require no similar commitment.[30] We've moved away from lifelong relationships with our employers to plug-and-play sorts of arrangements.

As Bill Clinton declared in his 1996 State of the Union address, "A hundred years ago we moved from farm to factory. Now we move to an age of technology, information, and global competition."[31] Today, the Second Wave's assembly lines have been replaced by the Third Wave's cubicles. But despite that transformation's dramatic effects on what we do for a living and how we access news and information, it represents only one piece of how our lives have changed over the last several decades. To build on our understanding of how life has evolved economically and technologically, we need to look at how the horizons of our mobility have changed.

A strange term has come to frame one of the most powerful effects of the Third Wave. As the gap separating America's richest and poorer citizens has widened over time, critics have been talking about the crisis of "social mobility."[32] Indeed, the suggestion that it's more difficult today to pull yourself up by the bootstraps hints at a fundamental chink in the American Dream. While it's impossible to deny that economic disparities have widened in recent years, or that it's become increasingly difficult for individuals to slide up and down the income ladder, the suggestion that American life has been confined confuses a central development: far from becoming more constricted on the whole, our personal horizons have actually widened considerably.

It's important first to acknowledge the widely noted reality: economic inequality in the United States has indeed exploded. The American Dream is defined, by some measure, by the promise that those who work hard and play by the rules can pass on to their children more than was passed on to them. Unfortunately, with very few caveats, more recent evidence suggests that that promise is under threat. We are now facing the very real possibility that future generations will see their quality of life diminish, rather than improve. But why?

For one thing, the spread of wealth in the United States has skewed to the top. Measured in real terms since the early postwar era, incomes for families in the bottom fifth of the scale have increased by less than $15,000, while those at the ninety-fifth percentile have grown by $130,000.[33] Between 1976 and 2007 alone, the share of national income claimed by the top one percent of households grew from 8.9 to 23.5 percent—meaning that every dollar of income growth over that period was divided such that the top 1 percent claimed 58 cents.[34] The rich have gotten richer.

The trend is even more dispiriting when you look at the very top of the income scale. Between 1979 and 2007, the disposable income of the top 1 percent rose three times over, while the figure for the bottom fifth of income earners rose only 40 percent.[35] Just as jaw-dropping: the top 1 percent of Americans saw their share of national income grow from 10 to 20 percent between 1980 and 2012, while the share going to the top .01 percent of American families grew from 1 to 5 percent.[36]

Nobel-laureate economist Joseph Stiglitz drove the point home recently when he wrote that beginning roughly during the Reagan era, "those with low wages (in the bottom 90 percent) have seen a growth of only around 15 percent in their wages, while those at the top 1 percent have seen an increase of almost 150 percent and the top .01 percent of more than 300 percent."[37] And this has wildly skewed the figures designed to measure economic inequality: the so-called Gini coefficient rose by almost a third between 1980 and 2012, after having reached a postwar low in the mid-1970s.[38]

The trend hasn't been uniform across the decades: it attenuated by several measures during the Clinton years. But the effect over the long term, as many have noted, has been to hollow out America's middle class. Between 1971 and 2012, those making between two-thirds and double the national median income shrank from 61 to 51 percent of the adult population. At the same time, those ranked in the upper-income tier rose from 14 to 20 percent, and the lower tier rose from 25 to 29 percent.[39] Geographically, the percentage of American neighborhoods within 20 percent of the national median fell by a third, as more communities tended to skew toward greater wealth or poverty.[40]

The temptation, when viewing the scene from above, is to blame the new middle-class hollow on some failure of public policy. And it's nearly impossible to deny that the nation's political leadership has contributed to economic inequality by failing, for example, to support unions. But by another measure, culpability falls more squarely on the changes discussed above: the realities of a Third Wave economy have eviscerated demand for the sorts of jobs that buoyed those once living in the counties situated between New York and Washington. The blue-collar jobs of the Second Wave have given way to the better-paying jobs of America's so-called creative class and the less well-paying positions available to those at the lower end of the income scale.[41]

The more troubling aspect of the nation's economic inequality concerns the question of whether those on the lower rungs can still find their way up the ladder. From that vantage point, the evidence is even more discouraging. As Stiglitz recently argued, Americans today are more likely to remain at the status they were born into—whether rich, poor, or in between—than the citizens of every other advanced economy.[42] And that argues for the sorts of public empowerment—massive investments in public education, for example—that are staples of the progressive agenda.

Fortunately, the march of economic inequality isn't the whole story, and American mobility isn't defined exclusively by our ability to jump from lower to middle to upper class and back. In fact, changing the economics of American mobility has been accompanied by an even more momentous shift: the removal of many of the limitations that once precluded Americans from going where they wanted to go, being who they wanted to be, and doing what they wanted to do. Indeed, much as it may be harder today to jump from one class to another, it's gotten significantly easier to make all sorts of other leaps. So whatever the dire state of America's Gini coefficient, the nation's social mobility, properly understood, has grown in ways most Americans have come to treasure.[43]

Nothing speaks more powerfully to the expansion of American mobility than the civil rights movement. Less than fifty years after

Martin Luther King delivered his "I Have a Dream" speech amid the injustices of Jim Crow, the United States elected an African-American president. That reflects a remarkable underlying shift. Although prejudice was blatantly woven into the rhythms of everyday life during the early postwar years, it would be unthinkable today, nearly everywhere in the United States, to prevent a certain race of people from taking a sip from a certain drinking fountain.

Of course, not all issues of race have been extinguished in twenty-first-century America. Even now, African-Americans have a median income well below that of whites. And more latent forms of discrimination still exist. But as the civil rights leader Reverend Joseph Lowery pointed out at the time of Barack Obama's inauguration, there were just a few hundred black elected officials in the United States when Martin Luther King was assassinated, and by 2009 there were more like ten thousand.[44] That is unmistakable progress.

Moreover, a raft of other rights—voting rights, women's rights, and LGBT rights among them—have emerged to strike at norms that once shuttered opportunity to broad classes of American citizens. The idea that an individual might be prevented from applying for a particular job, living in a fashionable neighborhood, joining an exclusive club, or striking up a friendship with a certain acquaintance is, in most circumstances, beyond the pale today. Many blatant prejudices have gone from the banal to the outrageous over just a few decades. And so, although we may be more limited in how much we earn, we are much more socially mobile today than we were in the years that followed the Second World War.

That points to a different aspect of mobility: our capacity today to move from place to place. We've already established that digitization has, as Thomas Friedman argued, "flattened" the globe. Today, I can read about what's happening locally in Cincinnati or Buffalo by clicking on a few Web sites; my wife can Skype regularly with her high-school friend in Malaysia. We needn't wait for newspapers to be heaved onto our front porches or for letters to be delivered by the Postal Service. But even beyond the virtual world, new technology and infrastructure makes us more *physically* mobile.

Consider the evolution of the airline industry. In the 1950s and '60s, plane flights were a sort of luxury: Americans, in 1954, flew, on average, only once every four years. By 2005, Americans had come to average two-and-a-half flights a year—a 900 percent jump over the course of a single half-century.[45] This speaks not only to an economic change but to a psychological one: to whatever degree we once felt stranded, we're now free to get away. Friends who live a few hundred miles apart—once considered to be a long way—can visit each other, at comparatively little cost, with much more regularity.

That's just the tip of the iceberg. While broadband penetration and cheap airfare winnowed the barriers that once limited American mobility, nothing has had as dramatic an effect as the automobile. The number of households with more than one car doubled to roughly 60 percent between 1969 and 2011, even as the percentage who survived without one dropped precipitously and the number of miles driven exploded.[46] To the extent that our grandparents were limited to shopping along the local strip—or maybe at the terminus of a public bus line—we now can select from a much wider range of retail options. In a way that would have been unthinkable a few generations ago, Americans rarely think twice about doing an errand across town.[47]

Cars haven't only changed our sense of where we can go— they've revolutionized where we live. Between 1950 and 2000, the percentage of Americans living in the suburbs doubled from a fifth to a full half, while the percentage living in nonmetropolitan areas plummeted from 44 to 20.[48] During the 1990s alone, nearly two-thirds of the growth in the nation's metropolitan communities involved those traveling from one suburb to another. Put in broader context, between 1990 and 2000, 83 percent of the growth in commuting was to a destination in the suburbs.[49]

So the Third Wave hasn't just marked a change from the old industrial economy to one defined by information. The very landscape in which we live has been broadened—even locally—to give us access to a much wider horizon. Limits to the average routine— where we could shop, what we might eat, whom we might know— are gone. And while some opportunities have been curtailed, the broad trend has been to slough off the barriers that defined early postwar life, providing younger generations with a much greater sense of freedom.

That brings us to the last set of upheavals wrought by the Third Wave—those that bear most directly on our lives at home. Conservatives in particular have long expressed concern that the nation's moral fabric is tearing. The two-parent, multi-sibling, one-breadwinner homes depicted in sitcoms like *Ozzie and Harriet* have yielded to a panoply of options. In much the same way that progressives blame economic inequality for America's problems, conservatives cite a sort of oozing depravity. And as with the left's focus on social mobility, there are elements of the conservative critique that demand our attention.

First, we should correct a misconception that drives scholars of the American family crazy: although we tend to assume that the broader narrative of the twentieth century was a decline in the prevalence of *Ozzie and Harriet*-style nuclear families since the 1950s, the truth is actually much more complicated. There's no denying that the percentage of American households structured in the Cleaver model has declined over the years. But the more dramatic shift has happened among those *not* living in what many people term a "traditional" family. The extended families that were common throughout so much of American history—homes that included grandparents, adult children, and cousins, for example—have more recently been replaced by single-parent families, and adults living alone.[50] For generations, the roles later thought to be the exclusive domain of parents were often shared by other relatives living inside any given home. Since then, however, the American family has evolved, first to the model now termed traditional, and then to something else. And there may be no better place to begin a survey of American home life than by spotlighting the roles filled now by American women.

Warren Buffett often highlights the changing place of American women with a paean to his childhood. As he tells it, when he was a boy, women working outside the home—many of whom would have thrived, as they do today, in diverse fields—were largely limited to positions as teachers, nurses, and secretaries. And that was, he points out, a real boon for the students, patients, and bosses who might otherwise have been taught, cared for, and served by a less talented pool of applicants.[51]

Today, while glass ceilings still exist, opportunities for women to work outside the home have expanded dramatically.[52] Between 1960 and the mid-1990s, the percentage of working-age American women engaged in work outside the home grew from roughly one-third to 70 percent.[53] That change—an indelibly Third Wave phenomenon—has become a broadly accepted norm of American life. By 2005, 81 percent of Americans approved of a woman working outside the home—even if her husband made enough to support the family alone.[54]

The birth-control pill has certainly played some role in women's emergence into the professional workforce. Fewer children—and children born at a more predictable pace—have reduced burdens that once compelled many women to stay at home. At the same time, the old burdens haven't been lifted entirely. As *New York Times* columnist Gail Collins has argued, the contemporary expectation that women will take a professional role outside the home has not diminished the pressure many feel to fulfill the domestic responsibilities their mothers and grandmothers shouldered.[55]

That said, new job opportunities do not account entirely for the flood of women in the workforce. Many have been pushed into breadwinning positions purely by a demand for income. Whether it's to keep up with the Joneses or to make up for the diminishing spending power of middle-class salaries, women who might once have chosen to work at home (or not at all) now feel compelled to earn a second household salary.[56] The composite result is clear: adults today spend more hours at work than they once did. Between 1968 and 2001, the number of combined weekly hours spent at work by husbands and wives grew by a full twelve hours.[57]

It doesn't end there. Beyond the changing role of women, American adolescence has also evolved—though few have explicitly noted the upheaval. Baby boomers grew up during an era when the typical coming-of-age story saw a clean break from childhood to independence: like Dustin Hoffman's character in *The Graduate*, adolescents were expected to remain tethered to their parents until they were thrust into adulthood upon marriage, the point at which men were expected to settle into a career and women were supposed to begin raising a new family. With the Third Wave a whole new process of maturation—one that has blurred the lines that separate childhood and independence—has emerged as the new norm.

Any effort to understand the transformation of American adolescence benefits from an analogy with the Amish tradition of Rumspringa. As Amish children come of age, they are cast out of their close-knit communities and required, for a time, to integrate into the modern world. After a period immersed in both the extravagance and turmoil of non-Amish life, the adolescents are given the choice to return to the communities where they were raised, or to abandon Amish life forever. The period outside marks, by some standard, the final step in an Amish adolescent's rite of passage. When (and if) they return, they are finally considered adults.

Non-Amish American adolescents may not be cast out so brazenly into a new and unfamiliar world, but they do experience some version of Rumspringa today.[58] It's fairly typical now to see young adults in their late teens and early twenties spend a few years trying on different hats, different relationships, and different ways of life—even if that leaves them tangentially dependent on their parents. Between 2005 and 2011, the percentage of American men between the ages of twenty-five and thirty-four living at home grew from 14 to 19 percent (many, of course, had no better option for lack of a well-paying job).[59] And as Princeton sociologist Robert Wuthnow has revealed, in a proxy for both the peak of adolescence and full immersion into the responsibilities of adulthood, the span between children's religious confirmation and their adult decision to join a congregation in their own right has widened, on average, by a matter of years.[60]

But it's not just that Americans are taking more time to become fully independent. Between 1970 and 2009, the average age at which Americans got married was delayed by five years, and between the mid-1970s and 2002 the percentage of twenty-one- to forty-five-year-olds who were married fell from nearly three in four to fewer than half.[61] By 2007, fewer than one-third of the nation's high-school senior girls thought that marriage was crucial to a life well lived.[62] Moreover, more Americans choose today not to have children until later in life: between the mid-1970s and today, the number of women between the ages of twenty-five and twenty-nine without children grew from 30 to 45 percent.[63]

Now not all households comprise married couples, and the prevalence of two-parent homes has also withered quite notably.[64] Much to the chagrin of the nation's conservatives, attitudes on sex have evolved. In the early 1960s, for example, 86 percent of married women responding to a Gallup poll indicated that it was not all right for a woman to have prenuptial sexual relations with a man—even one whom she knew she was going to marry.[65] But that attitude has since been turned on its head: today an increasing percentage of both men and women have had several sexual partners before taking their vows.[66]

Taken together, what now seems clear is that the period when young Americans float between outright reliance and utter independence has become a rite of passage.[67] A growing portion of Americans spend years "searching" for themselves. They bounce from job to job, and career to career. They cycle through a series of intimate relationships. They push off marriage and child rearing. And so, rather than following the model framed in *The Graduate*, we've evolved to accept a different norm—one more accurately depicted by Lena Dunham's cohort in *Girls*, where a group of college graduates move to Brooklyn and flail about in a sort of non-Amish Rumspringa.

This brings us to the prevalence throughout the United States of broken marriages and single parents. It was once considered scandalous to break the bonds of matrimony by choice, but now, with the near ubiquity of no-fault divorces, Americans end marriages that, a generation ago, likely would have persisted unhappily.[68] Divorce, which claimed one in six marriages in 1940, grew to end one in four in 1965 and one in two by 1975.[69] It has led to a sea change in our expectations of childbearing.

At the peak of the Second Wave, in the early postwar era, a stigma was generally attached to raising a child out of wedlock. But today, the rise in single-parent households has made the absence of a father or mother much more common. The percentage of all births to unmarried women grew from 3.8 percent in 1940 to one-third in 1999.[70] Between the early 1980s and the early 2010s, the percentage of births that occurred outside of marriage grew from 17 to 41.[71] Maybe most striking, in the period immediately following the Second World War, roughly 50 percent of American households had children—but by 2020, that number is slated to fall to 25 percent.[72]

Viewed collectively, changes in the role of women, the sanctity of marriage, the process of adolescence, the permissibility of divorce, and the proliferation of single-parenthood mark a veritable revolution in American family life. No consensus has formed on what it means: some see progress, others an abomination. But what's undeniable is that the lives we live at home have been affected dramatically. And the upheaval in this element of American life is a crucial feature of the Third Wave.

The three categories explored above don't cover all the changes evident in a brief history of the last several decades. For one, they don't delineate how advances in medicine and public health have lengthened and improved the quality of our lives. But it's clear that American society has undergone such a broad litany of changes that the real challenge isn't in drilling down on any individual item in particular, but in understanding how they have come together. Regardless of your opinion of any given development—the left's embrace of new family arrangements and aversion to economic inequality, the right's continuing embrace of the free market and concerns about decaying social mores—any comprehensive understanding of American society today must acknowledge the breadth of the alteration.

Before moving on, let's recognize at least one important caveat. As anyone who has been to an ocean beach knows, waves, the central metaphor of the Tofflers' grand theory, rarely emerge in any sort of neat progression.[74] And true to form, even after the Second Wave crested in the 1950s, First Wave society remained in much of rural America. The same sorts of overlap occurred decades later as the Third Wave began to crest over the Second—a process that continues today. Lewis Mumford, an early twentieth-century scholar who used waves to describe changing patterns of American life decades before the Tofflers, wrote in the 1920s that "the movement of population is not from farm-village to industrial town, to financial metropolis; the migrations rather come as successive waves, and while one wave recedes as the next comes foaming in, the first nevertheless persists and mingles with the second as an undertow."[75]

The enduring truth of Mumford's statement is plain again today. We don't all make our living from a corporate cubicle. Not every family has abandoned the one-breadwinner, two-parent norm of the 1950s. And not every aspect of American life has opened new opportunities. In fact, more recent literature has documented that as race and ethnicity have become less potent in determining how high any individual can climb up the ladder to the American Dream, education has emerged in their place to separate, in many cases, the wheat from the chaff; those of all races and ethnicities who progress further toward an advanced degree are now empowered to achieve even greater rewards than earlier generations with similar degrees.[76]

Setting that qualification aside, what's clear now is that the emergence of Third Wave society will be understood in the annals of history as the signature change of the second half of the twentieth century. Much as we're inclined to focus today on the effect of one change or another, the most remarkable element is how the changes have uprooted the foundations that girded life just a few generations ago.

3

THE CHINATOWN BUS
EFFECT

In the late 1990s, several Chinese-American businessmen—each owning separate going concerns that dotted Chinatowns throughout the Northeast—had fallen into the habit of shuttling their employees between various storefronts in Boston, New York, Philadelphia, and D.C. They had all run into the same frustration: the commute was terrible. The cheapest way to ferry an employee from Manhattan's Chinatown to its counterpart in Washington required her to catch a subway from Canal Street to the grungy Port Authority Bus Terminal in midtown, wait for a Greyhound motor coach, endure the ride down the New Jersey and Maryland turnpikes, navigate through the forlorn bus station tucked behind the capital's Union Station, and then catch a cab to the neighborhood just east of the White House. There had to be a better way.

Several of the businessmen decided, separately, to establish alternatives of their own. Their business plans were surprisingly simple: each bought a few used buses on the cheap and began running curbside service between Chinatowns throughout New England and the Mid-Atlantic.[1] The old beaten-up coaches weren't luxurious—but the direct routes cut hours off the trip and cost a fraction of the Greyhound fare. And while the "Chinatown Bus" didn't initially attract a wide range of customers, it eventually began to draw riders in search of adventure and a cheap ticket.

The secret of the Chinatown Bus's success wasn't particularly well hidden, even as rumors swirled that the proprietors operated at a loss. From the consumer's perspective, the rickety old coaches represented a better, cheaper way to get from one point to another. The service addressed an inefficiency in the market by eliminating hassle, craziness or nonsense—what is termed *mishigas* in Yiddish—from the journey. Soon enough the Chinatown Bus became something of an institution: those willing to forgo the luxury of Greyhound, Amtrak, or an expensive flight on the Delta Shuttle chose a quick service offered at a very low price.

In the annals of business-school textbooks, the story of the Chinatown Bus isn't particularly noteworthy. And what happened in the years that followed was fairly typical: after it became clear that sufficient demand existed for more convenient point-to-point curbside service, a host of other coach operators entered the market to compete with—and sometimes displace—their Chinese-American brethren.

But no matter how ordinary, the story offers an analogy for the composite effect of the Third Wave. The genius of the new commuter service, beyond its low price, was that it reduced the hassle of getting from one specific corner in New York to a counterpart in Washington. For each commuter, the bulk of the *mishigas* wasn't contained in the main journey—it was wound up in getting to and from each terminus. Would you need to take a subway to a bus terminal, and then take a cab once the bus dropped you off? Or could you sit in a single seat that took you from the grocery store across the street from your apartment to a drugstore a block from your destination?

By some measure, the idea that modern life is relatively free from hassle conflicts with our popular perception. More often we hear people complain that things have only gotten *more* complicated—that the simple life of *Leave It to Beaver* has fallen victim to progress. But beneath that conventional narrative is another, more important revelation: the things we *need* to do in order to get at the things we *want* to possess have successively been stripped away. And that marks the quintessential difference between life in a Second Wave society and the patterns that have emerged while surfing the Third.

In ways that were impossible to imagine in the early postwar era, we've been empowered to slice through the *mishigas*, and home in on what speaks to our particular taste. New Yorkers can get from their Chinatown to another without having to wend through the city subway system, bus terminals, and whatever else was once typical of the commute. That's been transformative not only because so much of what we want is more accessible today; it's been a revelation because, as we'll see, without having to deal with so much hassle, our opportunity horizons have widened considerably.

In at least one context, the effect seems entirely obvious: the digital revolution. The technological breakthroughs of the last several decades—the steady stream of improvements propelling us from snail mail to fax machines and from bunny ears to fiber-optic cable—have upended how we send and receive information. When considered in conjunction with the new ease with which goods and services from the far corners of the globe can be accessed, there are few better examples of progress trumping hassle.

Many of us may now take our newfound opportunities for granted, but it's not hard to discern how much things have changed. *Leave It to Beaver* characters intent on staying current would have had a handful of ways to keep up with the news. They might have been able to watch a program like *The Huntley-Brinkley Report* on NBC—but only if no one else had claimed the family television at the appointed time. Or they might have chosen to make a close read of the local paper—though, for lack of space, no publication could afford to give too much coverage to any single story. And so, beyond tapping into a few alternative possibilities—radio reports or weekly newsmagazines—those in search of more depth or breadth would have been compelled to head down to the local library, which, even then, would have had limited selection of additional periodicals.

The digital revolution has broken through the barriers that once limited our access to the news. June Cleaver's would-be grandchildren would now be able to watch any one of dozens of news channels broadcast from around the world, or stream any they miss over the Internet. They would be able to read the local newspaper if they liked—but if not, they could browse Web sites, blogs, and other reports on the Web. And should they miss a news report on the radio, they would be able to podcast it, listening through their mobile phones on the way home from school.

Changes in the way we consume news comprise only one sliver of the Chinatown Bus effect's impact. Two generations ago, a whole family was likely to gather around the television after dinner to watch *The Ed Sullivan Show,* a variety program targeting several audiences simultaneously. Everyone watched the same thing because each television set only received a handful of channels. Like the old Greyhound bus, the network executives shaping their prime-time lineups were compelled to capture a whole range of demographics with one uniform product.

Today, a family looking to relax isn't nearly so limited. Not only are there more televisions per household, but tablets, smartphones, and the like mean there are more screens across the board. Maybe even more important, there's a whole new universe of channels and networks generating content for much smaller niches. Consider how stark the change has been: on the day before John F. Kennedy's assassination in 1963, *The Beverly Hillbillies,* which was then the nation's top-rated television program, was watched in close to a third of the country's homes. But by 2010, *American Idol,* the nation's top-rated show, had a viewership of less than a tenth of all homes with a television set.[2] That's not a reflection of *American Idol*'s popularity so much as it is an indication that new programming has balkanized the television market.

The range of contemporary media choices would have been hard to imagine when Ed Sullivan dominated the airwaves. In 2010, there were almost 600 cable television channels, over 2,200 broadcast television stations, more than 13,000 radio stations, over 20,000 magazines, 255 million Web sites, and 26 million blogs on the Internet.[3] Most televisions hookups offered viewers scores of options, and because more and more viewers have begun to use DVR and on-demand services like TIVo to watch their favorite shows, we aren't even limited to what's playing when we want to be entertained.[4]

As powerful as the expansion of media has been in widening the options available to the average American, the world of software has been that much more revolutionary. Google, almost by itself, has sliced through the hassle that once impeded our ability to pinpoint particular bits of data. No longer do we have to trudge to the library and pull out a volume of the *Reader's Guide to Periodical Literature* to find an article detailing the electoral landscape in the panhandle of Michigan; with a few keystrokes from our living room couch we can call up every article ever written on the subject.

The advent of social networking has only served to press the point further. As Eli Pariser recently argued in *The Filter Bubble,* without our even knowing it, many software companies have found ways to predict the information we want and provide it to the exclusion of everything else.[5] As a further convenience (of sorts), the previous searches need not be related; it's now possible, for example, to associate our political sensibilities with our taste in restaurants and alcohol. As the Web site Buzzfeed highlighted during the run-up to the 2012 presidential election, the Obama and Romney campaigns were able to discern that Facebook users who "liked" Cracker Barrel's feed were highly likely to vote for the

Republican, while those who "liked" Jamba Juice were more likely to prefer the incumbent.[6]

The same trend can be discerned in what's happened in the world of advertising. As the *New York Times* recently noted, "Not so long ago, [companies buying Web ads] simply bought ad spaces based on a site's general demographics and then showed every visitor the same ad, a practice called 'spray and pray.' Now marketers can aim just at their ideal customers—like football fans who earn more than $100,000 a year, or mothers in Denver in the market for an S.U.V.—showing them tailored ads at the exact moment they are available on a specific Web page."[7]

The combined effect is clear: digitization has narrowed the chasm separating what we *want* from what we can *get*. Like the Chinatown Bus, technology is cutting through the hassle that once made it difficult for us to access information we desire. Now that we've been given the tools to zoom right to the news report, cable channel, or advertisements that line up with our individual tastes, we have the room to make more exacting choices.

As with the Third Wave, the Chinatown Bus effect hasn't simply been manifested in the digital realm—it's had a broad impact on the bricks-and-mortar world as well. That's plainly evident in the evolving patterns of how we shop. Consider, for example, how my mother's excursions as a child differ from those of my daughters.

In mid-1950s Cincinnati, when Mom needed a new article of clothing—or, more likely, when Meemaw (as my grandmother was known to her grandchildren) thought Mom's wardrobe warranted something new—they would drive down to one of the city's centrally located department stores. It wasn't an unusually arduous routine—but it wasn't seamless either. Once they'd parked, my grandmother would lead Mom through the various departments until they'd found the few racks of clothing appropriate to my mother's age and keen to my grandmother's taste. And then, like nearly every mother and daughter pairing, they'd argue about which outfits my grandmother was willing to purchase.

The story of those old shopping trips is anything but extraordinary. Mothers and daughters, let alone all parents and their children, still bicker about what the adults are willing to buy; it's an American rite of passage. What distinguishes the stories my mother remembers today is what shoppers had to trudge through to find the clothing they desired. Mom and Meemaw would walk through other departments and pass by other racks, each geared to a different market of shoppers. And only once they'd found their way to the appropriate racks could they begin to choose an outfit.

That routine was, by and large, the rule for most shoppers. During the early postwar era, stores geared to serve a variety of disparate consumers tended to congregate in the same area. Shillito's and its competitors around Cincinnati's Fountain Square served multiple demographics in the metropolitan area. It didn't matter if you were wealthy or middle class, Jewish, Catholic, or Protestant: as in other cities and towns throughout America, when you needed a new outfit, you headed downtown. Everyone was walking through racks of clothes being marketed to different kinds of people.

To be sure, it's not that America's commercial districts were idyllic melting pots. In most cases conventions, if not laws, kept the public balkanized—racial prejudice, class distinctions, ethnic and religious tensions often prevented different pockets of society from getting too cozy. But that shouldn't divert us from recognizing the point that downtown Cincinnati, like its counterparts across the country, served as a commercial focal point for a broad cross section of the local population. Even if you weren't sifting through the same racks of apparel, you inevitably walked among people who lived outside the bubble of your particular neighborhood.

Then suburbanization altered the landscape. As cars allowed

Americans to migrate out into the "crabgrass frontier," a term Columbia historian Kenneth Jackson once used to describe the new bedroom communities popping up outside city centers, the shopping patterns that had defined my mother's childhood disappeared.[8] New neighborhoods began to boast Main Streets of their own, obviating the need for residents to go downtown. In the decades that followed, outdoor shopping strips, enclosed malls, and big-box stores emerged as the nation's primary retail outlets.[9] The newer venues offered consumers the opportunity to shop without having to sort through racks geared for *other* demographics—it cut down the hassle of searching for a new outfit.

Years later Chris Rock would joke that in every town in America there are two malls: "they've got the white mall, and the mall where the white people *used* to go."[10] To an uncomfortable degree, Rock got it right. For one thing, the sheer volume of shopping centers—the immediate threat to downtown commercial districts—exploded. Between 1957 and 1976, the number of malls in the United States grew nearly nineteen times over.[11] And each individual strip tended to cater to a specific demographic, carving the *mass* market—a defining feature of Second Wave society—into the nichified parts that populate the Third.

Princeton sociologist Doug Massey, writing with two colleagues in 2009, put what was happening in the world of commerce in context. Noting that the transition that saw African-Americans move en masse from the rural south into the nation's big cities—a shift now known as the Great Migration—coincided with major upheavals in the residential patterns of American life, he differentiated between two effects. On a macro level, Massey argued, the nation had become less segregated because, as the statistics indicated, whites and blacks had come to occupy the same metropolitan regions. On a micro level, he determined, the Great Migration actually had the opposite effect. Americans had become *more* seg-

regated, as whites moved to the suburbs and blacks became isolated in the inner cities.

But, as Massey and his colleagues later noted, the story didn't
end there. More recently, census data revealed that socioeconomic separation—segregation along the lines of class—has begun
to overtake the racial divides that define much of American history: "Whereas the average poor family lived in a tract that was
14 percent poor in 1970, the percentage had doubled to 28 percent
in 1990." A similar sorting has played out at the other end of the
spectrum; wealthier and more impoverished Americans are less
likely to come into contact with one another on a regular basis.[12]

More recently, the swirl of digitization has merged with the long-
term trend toward geographic sorting to drive the Chinatown Bus
effect even further. In a throwback to the days of mail-order cata-
logs, online retail has chipped away at our need to leave the house
at all. Why go to the mall (let alone downtown) when Zappos will
send you any shoes you like? Why depend on the connoisseur running
the liquor store around the corner when better-quality wines from a
more extensive selection are available through a discounter online?

The combined effect has been to incubate a set of commercial
patterns that are entirely different from those that defined postwar
America. As Claritas, a firm that aims to subdivide the American
marketplace into niches, has noted, the number of discrete categories designed to define the various American consumer markets has
climbed from a mere forty in the 1970s to sixty-seven in 2005.[13] My
daughters, when they come of age, may fight just as much with their
parents about what they'd like us to buy them as my mother did with
Meemaw. But it will be easier for them to find things that suit their
tastes. Never before has it been easier to shop for exactly what you
want, when you want it, and with a minimum of hassle. Never before
have we had such expansive opportunities to satisfy materialistic
cravings.

Shopping may be one of the more identifiable features of American life, but it's hardly the most important. What's remarkable is that the Chinatown Bus effect has moved well beyond the rhythms of commerce, and into the sphere of intimacy. The nation's evolving view of homosexuality offers the most compelling evidence. The once widespread propensity to dismiss gays and lesbians as deviants forced generations of men and women into the closet. Fearful that they would be ostracized, or worse, many Americans lived large portions of their lives in a charade, letting their true identity emerge only in the shadows, if at all.

They were right to be fearful: the environment that prompted Americans to suppress or hide their identity included vile elements of hate and anger. If it hadn't been so uncomfortable, and frequently dangerous, to be identified as gay in previous generations, more men and women might have felt, as many do today, empowered to come out of the closet. But as recently as 1987, a majority of Americans believed that school boards should have the right to fire a teacher simply for having been discovered to be homosexual.

A quarter century later, the percentage of Americans who still believe homosexuality sufficient grounds to fire a teacher has dropped to little more than a fifth. More remarkable still, white evangelical Protestants, 73 percent of whom had believed that school boards should be able to fire homosexual teachers in 1987, have abandoned that view by half.[14] The nation's shifting view of marriage has been even more dramatic: in 2003–2004, less than a third of Americans supported gay marriage, and nearly 60 percent were outright opposed. By the time President Obama announced his support for marriage equality in 2012, a plurality were expressing support for the right of two Americans of the same gender to wed.[15]

By some measure, the movement for homosexual rights is unique, and deserves to be considered a standalone project. But by another, the nation's embrace of LGBT equality reflects the same trend defined by the Chinatown Bus effect. The institutions and norms that prevented Americans from zeroing in immediately on what they wanted (in this case an opportunity to live their sexuality) has been broadly stripped away. Without a doubt, the burden of shame and prejudice that spurred generations of gay Americans into the closet hasn't been eradicated. But the norms of life in Third Wave society are vastly more accepting, as evidenced by the It Gets Better Project, which has collected over fifty thousand online videos to support adolescents being harassed for their sexual orientation.[16]

While the changing acceptance of homosexuality in American society provides the most dramatic evidence, it's only one example of the Chinatown Bus effect's impact on intimacy. Rising divorce rates and the wide spread of single-parent homes suggest that the taboo conferred on those who deviated from the Cleaver family model has dissipated significantly. Americans stuck in dysfunctional relationships today are more likely to get out and move on. And taken together, these changes suggest something even more profound: the social conventions that acted as an extra barrier separating individuals from what they wanted—limiting each individual's landscape of opportunity—have experienced a massive erosion.

To what effect? You might have expected that greater freedom would have led to greater social diversity. But as Massey found with the Great Migration, the effects have been more nuanced. It turns out that as the strictures that limited the choices Americans had in whom to marry have worn away, we've sought out intimacy with people who fit our profiles more exactly. High-school dropouts, for example, now tend to end up with high-school dropouts; college graduates marry other college grads. That means that there's less educational intermarriage today. A study during in the early 1990s found that the odds a high-school graduate might marry a college graduate fell by a quarter between 1940 and the late 1980s.[17] Americans were four times more likely to marry someone with their same level of education in the early 2000s, up from three times four decades earlier.[18]

The same sort of evolution has also played out in other spheres. Extensive research by Harvard political scientist Theda Skocpol has revealed that the sorts of chapter-based organizations that were typical in the early postwar years—the Rotary Clubs and Elks Lodges that appealed to a broad cross section of the community— have been replaced by groups designed to appeal to smaller niches.[19] As Skocpol explained, mid-century organizations (as opposed to their contemporary counterparts) were, by and large, "fraternal or religious federations focused on celebrating brotherhood or sister- hood, or civic associations devoted to community service. . . . By the 1980s and 1990s, however, the goals of very large associations were much more narrowly instrumental or recreational."[20]

That shift offers a window into what has been an otherwise overlooked transformation. The membership organizations that were characteristic of Second Wave society demanded that adher- ents make long-term commitments. But as we've come to surf the Third Wave, that style of membership has begun to dissipate.[21] Two new patterns have emerged in its place: we now join local associa- tions established to pursue narrowly tailored purposes that, once accomplished, leave the organization without a mission. And to the extent that we join longer-term political causes, we tend to send checks to professionals working the issue from offices in Washing- ton, rather than participate in any integral way.

For example, instead of joining the Kiwanis Club's evolving efforts to improve our local communities, we're more likely now to sign up for a group designed to champion the paving of more bike lanes or to lobby against cuts to the state education trust fund. Because those efforts are often short-lived, the institutions that incubated deep connections have given way to more ephemeral relationships. The shift is most clearly reflected in the statistical profile of American membership: the sheer breadth of voluntary organizations has grown from fewer than six thousand in 1959 to more than twenty-two thousand in 1990. At the same time, the size of individual organizations has plummeted to a mere tenth of what it once was.[22]

In *Coming Apart,* the iconoclastic scholar Charles Murray offered a reflection that illustrated the very phenomenon Skocpol demonstrated through statistical analysis. Describing the small town of Newton, Iowa, where Murray grew up in the 1960s, he noted that local executives—many of whom worked at Maytag's nearby headquarters—had joined local organizations as a matter of course. A half century later, "fewer executives showed up at the local Rotary or Kiwanis Club meetings, and they were less likely to serve on civic boards of charitable drives. Their spouses were not as active in Newton's school affairs and church affairs."[23] But that did not necessarily reflect diminished civic commitment. In places all around the country, the same people who might once have been pillars of a town's nonprofit community have been pulled toward different sorts of organizations, many of which simply don't establish the same sorts of local roots.

There's a technological element to this story. Social networking sites like Facebook and Twitter have more recently made it possible for Americans to benefit from collective action without even shaking hands with their peers. Simply click on a Web site, send a small sum through PayPal, and you've joined a global association focused exclusively on a single niche. Angry at the proposal to build a power plant near the local high school? Sign an online petition. No longer do you need to work the channels of an existing bureaucracy, or go door to door for signatures; you can build the infrastructure required to promote a cause without much effort at all—even if it vanishes a second later or fails to achieve its goals.[24]

We've been empowered in nearly every aspect of our lives to move past many of the burdens that once prevented us from pursuing our personal interests and concerns. Americans of all stripes have been given the license to abandon the relationships that don't interest them for those that do; we've been given the opportunity to pick and choose the relationships we most want to maintain. And that brings us to the most significant evidence of the China-town Bus effect: the transformation of the local neighborhood.

In September 2003, *New York Times* columnist David Brooks published a long piece in *The Atlantic* magazine exploring an odd disconnect between what Americans said and how they actually behaved. Brooks had noticed that while we paid lip service to the benefits of diversity, Americans were often choosing to make "strenuous efforts to group themselves with people who [were] basically like themselves." In theory we were drawn to the idea of mixing with other people—but when push came to shove, we fre-quently demurred. That phenomenon, Brooks claimed, was play-ing out in all sorts of ways. As he wrote, describing a phenomenon he'd noticed in the communities around Washington where pro-gressives and conservatives tended to live in separate, if similar, pockets of suburbia: "If you asked a Democratic lawyer to move from her $750,000 house in Bethesda, Maryland to a $750,000 house in Great Falls, Virginia, she'd look at you as if you had just asked her to buy a pickup truck with a gun rack and shove chewing tobacco in her kid's mouth."

The effect, Brooks claimed, created parallel universes of homo-geneity. In a region where you might have expected a mélange of different Americans living in close proximity, residents chose to congregate among neighbors on the same political and cultural wavelength. The same pattern wasn't limited to the nation's capi-tal. Neighborhood by neighborhood, America wasn't embracing the legacy of Martin Luther King's "I Have a Dream" speech; it was becoming more intensely monolithic. Brooks asserted, "The

United States might be a diverse nation when considered as a whole, but block by block and institution by institution it is a relatively homogenous nation."[25]

Several years later, a veteran journalist named Bill Bishop took Brooks's observations a step further. He had noticed a similar trend during a move from Kentucky to Austin, Texas. When he and his wife began their search for a new home, he noted that they had inadvertently chosen one of the few sections of town where most residents shared their progressive worldview. And then he realized it had been no accident; the cultural landscape had, without being explicit, provided clues that made clear what kind of people were living in each discrete area. In Travis Heights, the part of Austin where they eventually decided to settle, the grafittied coffee houses, funky jewelry shops, and beat up old Volvos had given the neighborhood away.

Curious about whether something similar was happening elsewhere, Bishop enlisted the help of a retired University of Texas sociologist named Robert Cushing. What they uncovered is a telling consequence of the Chinatown Bus effect. Using presidential election return data, they discovered that progressives and conservatives were finding ways to congregate separately to a degree that hadn't been possible before. Little more than a third of American counties had voted overwhelmingly (with a margin of twenty points or more) for either Gerald Ford or Jimmy Carter in 1976; almost two-thirds of the nation's counties had been more or less competitive. A little more than a quarter century later, when John Kerry was challenging George W. Bush for the White House, the percentage of noncompetitive counties had grown to nearly 60 percent. An additional quarter of the nation's population had sorted itself into areas where one political liturgy prevailed. And that suggested that a much smaller slice of the population was living with any real exposure to people on the other side of the political divide.[26]

As Bishop and Cushing dug deeper, they discovered that same phenomenon—which they dubbed the "Big Sort"—playing itself out in other ways. For example, local churches once collected a diversity of believers, but younger adherents more frequently sought out houses of worship that spoke to their particular spiritual tastes. What's more, Americans were becoming less inclined to tolerate those who didn't share their point of view. One recent study has found that nearly a fifth of those who use social networks like Facebook have blocked, "unfriended," or hidden a contact based on a political disagreement.[27] It wasn't just, as Eli Pariser articulated, that corporations were manipulating what comes up in our news feeds and ad spaces. Empowered with the opportunity to connect with people who reflect our values and outlook, we've become more microscopically homogenous amid a sea of diversity.

In the mid-1990s, well before David Brooks had begun to note how neighborhoods were becoming monolithic and Bill Bishop had revealed the full extent of the Big Sort, a longtime editor of *Governing* magazine, Alan Ehrenhalt, published a book on an underappreciated shift in ordinary American life. Tracing changes in three separate neighborhoods of Chicago—one settled predominantly by working-class whites, another situated in the heart of the South Side, and a third in the more affluent suburbs—he noted one crucial similarity. During the 1950s, "day-to-day commerce was based on relationships—on habit, not on choice."[28] But by the mid-1990s, the reality Ehrenhalt described had been upended. A society coming to be defined by the Third Wave was awash in so much choice that the relationships that once circumscribed ordinary American life could be abandoned for something better almost as an afterthought.[29]

Ehrenhalt, Bishop, Brooks, and Murray all used their own terminology, but they were all describing the Chinatown Bus effect. The changes in America as we've transitioned from a Second to a Third Wave society have given individuals a chance to bypass the *mishigas* that might otherwise have suffused their daily routines. Institutions and limitations that compelled them to zigzag to get what they wanted have been cast aside. And without the same degree of hassle, new horizons have opened up: Americans can shop more discerningly for what they want; they can associate more freely with whomever they like; they can live more exclusively among the neighbors they prefer. Each individual American now has much more choice in crafting the life that he or she wants.

That then solves half of our mystery: by expanding our individual horizons, contemporary life provides us with much greater *opportunity*. The element that remains open to question is what we each *want*. What motivates us to select one option among the many now available? If our newfound capacity to sidestep *mishigas* has opened up new worlds of opportunity, which among that bevy of new choices are we likely to select? These are the questions we'll turn to next.

4

THE BIG CLIMB

"Are things better today than they were four years ago?"
That question has framed every recent first-term president's campaign for reelection, either as the mantra of
the popular incumbent, or as the indictment issued by a well-
positioned challenger. It's a question that gets right to the heart
of things: as we enter the ballot box, we have to decide whether,
on balance, things have gotten better or worse. And because it's so
concise—because it boils a whole range of issues down to a single
point of contention—it's worth asking the same question of longer
time frames. Do we believe that life in America is better today than
it was ten years ago? Or twenty? And how do things today compare
with the 1950s?

The preceding two chapters surveyed the upheavals of the postwar era. Whether you believe that changes like suburbanization or
globalization have been blessings or curses, the totality of transformation is overwhelming. What's less clear, however, is how those
changes have affected the trajectory of American life. As disruptive as the digital revolution (or the suburbanization of the American middle class, the embrace of gay marriage, or the Big Sort,
among others) has been, how have those trends, taken collectively,
changed our understanding of the good life? What do we most fear

today—particularly compared to the average American a few generations back? How have our hopes and dreams evolved?

As I've argued, despite evidence that the 1950s were far from
idyllic, the *Leave It to Beaver* era remains a paragon of American
history. Many of us believe that American life might improve if
only the norms that once kept things simple were reimposed. What
if we could take away the noxious stuff—the racism and sexism and
homophobia and poverty—and reenlist the optimism of the early
postwar years? Wouldn't it be better if Americans today were as
hardworking and conscientious as the Greatest Generation? Don't
we all want to re-create the cohesion of the Eisenhower years, only
with a few of the rougher edges shaved down?

The short answer to that last question is no—and unequivocally
so. Absent the blinders of nostalgia, there's no denying that life in
the United States has gotten better over the last several decades,
if often in ways we fail to appreciate.[1] Yes, there have been exceptions, as we've seen. But in the larger scheme, and despite the
widespread sense of pessimism, it's indisputable that the quality of
American life has improved.

Santayana is often quoted to the effect that those who fail to
learn the lessons of history are doomed to repeat its mistakes. The
truth is more nuanced. As societies overcome discrete challenges,
they tend to lose some in the rearview mirror. In some cases, as
with the civil rights movement, we celebrate those who strived to
overcome daunting hurdles even decades after their struggle. But
in other instances we've forgotten: now that children are inoculated against polio, for example, the disease rarely warrants a passing thought; now that the Soviet Union has fallen, the prospect of
nuclear apocalypse appears more distant.

For these reasons, any complete examination of American motivations demands a fuller understanding of the worries that defined
each generation. At any historical moment, what tragedies seem
likely to be lurking around the corner? What fears linger in the

recesses of the ordinary mind? Threats that are beyond our frame of reference today hovered over previous generations—even if the danger never came to pass. Not every kid contracted polio—but every parent was afraid. The Soviets never launched a nuclear warhead at the United States—but everyone knew that they might the day after next. As we try to get a better handle on how American desire has changed, we need to catalog both the fears that have faded from the American consciousness and those that have emerged in their place.

When delivering speeches in big lecture halls during the summer months, President Clinton often notes that if the air-conditioning failed, the audience would be shocked. It goes without saying in most of the United States that a large auditorium will be kept at a comfortable temperature. He goes on: "You would be stunned if the screen went out or the microphone failed or the lights went dark. You don't think about what it means to be drinking a glass of clean water. You know that you're not going to get sick."[2]

That level of comfort and security, which most Americans now take for granted, speaks to the most pervasive indication of how America's quality of life has changed: as John Kenneth Galbraith argued in the late 1950s—and as has become more apparent ever since— we've become the "Affluent Society."[3] The engine of America's newfound prosperity has surely been fueled by technological innovation. In an age of tablets, smartphones, and laptops, certain controls we once surrendered to big businesses, government, and bureaucracies—what to watch, read, and know, most notably—have been returned to us. Given that we Americans value liberty, we can revel in the fact that, of late, we have become much more independent.[4]

Beyond the technological revolution, our affluence has emerged from a panoply of more mundane improvements, many of which rarely receive proper notice. Our material affluence has been generated by the explosion of American productivity: there's more to enjoy today because what we want costs so much less to accumulate. And because our more basic needs are met by a more limited pool of labor, a greater proportion of the American workforce—most of whom, in previous eras, would likely have toiled on farms and assembly lines—have been empowered to earn their livings by satisfying more fleeting demands. The guy who once might have worked in a steel mill now earns a living making custom window treatments. The woman who once would have done backbreaking labor on the family farm now works in the relative comfort of a telemarketing call center. Say what you will about which job you'd prefer in a perfect world, two things are true: food and steel satisfy a more basic need than window treatments and customer service, and the latter two jobs are significantly less taxing and dangerous.

It wasn't always obvious that things would turn out this way. In fact, John Maynard Keynes, arguably the most influential economist of the twentieth century, predicted decades ago that gains in productivity would drive the expansion of leisure.[5] He worried about what the average worker would do with the extra time. But fortunately or not, we've never had to answer that question. On the whole, we've chosen to fill those additional hours with more work. As the nation's gross domestic product per capita doubled between 1960 and 2000, Americans actually began to spend *more* time at the office.[6]

As a result, American purchasing power has exploded. In the first decade of the nineteenth century, a manufacturing worker needed a half-hour's wages to buy a pound of bread and an hour for a half gallon of milk. By 1970, that was down to five and twelve minutes respectively.[7] And because our dollar goes so much further, we've developed a taste for new products and services. You no longer get a plain cup of coffee from a pushcart—you get a Starbucks latte with a shot of vanilla. You're no longer satisfied with a cape-style bungalow—you want a McMansion. Over the years middle-class life has gotten better and better: products that seemed like luxuries during the early postwar years have become standard fare. And as a result, accoutrements once reserved for the rich and famous have become increasingly pedestrian.

Even better, the blessings of American prosperity haven't been limited to the upper crust and those aspiring to get there. Earners at the lower rungs of the nation's income ladder have benefited as well. The percentage of Americans living beneath the "poverty line" fell precipitously, dropping from roughly 41 percent in 1949 to roughly 20 percent in 1963 and to little more than 15 percent even in the wake of the Great Recession that began during the last months of George W. Bush's administration.[8] Over that period, the working class's quality of life has only continued to improve: second cars, multiple televisions, bigger homes, less-expensive furniture, more exotic vacations. Many things that would have seemed extravagant in the immediate aftermath of the Second World War are much more typical, even among those with less financial security.

What's more, American affluence has spurred a broader upheaval in the nation's attitude toward money—a fact made most evident in the transformation of conventional attitudes towards debt. Once thought to be taboo—as recently as the period that immediately followed the Second World War, many considered it dishonorable to be found in arrears—we've since become much more comfortable spending tomorrow's earnings on today's comforts.[9] In 1974, household debt amounted to a mere $680 billion; by 2008, it had exploded to roughly $14 trillion.[10] And that speaks to something profound: Americans are frequently so confident in the future—the risk of destitution seems so remote—that they're willing to risk bankruptcy.

There are exceptions to the rule, and America's increasing affluence hasn't been without shortcomings. One need only read the *New York Times*'s 2013 profile of a homeless girl living in the Big

Apple to realize that many have been left out.[11] The discretionary income of many middle- and lower-income families, measured in real terms, has declined.[12] The three decades preceding the Great Recession of 2007 saw wages stagnate for full-time male workers, particularly those doing blue-collar work.[13] And retirement security remains a real worry for many Americans, even as few have embraced strategies that would help to finance the elderly lifestyle they dream of enjoying.

Nevertheless, in the aggregate it's almost impossible to deny that the goods that define the average American's material life have improved. The destitution that was so palpable to even middle-class adults who survived the 1930s and 1940s—the scenes described in *The Grapes of Wrath* and typical in the nation's Hoovervilles— have been pushed further to margins. So even while critics complain that we've become more materialistic and that prosperity has corrupted our underlying moral fiber, worries that were in the forefront of previous generations' minds have faded from contemporary focus.

Better *stuff* is hardly the only thing that has marked American affluence. Americans today are also safer than they've ever been. The fears lingering in the background of everyday life through the early postwar years—of both nuclear war and rampant street crime—have diminished. To a degree that would once have been a fantasy, many of us take our security for granted.

It's not that we've become immune to the threat of violence. Indeed, the threat of terrorism has become more palpable since the Twin Towers fell in 2001. The pervasive fear that compelled the authorities to shutter the Boston region in the aftermath of 2013's Marathon bombing speaks to the sense of vulnerability Americans still feel, particularly as pernicious ideas that were once kept safely offshore are now accessible across the sea of new digital media.

The specter of a random attack rarely escapes the rational mind—and for good reason.

Nevertheless, we ought to put our newfound sense of vulnerability in the proper perspective. Although jihadists menace our sense of security, it's difficult to equate the perception of our susceptability today with the danger evident during Cold War flashpoints like the Cuban missile crisis. Americans had good reason to be frightened when grainy videos of Osama bin Laden were rebroadcast repeatedly on cable news networks. But al Qaeda's capacity for destruction—to pinpoint a few choice targets—cannot be compared to Nikita Khrushchev's nuclear arsenal, which pointed thousands of warheads at America's metropolitan centers. Frightening as terrorism may be, the prospect of World War Three was, in practice, much more menacing.[14]

The diminution of danger doesn't end there. Domestic crime rates rose steadily from the mid-1960s through the late 1980s, becoming crucial determinants of the presidential elections of 1988 and 1992, when opposition to the death penalty virtually ruled candidates out of contention. As well-to-do Americans fled the nation's cities for the suburbs, the urban landscape became more terrifying, suggesting a sort of rampant lawlessness. And as drug abuse spread through the 1970s and 1980s, it wasn't entirely clear that the nation would ever emerge from the menace of criminality.

Since then, however, beginning really in the 1990s and extending for more than two decades, crime rates have fallen dramatically.[15] The worst of the nation's drug epidemics—that of crack cocaine—largely burned itself out even as the spread of methamphetamine abuse took hold in certain, mainly rural, pockets of the country. Many city neighborhoods that appeared as virtual wastelands have since been gentrified by middle-class families. While debate continues about why crime has fallen—conservatives usually cite higher incarceration rates, and progressives the combined effects of "community policing" and economic growth—what may be most remarkable is the fact that an issue that once seemed intractable has receded from the front page.[16] And that then speaks to what may be the truth: as with the nation's concerns about nuclear annihilation, the once pervasive fear of victimization has been diminished.

Despite our heightened affluence and security, neither indicates the most powerful improvement to American life. Breakthroughs in research labs around the country and the globe have been translated into an unprecedented boon to the health and longevity of the average citizen. Between 1900 and 2000, the life expectancy of a baby girl rose from forty-eight to seventy-nine.[17] And that's had an ever more profound effect on the way we map out our lives: we now expect, in most cases, to live to old age with a fair degree of physical independence.

Compare that expectation with the presumption of the early postwar period. Back then, it wasn't nearly so uncommon to be struck down in middle age. Today, many fewer people pass away in their prime. Mortality rates dropped by 60 percent between 1935 and 2010, driving down the day-to-day concern that we'll lose someone we love to an accident or an incurable disease.[18]

Two primary developments are responsible for the vast expansion of American longevity. First, those alive today are the unwitting beneficiaries of incredible advances in the field of public health (the bulk of which, it's worth noting, preceded the Second World War).[19] Breakthroughs fighting disease by improving clean water, sanitation, immunization, nutrition, education, and environmental preservation have combined to cut drastically the likelihood of premature death.[20] And here, to a greater degree than in most other realms of American life, our newfound prosperity has been hidden from common appreciation.

Consider how the routines of an archetypal middle-class family have changed since the 1950s. Back then, Mom and Dad would wake up to savor a leisurely cigarette in bed before waking the kids. (Cigarette smoking, which was later revealed as "the single greatest contributor to premature death," peaked in 1963.[21] Between 1972 and 2000, the decline in smoking contributed to a 51 percent decline in coronary heart disease.) Then Mom would head downstairs to the kitchen to whip up some breakfast, maybe with some white toast or cereal that had likely not been fortified with the micronutrients that are laced into today's food supply—ingredients that have virtually eliminated diseases like rickets, goiter, and pellagra.[22]

Dad would then head off to work, driving a car without a seat belt, air bags, antilock brakes, or a host of other technologies that have reduced highway fatalities. (The number of highway deaths in 2010 was the lowest of any year since 1949.)[23] At work, he would hop onto a line without all the safety improvements that are standard in industrial plants today—safety goggles, fire extinguishers, protective gloves, and handrails. (Between 1980 and 2000 alone, incidents of fatal occupational injury fell by roughly 40 percent.)[24]

And that points to the second development responsible for our expanded longevity—an advance best illustrated by the story of Dwight Eisenhower's 1955 heart attack. Upon finding the president in cardiac arrest, his physician recommended that the First Lady "snuggle" with Ike. He received no heart-specific drugs, nor any treatment to address his falling blood pressure. The vanguard of medical care just a few decades ago prescribed simple stillness and warmth to someone undergoing a major health crisis.

Today, almost any American suffering in the same circumstances—or in any number of other crises—has access to a whole world of improved interventions: lab tests, CT and PET scans, better nursing care, antibiotics, blood transfusions, 911 services, round-the-clock monitoring, organ donation, diuretics, angioplasty, stents, bypass surgery, artificial joints, radiation, defibrillators, and pacemakers are common almost everywhere across America. And that range of tools has made all of us less susceptible to medical conditions that would likely have taken our lives in an earlier era.

Together, this host of advances, taken in combination with the waterfront of other advances in modern care, spurred the *New York Times* to conclude that "medicine has advanced more since World War Two than in all of earlier history."[25] The statistics bear that conclusion out: the number of FDA-approved prescription medications had jumped from roughly 7,000 to more than 11,700; the five-year survival rate for children diagnosed with cancer grew from 58 to almost 80 percent between 1975 and 2005.[26] In addition, children born today benefit from recently discovered vaccines to many of history's most debilitating illnesses—not only polio, but chicken pox, two forms of hepatitis, measles, and mumps among them.[27]

Maybe most remarkable, while we haven't been able to find medical cures for many frightening illnesses—more than one million Americans are fighting HIV or AIDS today—most residents of the United States (including those without health insurance) now have *access* to medical care.[28] A complicated mélange of programs make expensive treatments available to many of those who would be unable to afford them. And while gaps still remain, the health-care reform law President Obama signed into law in 2010 promises to expand coverage even further.

Taken in isolation, the three remarkable sets of advances listed above—improvements to our prosperity, security, and longevity—might have transformed the rhythms of American life entirely on their own. Books and articles weighing their respective impacts continue to be the subject of debate and examination. But taken together, there's no question that the advances have helped to cement the transformation in the way Americans have come to understand the good life. Amid widespread expectations that we'll live to old age, we focus a great deal of our adult lives building a comfortable retirement. And if there's any doubt of just how powerfully we've reoriented our priorities, cast a discerning eye on the television commercials broadcast during any major sporting event.

By now, we barely register the scenes of fit, happy, well-to-do retirees fishing in the wilderness, visiting grandchildren, and traveling around Asia and Europe. But it's worth noting what a revolution the *idea* of a "golden age" represents in American life. In 1900, most men worked until their death. A half century later, a sixty-five-year-old was likely to be frail, often hobbled by a chronic or acute condition. Today, the broad majority of sixty-five-year-olds are sprightly enough to live another two or three decades with a fair degree of freedom and independence. Between 1950 and 2000, the percentage of elderly men who were retired grew from 50 to 80 percent.[29] For the first time in American history, an adult's mandate isn't simply to enjoy a productive career—it's to make it to the promised land of his or her senior years.

If nothing else, this is likely the most powerful indicator of just how much better American life has become. Having vanquished many of our earlier fears of premature death in a nuclear war, from an infectious disease, or at the hands of a neighborhood hooligan, many of us have shifted our worries from the present to the future. As never before, the question many Americans wake up to—excepting those who are struggling to enter or keep themselves among the ranks of the middle class—is less whether they'll do well enough now, and more whether they'll be able to save enough for later. That's not a tangential issue, and few Americans are saving as they should.[30] But as things go, that's a high-class concern—and certainly a good shot better than what kept adults up in the decade that followed the Great Depression and Second World War.

———

Around 1940, a young professor at Brooklyn College worked up the gumption to act on a growing frustration. The field of psychology, Abraham Maslow believed, had become too focused on addressing mental disorders. At a moment when most American adults had suffered the ravages of the 1930s and 1940s, he thought more mind ought to be paid to other end of the psychological spectrum. How, he wanted to know, did healthy Americans reach their fullest potential? What was it that had enabled the most successful among us, giants like Albert Einstein and Henry David Thoreau, to flourish?

In an attempt to draw research into those questions, Maslow published an article in which he unveiled what is now known as "Maslow's hierarchy of needs."[31] His theory posited that individual desires flow in rough sequential order: once more basic needs are satisfied, we move onto the next set of concerns; and if you keep ascending the hierarchy, you eventually reach what Maslow termed "self-actualization."

This basic premise makes intuitive sense. No one can survive without food, water, and shelter, so the drive to secure those more basic concerns comes before anything else. Those elements comprise the bottommost rungs of the ladder. But once those desires are sated, humans generally focus on the next set of cravings—the desire to achieve some level of safety (lest they fall back into needing food or shelter). From there, the rungs in the hierarchy became more ephemeral: with our bellies full and the risk of violence diminished, we begin to desire things such as recognition from our peers and the opportunity to express our creativity. Address those higher-level concerns and one can become, in Maslow's view, self-actualized.

While Maslow's influence within the field of psychology has ebbed in the years since his death—it's not entirely clear that the barriers to happiness can be addressed quite so sequentially, for one—the theory of a stepladder of desires remains a powerful tool for thinking about how society develops.[32] In particular, his hypothesis offers us a helpful way to interpret the vast improvements in the quality, length, and security of our lives. We have satisfied many of our most fundamental concerns, to the point that many American can focus on higher-level yearnings.

This is not to suggest that some Americans aren't trapped trying to meet their most basic needs. As Joel Berg, a senior fellow at the Center for American Progress, wrote recently, "Even before the worst of the economic downturn in 2008, 16.6 million American children lived in homes that couldn't afford enough food for their families."[33] Too many Americans remain homeless, and far too many, particularly through the Great Recession, found themselves without work.

But with those exceptions, the broader trend is clear: the prosperity, security, and longevity offered to those surfing the Third Wave have propelled us to higher-level concerns. To the degree that life has gotten better—that American society has benefited from a big step up the hierarchy of needs—we have a new series of hurdles to face.

It appears then that our *motives* have also been affected by the developments of the last several decades. The Chinatown Bus effect has expanded our horizons. But we also now want different things from what previous generations desired. With a better handle on how *motive* and *opportunity* have each evolved, we can begin to examine exactly where they intersect.

CONFORMITY COMES
FULL CIRCLE

More than two decades after MTV's *The Real World* sparked the creation of a whole new genre of "reality" television, reality-style competitions have become a staple of network and cable programming.[1] *Survivor, Top Chef, The Bachelor(ette)*, and *Project Runway* all trace the same basic arc. In the first few episodes, cast members begin to develop a comfortable rapport—but then something happens: someone refuses to wash the dishes or gets a little too friendly; two friends realize they're each the other's most capable opponent. Eventually, the spirit of competition butts up against the prevailing decorum. Personalities begin to clash, and someone invariably turns to the camera and throws down the climactic gauntlet: "Look, I came here to win, not to make friends . . ."

Of course, that's not the only element of contemporary television that's become cliché. It may not even be the most universal. Today, spliced into nearly every after-school special, public-service announcement, professional sports interview, and reality television series is a phrase so frequently invoked that few give it much thought. The admonition that "you just need to be yourself" is now more ubiquitous than catchphrases like "there's no such thing as a free lunch" and "think outside the box." But innocuous as it sounds, that simple phrase embodies a very specific ethos—and one that just may be the defining feature of contemporary American culture.

The need to "be yourself"—frequently uttered interchangeably with "just follow your heart" and "don't pay attention to what other people think"—has emerged as the preeminent way to endorse what many might term personal authenticity. Americans now celebrate, more than nearly anything else, an individual's capacity to resist the pressure to put on airs. You might be poor or lonely; you may have lost your job or your marriage. But what's important is that you not lose yourself. That's reflected in the personalities who have become our role models: Steve Jobs for steering Apple in its own direction; Paul Farmer for taking the road less traveled in Haiti; Aung San Suu Kyi for standing up to dictators in Burma. Our heroes remain steadfast in what they believe despite overwhelming pressure to change or back down.

That's why the struggle to "be yourself" resonates with television audiences. Amid the tension that develops between reality-show cast members, viewers are eager to see how people from different backgrounds will resolve their disagreements. How will the flamboyant restaurateur deal with the conservative Sunday school teacher? How will the hard-working truck driver handle the lackadaisical dilettante? As a writer in the *New York Times Magazine* wrote in November 2012 about what may be the most popular reality television series in history, "What 'Survivor' is really about is the inescapability of your being yourself, even when you have told yourself you can be someone different for 30 days."[2]

We should be careful about reading too much into any premise gleaned from a genre of television programming. The contrived dramas network executives use to drive up Nielsen ratings are not designed to reflect a true sense of reality. But the fact that "being who you are" has become synonymous with the American ideal— the fact that few of us, if anyone, think twice about whether we ought to hold "true to ourselves"—is remarkable. What specifically does it even mean to "be yourself"? Who else, in the end, could you possibly be?

It's tempting to argue that the aphorism is as vapid as it sounds— a throwaway tautology like "it is what it is." And maybe, in some cases, it's not meant to be more substantial. But examined more closely, our endorsement of authenticity speaks to something else. It suggests that we ought to listen to the voice from within, rather than accept received wisdom. It urges us, in clichéd form, to cut against the grain and to strike out on our own. The surest path to the good life demands that we cast aside the distracting influences of the outside world. Conformity, this particular creed suggests, runs counter to the American ideal.

Authenticity was not always the watchword of the American Dream. In fact, we can only imagine what a relief our celebration of individuality might have been to the group of scholars who fretted about America becoming a milquetoast nation during the 1950s. In those very early postwar years—during the Truman and Eisenhower administrations—David Riesman, William Whyte, and others sounded an alarm; future generations, they feared, were destined to be limp noodles.[3] To their way of thinking, it might seem a blessing that today, rather than becoming a nation beset by conformity, individualism has emerged as the country's abiding ethic.

It's less clear whether they would have believed you could have too much of a good thing. That was the issue that spurred Berkeley sociologist Robert Bellah to write *Habits of the Heart* roughly thirty years after *The Lonely Crowd*. Working with several colleagues, Bellah reached a very different conclusion: by the early 1980s, rather than projecting any eagerness to blend in, Americans seemed to be abandoning the ties that bound them together. Far from being too willing to conform, Americans seemed too eager to express their individualism.

It was a remarkable turnaround. Merely three decades after scholars feared that Americans were too attuned to the reactions of others, they now seemed to be more focused on "cultivat[ing] their own emotional gardens," as Johns Hopkins sociologist Andrew Cherlin would later describe Bellah's analysis.[4] The new ethic celebrated the authentic individuals who followed their own dreams— even if that frayed the ties of their communities. The admonition to be yourself had found its way, to Bellah's horror, into the center of American life.

Today we are left to consider where things stand yet another thirty years on. As we try to piece together how motive and opportunity have contributed to the transformation of American community, the final question we need to answer involves what exactly we each *want*. In the last chapter, we saw Americans take a big leap up Abraham Maslow's hierarchy of needs: because we're less focused on fulfilling our more basic demands, we've attained the freedom to focus on higher-level concerns. But that raises the issue of what the giant leap has meant for the battle between conformity and authenticity. Have we become more disposed to seek the approval of others, as seemed be the case in the 1950s? Or are we more inclined to seek our heart's desire despite what others might say?

The answer, we'll find, is both. Americans have always struggled, as Tocqueville noted more than a century ago, to balance competing impulses toward individualism and community, authenticity, and tolerance.[5] But more recently, we've been given the tools to satisfy both desires. How? To answer that question, we need to take a quick detour into the world of political science, where scholars have recently been able to unearth a deeper understanding of the connection between our everyday footing and our political desires.

A growing body of research now reveals that we tend to think about the relationship between politics and circumstance in the wrong order: it's not, as we tend to assume, that democracy begets prosperity as much as that greater affluence and security spur individuals to put different emphasis on disparate sets of desires. And that suggests that much as certain elements of the American character have remained constant through our history, the remarkable changes that have defined the last several decades may have also had an impact on what we want both from our government and, more broadly, from our interpersonal relationships.

Getting to the bottom of the relationship between governance and circumstance has been a central issue for University of Michigan professor Ronald Inglehart for several decades. His research has focused on which foundations offer the most fertile environment for freedom and the rule of law. To that end, Inglehart helped to devise, promote, and expand what has come to be known as the World Values Survey, a global opinion poll that for thirty years has compared personal attitudes against more traditional indicators such as economic growth and political stability.

Inglehart's work has rendered some remarkable conclusions. Maybe most important, it largely buttresses the anecdotal observation that was made so plain after Saddam Hussein was deposed in Iraq: representative government often takes hold only after a society has satisfied many of its citizens' more basic needs. Democracy doesn't emerge, as the Bush administration hoped, as the result of pressure from above; it's not a plug-and-play utility. Rather, representative government is more like a flower that needs to be nurtured before it blooms. And amid the sectarian conflagration that emerged in the aftermath of the American-led invasion, it was almost impossible to stand up the kind of dominion many of the operation's proponents had envisioned.

Specifically, Inglehart's analysis of World Values Survey data reveals that democracy is properly understood as a stop along a continuum that tracks a population's economic development. As he and his colleague Christian Welzel have argued, once basic concerns about safety and security are satisfied, societies develop an increasing taste for "choice, autonomy, and creativity."[6] By some measure, that insight can explain the broader sweep of American history. Another sociologist recently pointed out that as life in America has become more stable and prosperous, Americans have embraced "an individualistic view of family life that emphasizes personal growth."[7] And that shift was reflected in the progress of the most heroic story in twentieth-century American social history: our attitudes on race.

In 1972, when the Great Depression and the Second World War were fairly fresh in the public's mind, the portion of the country that opposed laws to ban interracial marriage—in effect, the percentage who believed a black man and a white woman should simply be allowed to get married—was just 63 percent. Think of it: at a moment when the tumult that had begun during the late 1960s was still front-page news, more than a third of Americans weren't sure that intermarriage should be legal. Since then, however, the nation's attitude has changed. In 2002, nine of every ten Americans believed there should be no legal prohibition preventing a loving mixed-race couple from getting married.

The same shift in attitude has been reflected in who has, in fact, gotten hitched: in 2008, 15 percent of marriages in the United States were between spouses of different races, a figure six times over the percentage in 1960.[8] The question is whether this wholesale evolution of American opinion—one that celebrated "choice and autonomy" unlike the previous bigotry—would have emerged without the growing prosperity of American life. We can hope so. But as the World Values Survey reveals, our improving circumstances almost surely played an important role. Had Americans been preoccupied with a different set of worries, the iniquities that prompted the civil rights movement might well have been left unaddressed, as they had been for decades before.

Demographic snapshots bear out this distinction, with people living in more and less prosperous circumstances embracing entirely different political agendas even beyond fiscal concerns. In the early 1990s, a sociologist at the University of Virginia named James Davison Hunter coined the term "culture war" to describe a deepening cleavage in the United States.[9] The residents of wealthier neighborhoods, he noted, were generally more supportive of efforts to expand opportunities for what Inglehart would call "self-expression." Those in households further down the socioeconomic ladder were generally focused on a different set of political concerns. And conflicting points of view on a range of issues—abortion and flag burning among them—seemed to track the demographic spread.

No one, including Hunter, has argued a one-for-one connection: plenty of wealthy Americans oppose marriage equality and abortion rights, for example, and large swaths of the working class support gay marriage and the right to choose. But as with issues of divorce and abortion, the general trend holds: demands for new rights typically emerge from pockets of society that feel less vulnerable on more basic issues.[10] And so, to get a comprehensive understanding of how American motivations have changed, we must gauge how the "big climb" has laid the groundwork for us to make new choices. To begin, let's stick with the same basic category: what factors determine who the typical American chooses to marry?

The kitschy song sung by the matchmaker in *Fiddler on the Roof,* the popular musical depicting the struggles of a Jewish family in early twentieth-century Russia, could well be the refrain for any of the online dating services that have become popular a century later. Indeed, Americans are now more prone than ever to rely on the expertise of strangers to find a life mate. EHarmony, one of the more heavily publicized contemporary matchmaking services, claims to use sophisticated criteria to determine who is best matched with whom. And as with the matchmaker eager to find a good mate for one of the daughters in *Fiddler on the Roof,* the hope is for compatibility that will ground a lasting relationship.

Beyond the fact that one is done in person, and the other online, there is another distinction between the matchmaking services of the early twentieth century and today: while the matches of couples brought together a century ago were geared toward the practical, the hope today is that a match will be satisfying. It's not that breadwinning isn't important today to some potential spouses, or that parenting acumen holds no allure. But today Americans want "chemistry." They not only expect a partner—they want a soul mate.

What may be most remarkable about that transformation is that our contemporary impulse to expect love to go hand in hand with marriage is a fairly recent phenomenon. Until the early twentieth century—and, for many couples, until decades later—marriage was more about material compatibility.[11] At a lower rung on the hierarchy of needs, the value of a marriage isn't romance; it's whether the partnership will provide stability. Will a prospective husband make a salary sufficient to support a family? Will a prospective wife be capable of raising well-balanced children? It's not that sexual attraction wasn't an issue in earlier eras—it was just a more peripheral concern. As Tom Brokaw described the marriages of the Greatest Generation: "These relationships were forged when the world was a dangerous place and life was uncertain. Couples were forced to confront the profound emotions—and passions—that come with the reality of separation and the prospect of death. If their relationship could withstand the turmoil and strain of the war years, it should only get better after that."[12]

Then something changed. Andrew Cherlin, maybe the leading scholar of marriage in America today, puts it this way: "Beginning in the 1960s people began to judge the success of their marriages not by the material standard of living or how well they raised children but rather by whether they felt their personal needs and desires were being fulfilled." No longer fearful that life outside matrimony would leave them as vulnerable as they might have been during previous eras, Americans wanted something more from their most intimate relationships: personal satisfaction. Marriage became as much about romance as it was about partnership—more about sparks than stability.[13]

It was a striking, if underappreciated, change. But the world's marketers have not only noticed the difference—they've adapted to it. The proportion of articles in women's magazines that offered advice on how to spice up the romantic element of a woman's marriage grew from a third in the first part of the twentieth century to two-thirds by the 1970s.[14] And as we've seen, divorce rates grew for similar reasons: individuals who two or three generations earlier might not have expected their partner to fulfill their romantic desires began more frequently to exit the marriage and try again with someone else.[15]

The evolution of American desire wasn't limited to the matrimonial sphere. Something similar has become evident in the nation's spiritual life. Much as it's common practice now to decry the loss of religion in contemporary American life—right-wing radio loves to complain about the supposed "war on Christmas"—the truth is that the United States has actually remained remarkably religious over time: a Pew Forum on Religion and Public Life survey in June 2008 found that 92 percent of Americans expressed a belief in God.[16]

While many scholars tend to focus on our migration from mainline Christian denominations (Episcopalians, Presbyterians, Methodists, and others) to evangelism, what may be more remarkable is the evolution of what Americans, on average, seek from spirituality. Where religion once acted as a sort of social obligation passed down from generation to generation, we now view piety as a route to personal expression. We have moved from a sort of institutional religiosity to what Princeton sociologist Robert Wuthnow has termed a "spirituality of seeking."[17] Americans today choose much more frequently to abandon their parents' liturgy in favor of a spiritual journey that feels more individually fulfilling.[18]

Moreover, while we're less likely to attend religious services, when we do choose to frequent a house of worship, we're much more likely to travel to attend the services we like best.[19] That being the case, we've abandoned the spiritual diversity that once characterized American congregations: churches today are full of people attuned more perfectly to their own devotion.[20] The growth market in spirituality is among those movements that offer less dogma and more practical advice.[21]

That's evident in the sermons Rick Warren delivers at his Saddleback Church and that Joel Osteen offers in his national broadcasts. In each case, listeners are offered less an indoctrination into a specific liturgy than pointers toward a more spiritual guidepost. The title of Osteen's book, *Your Best Life Now,* suggests that the spirituality he preaches steers individuals to a higher level of self-fulfillment even more than a path to salvation.[22] In essence, as we've moved up the hierarchy of needs, our focus on living the good life after we're gone has been subsumed by a greater desire for a satisfying existence here on earth.

Taken alone, these changes may seem incidental; they might appear as simple snapshots of the changing American experience. But a more holistic view reveals a broader and more profound pattern. When an octogenarian shakes his head and gripes that "Americans aren't what they used to be," he's not just indulging in nostalgia—he's noting something very real. The very timbre of America's social character has been transformed as Americans have climbed the hierarchy of needs. The objects of our desire have been displaced by the prosperity and security of contemporary life.

And this points to an interesting wrinkle—one that we can appreciate only if we take stock of earlier analyses of the American character. Recall that in the immediate postwar period, David Riesman and his colleagues had been concerned about American conformity. Their central gripe was that young people were too willing to follow the crowd and too reluctant to cut across the grain. It seemed at the time as if the gumption that had propelled previous generations had been engulfed by a desire to fit in.

Thirty years later, Robert Bellah's concerns emerged from the opposite pole. Americans' eagerness to express their individualism had distracted them from the bonds of community. As subsequent research has made clear, that might not have come as such a surprise: Ronald Inglehart's analysis of World Values Survey data has made it plain that as life gets better, humans focus more on "choice and autonomy."[23] Between 1982 and 2008, the percentage of students who scored above average on a standard test of "narcissism," a more clinical word for what most of us would consider self-centeredness, rose by 30 percent, to nearly two-thirds.[24] American *motives* have indeed evolved over the last several decades.[25]

Which brings us to the final challenge of squaring our new motives with our new opportunities. As delineated in earlier chapters, the range of choices we can now make about where to live, what to read, whom to befriend, and how to earn a living has exploded—largely because the Chinatown Bus effect has removed the *mishigas* that once circumscribed our opportunities. So where do contemporary motive and opportunity now meet? The answer echoes the abiding ethic of the 1950s and the creed of conformity.

The social character that has developed in the last several decades has had the counterintuitive effect of driving us into isolated corners of society full of people just like us. Our desire to "be who we are" has morphed into a desire to "be among people just like us." And our wider horizons act on that impulse. Once we find our niche, we want desperately to fit in. If being yourself means loving old country-music records, you can find people who share that interest anywhere. If you're defined by your love for the Philadelphia Eagles, you can follow them intensely—even while living on the West Coast. In both cases, once you've you tapped into who you "really are," you seek out an environment that offers you comfort among like-minded companions. Instead of an outlier, you become a face in the crowd.

There are, of course, some key differences between the conformity of Riesman's era and today's. In the 1950s, the concern was that too many Americans were conforming to the *same* standard: we were becoming a Wonder Bread nation. Today we don't aspire to meet any one standard but are driven into pockets of conformity, each of which is centered around a different identity. We want to join religious congregations that speak exactly to our spiritual point of view. We want to marry spouses who feed our sense of romantic compatibility. We want to live in neighborhoods full of people who vote and shop and eat and play in the same way we do. We want to watch news programs that explain contemporary events through the lenses that frame our existing assumptions about what's happening in the world.

The end result is the same: today, as in the early postwar period, American motives and opportunities drive us to conform. We're not a nation of free agents who don't care what others think of us; we aren't simply out to express our individualism. We're better equipped today to find the people who will tell us we belong. In essence, we've come full circle. This time, however, Americans are less desperate to conform to some national standard than they are to fit into their own.

Typically, books that explore upheavals in the landscape of American life identify a single factor and trace its ripples over the whole of society. How did the fax machine change the world? What's the impact of money in politics? Would new investments in education really extinguish poverty? Those are important and worthy questions. And they all deserve further exploration.

But our desire to uncover the hidden effects of any single change too frequently forsakes a broader appreciation for how the pieces fit together. Too often, after diving into a specific subject, we are tempted to pick sides, ascribing blame or credit to individual elements of modern life. I've tried here to take a different approach. Rather than press the case for good or ill, the first section of this book has simply explored, in what I hope is a disinterested way, how the changes that define the last several decades have revolutionized the mundane routines of our everyday lives.

We have mapped out the several elements that determine the structure of any given social environment. As in a crime story, motives and opportunities determine which connections we choose to harvest, and which we leave behind. The Third Wave and the Chinatown Bus effect have broadened our horizons; our steady progress up the hierarchy of needs has altered what we want. And that leaves two glaring questions: How, exactly, has the architecture of American community changed? And what do these changes augur for the American Dream?

Part 2

The Missing Rings

A BRIEF HISTORY OF
AMERICAN COMMUNITY

In the spring of 2012, Canadian radio host Eleanor Wachtel asked Toni Morrison to describe what it was like growing up in the industrial town of Lorain, Ohio, during the 1930s and '40s. The Nobel and Pulitzer Prize–winning novelist explained:

> This was a working class town, a steel town, with shipyards, and it was not segregated. People came from Poland and Italy and Mexico and I even knew black people who came from Canada who had escaped there during the 19th century and had come back. So it was a big mix of working class people, mostly union-ized, and we had different churches . . . but one high school. . . . Together we just worked it out. I mean the Golinis lived next door, some Czechs lived next door. They gave my mother beef wrapped in cabbage. They traded recipes. It was sort of like the women in [Morrison's novel] *Home*, but they were all races and religions.[1]

Not every community in America was akin to the Lorain, Ohio, that Morrison described. Other towns and cities in other parts of the country were more explicitly divided by race, ethnicity, and class, among other distinctions. However successful the working-class residents of northern Ohio might have been in cobbling together a fairly idyllic, if impoverished, communal existence, life throughout the United States was not so uniformly tranquil.

Nevertheless, the sense of interconnectedness so colorfully portrayed in Morrison's memory does describe an American archetype—one that connects back to the seedbed of our nation's independence. When traveling through the United States on the journey that would inspire *Democracy in America,* Alexis de Tocqueville found that, among the host of elements that differentiated life in Europe from the New World, one of the most important was the way in which community emerged from the routines of everyday life. For all the distinctions Tocqueville is famous for exploring—the alacrity with which Americans formed voluntary organizations, the unique "quality" of American women—the social bonds of American life were among the first to catch his eye.

Most important, Tocqueville noted, American communities were oriented from the bottom up—a feature that contrasted drastically with those in France, where they were preponderantly structured from the top down.[2] That distinction was most evident in their respective systems of government: French power flowed from the central government in Paris to leaders deputized to run each municipality; in the United States, local residents selected their own representatives, and power bubbled up from the municipal to the state to the federal level.

That difference spoke to an underappreciated distinction. In the New World, towns and neighborhoods weren't just clumps of residents sectioned off into bureaucratic wards. Quite the opposite, "townships," as Tocqueville and others termed them, were of a more organic quality.[3] Municipalities were integrated units determined not by a remote central authority, but by the realities of everyday life. Through their typical routines, neighbors were accustomed to hashing out their differences.[4] The effect was to force Americans of differing stations to interact. Whatever they thought of one another, those who lived nearby were compelled to feel connected, both for good and for ill.

That's a crucial point. When eighteenth- and nineteenth-century Europeans thought of their "little platoons," they tended to group themselves among cohorts of their class or rank. Indeed, Edmund Burke, who coined the term, was referring to distinct economic classes.[5] Americans, by contrast, viewed the world through the prism of their villages and towns—each of which often contained its own diverse mix.[6] Doctors, teachers, bankers, policemen all knew each other and interacted. Appropriating Tocqueville's famous phrase "habits of the heart," Robert Bellah argued more than a century and a half later that the same social architecture had defined America's sense of community throughout the bulk of its history.[7]

That Americans had embraced a different sort of social structure during the colonial period marked what some consider the central backdrop for the American Revolution. As Gordon Wood revealed in *The Radicalism of the American Revolution,* America's emancipation from Britain wasn't just a political upheaval—it marked a break in the very structure of community.[8] The incumbent model of organizing American society—drawn mainly from the patterns of English manor life and, by extension, the plantation society of the antebellum South—had initially been mapped onto the New World. But the seeds of the "townshipped" social architecture that Tocqueville would explore roughly a half century later were planted in the small towns of Puritan New England.

Recall the backdrop. Through most of the eighteenth century, monarchies still governed Europe, even if the facade of royal despotism was beginning to crack. And there was a reason that despotism endured in the "Old" World: kings and queens often served as the mortar that held fragmented societies together because classes of citizens with nothing in common could be forced to swear allegiance to the same royal family.

Americans, by contrast, had become accustomed to a different way of doing business, and couldn't abide the same fealty. Colonists' ordinary lives were awash in the expectation that they, along with their neighbors, could work things out in a more collaborative and easy-flowing way. And so the impetus to secede wasn't just driven by a parochial interest in avoiding the Stamp Act. It wasn't even exclusively propelled by the thirst for "liberty," though that certainly played an important role. Beneath it all was a desire to match the New World's governing institutions with the realities of regular American life. America needed a political dynamic that worked with the unique architecture of colonial community.

Consider what that means. Foremost among the distinguishing characteristics of American exceptionalism (our historic fealty to property and free speech rights, our sense of optimism and entrepreneurialism, and our commitment to federalism among them) was a different way of organizing its towns and neighborhoods. None other than James Madison cited "the spirit of locality" as the basis of eighteenth-century American political life. And in 1807, an Englishman trying to explain the differences between the old and new worlds noted that while Englishmen thought in terms of "church and nation," Americans tended to sort the world by "village and congregation."[9] That distinction isn't simply a difference in perspective; "townships," properly understood as the rudimentary building blocks of American society, were a crucial force in driving the birth of a new nation.

Writing in 1925—a year shy of the nation's 150th birthday—the philosopher, historian, and sociologist Lewis Mumford published an essay arguing that American history had been defined by four major migrations.[10] The first was westward expansion of the frontier, and the second our economic transition from farm to factory. The third migration saw the arrival of millions of European immigrants in the nation's metropolises. And the fourth, which had only begun when Mumford was writing his essay, was the exodus of well-to-do city dwellers from the urban core—an evolution propelled by the pull of the single-family homes being constructed on city outskirts around the country.

Mumford's contemporaries in the world of sociology—or, at least, those who came to be known as members of the Chicago School—were largely preoccupied with the effects of that third migration, from town to city. Believing that distinct social environments shaped disparate social outcomes, they worried that the depravity of urban life might breed generations of social misfits.[11] They feared that absent the warmth and comity of small-town America, the children of urban factory workers would mature without the decency required to sustain a modern, civilized society. The American Dream might eventually be extinguished amid the crime-ridden and poverty-stricken streets of America's overcrowded cities.

By the end of the 1900s, with cities awash in the affluent crowd Richard Florida termed the "creative class" seeming safer and more prosperous, a look back might have concluded that the Chicago School's concerns were absurd.[12] But a snapshot of life back then reveals the roots of their worry. America's big turn-of-the-century metropolises were nasty places. The nation's new mills and factories polluted the surrounding areas. Crime was rampant—at least by the imagined standards of idyllic small-town life.[13] The political issues of the day were largely understood through that prism: the push for prohibition, for example, was at heart an effort by the nation's more staid rural population to impose a sense of decorum on raucous and unhinged masses.[14]

As New York University historian Thomas Bender noted in an important book published decades later, a subtler change was also at work: the growing separation between home and neighborhood. The totem that many of us ascribe to the whole of American history—that the nuclear family is a refuge from the frightening world beyond our front door—was unfamiliar in agrarian America.[15] Quite the opposite, nineteenth-century towns involved a much closer set of nonfamily ties. Meals were often communal, neighbors were much more intimately familiar with one another, and the phrase "it takes a village" was more literal when it came to raising children.[16] It wasn't that the United States was a nation of kibbutzim. But the exalted place family life began to play after the Second (industrial) Wave had enveloped American society was, up to that point, fairly novel.

Today, it's hard to identify with those early industrial era concerns. New York, Boston, and Chicago are now thought to be among the safer places to raise a family—certain neighborhoods excepted. Tenement buildings that once housed dozens of families have been converted into multimillion-dollar lofts. And among those living along the coasts, the vast expanses of rural and suburban America now seem the more likely venues for wanton behavior.

This flipped view of urban American life is a recent phenomenon: the sense that depravity lurked in the dark corners of the nation's cities persisted throughout most of the twentieth century.[17] When, in March 1964, a twenty-eight-year-old bartender named Kitty Genovese was raped and murdered in a working-class neighborhood of New York, the story of her demise seemed to confirm the nation's underlying fear that urban life sucked the morality out of its residents. As reported at the time, even as Genovese screamed for help in an alley, none of the thirty-eight people within earshot took the trouble to call the police.[18] The horror of the attack, and the blithe decision of those nearby to turn away rather than help, suggested that inhabitants of America's cities had been stripped of the innately human instinct to be their brother's keeper.

Genovese's story, however apocryphal, reinforced what sociologists associated with the Chicago School had argued decades earlier: urban America was a place where few people knew your name.[19]

The Industrial Revolution, the sociologists concluded, hadn't simply changed the sorts of professions driving the economy—it had disrupted the very fabric of American community. Americans had moved to cities, taken jobs on assembly lines, and begun to raise their children in the hustle and bustle of city life. The result, they complained, was that an urban American society would see its citizens lose any devotion to community, impelled instead simply to coexist for material convenience.[20]

What could be done to reacquaint the American public with the character bred by the rhythms of nineteenth-century life? How could cities be reformed to eliminate the degeneracy that had seemed to infect the teeming masses? What could be done to sand down the rough edges of the industrial era? For the better part of the next several decades, right through the Great Depression, the Second World War, and the postwar era that raised Kitty Genovese, answering those questions became one of sociology's most important projects.

Then two things happened. First, in 1961, a transplant to New York City from Scranton, Pennsylvania, published arguably the most important twentieth-century treatise on American community. Jane Jacobs's *The Death and Life of American Cities* offered a wholly new understanding of municipal success. Conventional wisdom argued that city problems were driven by the chaos of urban life; but Jacobs thought just the opposite. It wasn't that cities alienated people from one another; quite the opposite, efforts to clean up the nation's metropolises were sterilizing their streetscapes. The key to a vibrant city, in her view, was to maintain the familiar relationships that arranged neighborhood routines into an intricate ballet. The challenge was to harness the vitality of neighborhood life without stifling it.

Upon observing the mundane patterns of New York's Greenwich Village, Jacobs concluded that the sense of interdependence and fellowship so frequently ascribed to smaller towns, known as gemeinschaft in the world of sociology, had survived the Industrial Revolution. It was difficult, perhaps impossible, to see from afar, but in the daily interactions of neighborhood life—shopkeepers holding a spare key for the tenants upstairs, mothers keeping an eye on the gaggle of children playing in the alley—a web of social interactions grew organically. And beyond any seeming messiness, the familiarity that arose out of those interactions was the most effective salve for social isolation.

Jacobs wasn't arguing that any mass of people would develop a sense of community naturally; that, she contended, was the problem with bad urban planning. Certain structural elements were necessary, if not sufficient, to cultivate gemeinshaft. At the core, she argued, well-functioning cities needed to be divided organically into internally diverse districts of between eighty thousand and two hundred thousand people. "The chief function of a successful district," she wrote, "is to mediate between the indispensable, but inherently politically powerless, street neighborhoods, and the inherently powerful city as a whole."[21]

The success of each district hinged in turn on its capacity to embrace several axioms of vibrant urban life. First, Jacobs argued, flourishing neighborhoods needed to fulfill at least two primary functions—they had to be both residential and commercial enclaves, since the layering of different populations was what created textured community. Second, they had to be composed of short blocks, frequent intersections being a key to cultivating pedestrian traffic. Successful neighborhoods needed to contain buildings of both new and old stock, allowing a diversity of businesses and tenants to interact. Finally, each community needed a dense concentration of residents—a critical mass that would keep streetscapes lively.[22]

Jacobs's approach was soon followed by more academic studies. Several decades removed from the Dickensian world of early twentieth-century American metropolises—and in the aftermath of the urban decay wrought, in some circumstances, by the successive riots of the late 1960s—Claude Fischer, a sociologist at Berkeley, decided to take a second look at the Chicago School's assumption that the bonds of community were undermined by the process of industrialization. What he found largely contradicted the conventional view. The sorts of relationships found in small towns might not have mapped one for one onto the routines of urban neighborhoods, but cities were nevertheless helping to cultivate ties between people who had particular interests in common.

Across the country, gays and lesbians living in urban areas were developing clusters of relationships that separated them from their counterparts around town. Quite frequently, communities of Puerto Ricans, WASPs, and Orthodox Jews lived nearby. Together they comprised a huge mass of people. But while many of them lived in crime-ridden and squalid circumstances, it didn't follow that they were all lost amid a sea of isolation. Smaller pockets were developing the sort of warmth and familiarity often assumed to exist in small-town life. Fischer labeled his new approach a "subcultural theory of urbanism," and argued that a closer look at the lives of city residents revealed a rich tableau of smaller groups all living among one another.[23]

Admittedly, relations between various communities were often strained. But Jacobs's observations and Fischer's new scholarship suggested that far from being monoliths of despair—the view often held from afar—the vibrant interactions within the discrete communities contradicted notions that cities were dens of anomie. The metropolises, each an intricate tapestry of disparate factions, comprised, in and of them themselves, lively neighborhoods. And while they differed unmistakably from their small-town brethren, the presumption that industrialization was eroding the ties that kept American society together had broadly missed the mark.

Through all the changes wrought during the first two hundred years that followed independence, the essential DNA of our national society managed to survive in one form or another. Through the turmoil of the battle over slavery, the drive westward, and what the Tofflers had deemed the Second Wave, the Tocquevillian "township" persevered. No matter whether in colonial villages, frontier towns, urban tenements, or, as Fischer noted, the distinct pockets of life that persevered even in the darkest days of American city life, the township remained the core building block of American community.

It's not that the disruptive elements of the nation's past didn't have dramatic effects. Undoubtedly, cities experienced growing pains around the turn of the twentieth century. But Jane Jacobs's work illustrated clearly that the connections that represent the core ties of any township remained a central feature of successful twentieth-century American communities. Whether or not neighbors were socializing with more circumscribed groups of people—if the Italian immigrants largely kept to themselves, or the gay community cocooned in one part of a city—they were carrying on the tradition.

That means that for more than two hundred years, Americans emerging from different experiences and with disparate roles to play in their everyday lives—bankers and lawyers, policemen, and teachers—could not escape some element of interaction with one another. Not everyone maintained such relationships; Americans were frequently limited by their own prejudices. And not everyone got along, as any narrative of American community reveals. But Americans throughout their history have been unable to avoid the fairly unique circumstance of becoming familiar with one another over the course of their daily routines. The township structure, through all the other changes woven into American history, engendered an element of mutual understanding.

What has happened to that basic building block of American community over the course of the last several decades? If the township model survived the crest of Toffler's Second Wave, has it survived the Third? This isn't the first time that Americans have asked if some big paradigm shift was going to undermine our habits of the heart. A fair bit of literature over the last several years has asked whether American community is on the ebb. The truth, as deciphered in the following chapters, is neither here nor there; something very different has emerged. But to understand it, we first need to develop a new way of interpreting how our individual routines, when taken together, contribute to the process of defining the particular architecture of each community.

BANDS, VILLAGES,
AND TRIBES

At some point in the late 1980s, a group of anthropologists took up an enduring evolutionary conundrum. Conventional wisdom to that point had suggested that the sheer capacity of the human mind had propelled our species to the top of the evolutionary food chain. By whatever accident of biology, our ancestors had developed the overwhelming cognitive firepower that enabled them to dominate the globe. Big brains begat better tools, and better tools had vanquished the competition.

Unfortunately, that story didn't square entirely with the archaeological record. It wasn't entirely clear why humanity's ancestors—who had been using tools for at least a couple million years—had seen such dramatic brain development only a few hundred thousand years before modern day. Beyond that, there was no satisfying answer as to why natural selection, at that point, would have favored the bigger brains among us. By most measures, it seemed heavy craniums would have been an evolutionary disadvantage rather than a leg up.

Gray matter, after all, is calorically intensive, draining as much as a fifth of a contemporary human's energy intake. Our bigger-brained ancestors would have had to consume significantly more food than their smaller-brained brethren.[1] The smart money, back in the day, would have bet that some other branch of the evolutionary chain—maybe a faster species with a smaller brain, or a more powerful mammal without so much gray matter—would emerge to rule the animal kingdom. So what was it that propelled humanity to the top of the food chain?

That enduring question spurred Robin Dunbar, an anthropologist now at Oxford, to develop a theory that has since come to be known as the "social brain hypothesis." His argument was that the big burdensome brains our ancestors lugged around equipped them with an advantage that outweighed its liabilities: the ability to coordinate.[2] More sophisticated minds, he contended, had enabled humanity's ancestors to choreograph attacks, warn one another in the event of danger, and harmonize their lives in ways that other species—even those that traveled in packs—could not. Our emergence as the globe's most powerful species had hinged most directly on our ability to communicate.

Dunbar went further. Not only did the social brain hypothesis explain why our ancestors were able to overcome the disadvantage of lugging around a big head full of gray matter; it suggested that there was (and is) a direct relationship between the size of an animal's neocortex and the size and complexity of the social network that animal can maintain.[3] As brains got bigger, Dunbar's research revealed, our ancestors had become more adept at organizing larger groups of their peers. No longer limited to recognizing a handful of neighbors from nearby caves, an individual might have been able to distinguish among several dozen. And the larger the network, the more advantages conferred: the more complex the hunting group, the more sophisticated the warning signals.[4]

That relationship between the mammalian neocortex and network size opens a window onto human sociability. Even today, our capacity to keep tabs on our friends and acquaintances is limited by the size of our brain. By some measure, that's obvious—none of us can remember everyone we meet (though, as Malcolm Gladwell has pointed out, some of us are better at keeping names and faces straight than others).[5] But while we may presume that our limits are determined by the choice of whether to pay attention, biology actually plays a fundamental role. And that led Dunbar to wonder how many acquaintances a contemporary human might really hope to have.

Dunbar wasn't trying to determine exactly how many acquaintances we might have were we to spend all our time with facial flashcards. Nor did he mean to suggest that every human being has exactly the same social capacity. But, accepting some reasonable variation among individuals, he wanted to know if there were patterns to suggest the limits of our ability to keep tabs. After gathering and analyzing all the data he could find on the nearly two dozen modern hunter-gatherers and "settled horticulturalists" around the globe—societies including the !Kung San of southern Africa, Australian aborigines, various Eskimo societies, North American Indian tribes, and Congo pygmies—he discerned a pattern.[6]

Each society was unique, just as each individual has his or her own social limitations. But what emerged through his research was that nearly every society had developed a structure that grouped relationships into roughly three categories. First, individuals in each society tended to associate most intensely with a group of roughly thirty-five to fifty people, all of whom who slept in close proximity. Dunbar labeled these groups "bands" or "overnight camps" and associated them with the fairly close relationships you would expect among any small group that lived together, ate communally, and coordinated their activities (hunting, gathering, etc.) on a daily basis.

Next, he noted that individual bands tended to develop special ties to a small number of the bands nearby. Together, these hundred- to two-hundred-person "villages" didn't necessarily have any set manifestation—it wasn't that everyone slept or worked or ate together. But, invariably, certain rituals brought the village together: a feast or a dance or a procession. And while village neighbors didn't know one another as intimately as those who lived in the same band, it was likely that each villager would know most of the rest of the village by name. Moreover, in most cases, villagers were intimate enough to develop a sense of mutual trust. As Dunbar put it, each village defined "a subset of the population that interacts on a sufficiently regular basis to have strong bonds based on direct personal knowledge."[7]

Finally, Dunbar noted that the villages tended to be grouped into larger "tribes," ranging from roughly five hundred to two thousand people. The tribes, of course, shared certain common traditions—languages, rituals, celebrations—but the relationships between individuals living in disparate bands and villages of the same tribe were likely to be tenuous. An individual in one band might know an individual in another, or a particularly attentive member of the tribe might know the names of lots of people throughout the group. But on the whole, the relationships among people in disparate bands tended to be superficial.

Having sketched out three separate rings of acquaintances— bands, villages, and tribes—Dunbar began to wonder what more could be gleaned about each category. What could the data tell us about our biological capacity to maintain relationships? First, as he noted (and is obvious), there's a limit to the number of intimate (band-like) and more superficial (tribal) relationships any individual can maintain: while the exact figures certainly vary, you can only have so many close friends, and you can only remember so many names and faces.

But the data also suggested something not nearly so intuitive: the human brain also has a limited capacity to compile contacts at the middle level; we're intellectually incapable of maintaining any more than a certain number of friendly but not intimate relationships. None of the societies Dunbar had studied included villages much larger than 200 individuals, and no typical village was much smaller than 100. And when he averaged the individual figures out, Dunbar discerned a number that suggested a biological limit on village-level acquaintances: 150. That figure came to be known among anthropologists and other scholars as "Dunbar's number."[8]

What's more, Dunbar found that his number reverberated through patterns of historic and even modern-day human interaction. Militaries, dating back to the Roman legion, for example, often organized into discrete units of roughly 150, the size that most perfectly harnessed the uniquely human capacity to coordinate. Smaller groups could not so effectively channel the capabilities a "village" of soldiers might boast, and larger groups frequently proved too hard to manage in combat. By contrast, 150 seemed to mark a happy medium: a unit of that size could exploit the benefits of diversity without becoming unwieldy.

The presentation of 150 in the history of human interaction didn't end there. Small farming communities, such as the Amishlike Hutterites in the upper Midwest, unknowingly embraced the 150-person standard, requiring communities that grew larger to subdivide in the maintenance of self-sufficiency. Maybe most startling, Dunbar determined that across various societies humans tended to maintain holiday-card lists of about 150 people, confirming his supposition of a natural human tendency to maintain familiarity with only a set number of acquaintances.[9]

It's not that human beings are incapable of maintaining ongoing personal relationships with more than exactly 150 people. Rather, what now seems clear is that some number represents the ceiling above which an individual cannot maintain more village-level relationships. And those limits aren't just a function of our attention, they're determined by the mass of our gray matter. Our brains, in the end, only have so many social slots to fill.

To date, scholars of American community have only taken cursory insights from Dunbar's research, most likely because the trend among scholars of contemporary social ties has been to look at our networks from the top down, rather than from the individual out. When pundits decry the tribalism of American life, their concerns generally center on observations like those that spurred Bill Bishop to write *The Big Sort*: they worry that America is becoming balkanized. Indeed, the bulk of network theory, the growing body of literature that discerned, for example, that most humans are only separated by some set number of "degrees of separation," focuses more on whether individuals are connected, and less on the nature of those relationships.[10]

It's not that there isn't a lot to glean from studies that track how the nodes of American community have been re-sorted. Bishop made plain how circumscribed our social spheres have become. But our point-to-point connections hardly mark the *only* way to understand community; our social lives are also defined by how much time and energy we invest in each different relationship and how, collectively, those choices make up the social fabric. Any comprehensive understanding of what's happened over the last several decades requires that we look beyond nodal connections to the state of America's bands, villages, and tribes.

That may seem like a silly proposition. After all, few of us today sleep in overnight camps or identify with a particular tribe. But by the same token, we can certainly distinguish between our most intimate friendships, our most ephemeral acquaintances, and those in between. In that spirit, we need to figure out a way to map the social distinctions Dunbar identified in the "settled horticultural" societies onto modern-day life. How have the patterns of sociability engrained in the human mind manifested themselves?

Conjure up an image of the planet Saturn. As you may recall from the diagram on the wall of your third-grade classroom, the solar system's sixth planet is orbited by a series of gaseous rings, each of which extends on what appears to be a single plane. That image offers a perfect way to imagine how individuals sort their family, friends, and acquaintances.

In the Saturn model, the planet is a person, and the rings his or her acquaintances in a succession of diminishing intimacy. Some sociologists might suggest that the distance between the globe and each ring represents a measure of "multistrandedness," a term they use to describe how many disparate subjects define the bond between two individuals.[11] But the essence of the model is simple: our most intimate relationships—whose orbits form the innermost rings—are distinguished from those that are, successively, less and less familiar.

Consider an ordinary American adult—let's call him Joe. The very first rings out from Planet Joe might comprise his wife, for example, and maybe his kids. The rings just beyond those might represent the childhood buddies he still calls once a week—maybe the guys he hung around as a young man. These are people who know the full spectrum of what's happening in Joe's life; they'd be aware, most likely, if his dog were sick or if his son were struggling in algebra. Together, these acquaintances make up Joe's Dunbarian "band."

Anthropologists would likely think that the inner rings resemble a combination of what some scholars have termed an individual's "support clique" (by definition, the people she would turn to in a moment of distress) and her "sympathy group" (the ten or fifteen people with whom she visits at least once a month).[12] Without a doubt, they would include the four people Harvard professor Nicholas Christakis and University of California–San Diego professor James Fowler found the average American claims as a "close contact."[13] But they would also include the twenty-three ties that University of Toronto sociologist Barry Wellman found, in a landmark study, to define the average number of acquaintances with whom an individual claims to be "close" or "somewhat close."[14]

At the other end of the spectrum—corresponding to the relationships that Dunbar associated with the tribe—the outer rings harbor Joe's most ephemeral acquaintances. The eBay vendor who sold him an iPod cover or an unremarkable cashier at the grocery store would be prime examples. The outer rings also include the long-lost elementary-school friend whose updates show up on Joe's Facebook feed and the guy he nods to when passing in the lobby of his office building, without ever pressing for an introduction.[15] These relationships range from passing to transactional. Most are forged across a single shared interest or experience. They represent the sorts of ties that would have bonded two tribesmen from disparate villages: the two might have acknowledged one another when their paths converged, but neither would have had any real sense of what was happening with the other.

Finally, there are the relationships in between—those that correspond to the Dunbarian village. The middle rings comprise ties between people not as close as kith or kin, but not as distant as a mere acquaintance. These rings, for Joe, might begin with members of his extended family, work buddies he meets semi-regularly for lunch, or neighbors he knows from community meetings. They might include the tailor who has hemmed his pants since middle school or the diner waitress who serves him pancakes every Sunday after church. Middle-ring relationships are defined by a familiarity that allows acquaintances to carry on conversations about personal subjects even if they aren't entirely private: the birth of a child, for example, an ongoing illness, or a funny coincidence from a few years back.[16] They represent, in essence, the people with whom an individual is familiar but not intimate, friendly but not close.

It was middle-ring relationships that Robert Putnam lionized in *Bowling Alone*: bridge partners, brothers in the Elks Club, fellow members of the PTA. The middle rings would also include the neighbors my father remembers from his childhood in Cincinnati and that sociologist Sean Safford's father still knows in Buffalo. Over time, the middle rings have become what most Americans consider "community." And inasmuch as Dunbar's research revealed that our brains only provide so many slots, it's in the middle rings where Dunbar's number most aptly applies.

The three categories I've described can't be thought of as perfectly distinct buckets, and there are gradients within each. Certain sorts of relationships can straddle any hard definition, and reasonable people might argue about where certain ties might most properly be placed. But the broader point is still apt. Whether we set out to do so or not, each relationship we maintain is assigned a certain role in our social constellation, and each has its own rank of familiarity. What's less clear, however, is how recent changes to American motives and opportunities, outlined in the first third of this book, have affected the way we fill our limited supply of social slots.

In 1988, one of the leading lights of mid-twentieth-century American sociology, a University of Chicago professor named James Coleman, published a paper that changed the way academics approached the study of community. Having spent the bulk of his career examining the dynamics of interpersonal relationships, he argued that social ties ought to be understood as a form of "capital." Like human capital or physical capital, Coleman contended, social capital "is productive, making possible the achievement of certain ends that in its absence would not be possible."[17] The fact that you know the woman next door makes it more likely you'll be able to borrow her electric drill. And so the impact of community life needed to be studied and celebrated the same way other forms of capital had become staples of academic literature.

Coleman's focus largely centered on the value of interpersonal trust, and he made his point with a now famous example.[18] Among those who bought and sold large quantities of jewels in the Diamond District of Manhattan, he noted that most were Orthodox Jews from certain pockets of Brooklyn. For the most part, they attended the same synagogues and sent their kids to the same schools. And because their lives were so intertwined, they'd developed a series of norms that, taken out of context, might have appeared reckless. For example, when one dealer wanted to sell a bag of gems to another, he generally offered the prospective buyer an opportunity to examine the stones in private.

To most outsiders, that tradition might appear to be an invitation to theft—the buyer, after all, would then have a chance to replace the stones in question with less valuable impostors. But the sellers were rarely snookered—and for good reason: if a buyer tried something sneaky, he faced the wrath of the neighborhood back home. It's not just that a thief would be shunned from future business transactions in and around the Diamond District—he'd be ostracized from community gatherings, subjected to glares at shul, and offered the cold shoulder on the street. Integrity in the Diamond District wasn't the issue it might have been because good behavior was enforced through shame.

Coleman's explication of social capital contended that interpersonal connections couldn't be discounted as leisurely pleasures because, in reality, they harnessed very tangible economic value. Without the norms of trust established within the Orthodox community, it would have been much more difficult and expensive for New York's jewelry trade to flourish. Sellers would have insisted on being present when buyers inspected their stones. Whole new levels of security would have required burdensome outlays of money. And the alacrity with which gems could be sent from one vender to the next would have been seriously imperiled.

Bowling Alone, which Robert Putnam published roughly a dozen years after Coleman first articulated his theory, broke new ground by tracing the ebb and flow of social capital through the latter half of the twentieth century. What Putnam concluded, after culling a seemingly endless trove of source data, was that American social capital was evaporating. Our propensity to join clubs, participate in civic organizations, vote, or even simply to have friends over for

dinner had declined in the decades that followed President Eisenhower's retirement from office.[19] It wasn't just an academic observation; *Bowling Alone* became a sensation because, on a visceral
level, it rang true for ordinary Americans.

What's since come into clearer view is that the category of
social capital that became Putnam's focus—the middle-ring
relationships that constitute our traditional understanding of
"community"—don't constitute the whole of our social lives. As
compelling as *Bowling Alone* was, it left beyond the scope of its
analysis all the new ways Americans had begun to connect outside
the institutions that defined life in the 1950s. As we've seen, the
patterns that defined American life in the early postwar period
no longer exist. Nevertheless, to date we've not yet sorted out how
the effects, placed in the context of the trends Putnam identified,
have changed our individual portfolios of both intimate and more
casual relationships.

For that reason, as illuminating as Coleman's definition and Putnam's research are, it's time to repurpose the term "social capital."
Rather than imagine it as a gross measure of a society's connective tissue, we should think of it as we think of, well, capital. Social
capital should be defined quite simply as the amount of time and
attention an individual devotes to a range of human interaction.
We should think of it as something that, like money, we control
and invest.[20]

Whether or not, as academics sometimes say, we have "agency"
over our social capital—whether we're actively manipulating our
investments or, alternatively, outside circumstances define our
portfolios—we need to recognize that social capital does not emerge
from the ether; it's something that we each possess individually,
and then divvy up. By some measure, that's a more intuitive way
of thinking about our individual social constellations. After all, no
one would suggest with a straight face that all relationships are
interchangeable—that an acquaintanceship, as measured in typical

analyses of social "networks," can be automatically swapped out one for another.

We also know that our social investments change over time—that certain periods of our lives are focused on certain ties, and that other periods compel us to make different decisions. Studies have shown, for example, that individuals who get married tend to pull social capital away from their friends by a factor of 30 percent.[21] The parents of a newborn, suddenly stuck at home, typically shrink away from the friends they had once seen nearly every weekend.[22] We can imagine all sorts of different factors—the geography of a given neighborhood, the rhythms of a career, the vitality of a family member's health—that might affect how any individual invests his or her own lot of attention.

What's less clear—and what we need to tease out—is how the Third Wave, the Chinatown Bus effect, the big climb up the hierarchy of needs, and our new impulse to conform have changed how Americans choose to spend their time. Are there certain types of relationships that have come to claim more attention while others lagged? Which rings have "thickened," so to speak, and which in turn have withered?

In some instances, quantifiable evidence can help us uncover the truth. But in the absence of hard data, we need some sense of what's happened because, as we'll discover, the way we distribute social capital holds the key to understanding the evolving architecture of American community. Our temptation has long been to assume that big changes from up above—namely, the decision made by political leaders and corporate titans—filter down to shape the rhythms of everyday life. But what will become evident is that things also work the other way: subtle disruptions in the way each individual invests his or her social capital can collectively play a much more powerful role in changing the fabric of American society.

8

———

THE SEARCH FOR AFFIRMATION

To wrap your mind around what's driving us to choose certain friendships over others, consider a recent television advertisement for Dr Pepper.[1] Set to a song titled "I Gotta Be Me," the sixty-second spot opens when a young man exiting a commuter train is overcome by the desire to break free from his daily slog.[2] Springing to life, the twenty-something rips off his button-down to reveal a tee shirt with the words "I'm One of a Kind" emblazoned on the front. His gumption spreads like wildfire: legions of other commuters begin ripping off their business suits and uniforms, revealing similarly hidden taglines: one's a fighter, one's a momma's boy, one's a rebel, etc. As the movement to "be me" sweeps across the city and each commuter reveals his or her unique tagline, the whole lot of freedom lovers begins to walk across the town square almost as a synchronized mob.

The nearly perfect coordination might make you wonder whether the "rebels" are really expressing their individuality or—quite the opposite—whether they're reveling in the harmony they've found among their peers. After all, if they were faithful to the principle of "being yourself," wouldn't you expect at least some of them to be wearing tee shirts with different color schemes? Moreover, might not some people "being themselves" prefer a cola or root beer to the refreshing taste of Dr Pepper?

The marketing executives who produced the spot weren't trying for profundity—they just wanted to sell soda. But the underlying message suggests something important. As we explored in chapter 5, our desperate desire to avoid being judged has come to propel us not to be true rebels—but to seek out peers who celebrate us for "who we are." We've developed an intense if underappreciated need to have our worldviews affirmed by those on the receiving end of our social capital. And so we've become more eager than ever to invest the bulk of our time and attention in relationships that provide just that kind of comfort.

Combined with the expansion of social opportunities delineated in Part 1—the fact that we have so many more options when deciding where to devote our attention—it's not difficult to see why American investment portfolios might have shifted over time. Different kinds of relationships provide different sorts of feedback. The question is how the constellation of rings that surrounds the typical American differs today from what predominated in the early postwar years.

It's difficult, of course, to measure precisely how social capital is distributed, or whether we're choosing to invest more time and attention in one category of relationship or another. But the prima facie evidence suggests first that Americans have chosen to invest more time in the inner rings. Desperate for affirmation, and equipped with new tools to keep in touch with a few prized connections, we've chosen to double down on the small group of people we hold most dear.

The best indications may come from analysis of the digital revolution. Although we often assume that information technology serves primarily to expand our horizons, several of the advances that mark the last few decades have actually served to deepen the connections we already treasure. Studies have shown, for example, that the majority of cell phone conversations are actually sent to our most intimate three to five associates.[3] So much as we imagine that mobile technology connects us more closely to the wider world, more often it's just used to call Dad for a ride.[4]

Our propensity to use technology to buttress our closest ties has had far-reaching implications, though some of the effects have been lost amid subtle changes to the routines of everyday life. Today, for instance, the morning kiss goodbye need not signal hours of separation: husbands and wives can text one another while commuting (if not while driving) and instant-message from their respective cubicles. College kids can call their parents about what to grab for lunch between classes, then "e-whine" for more generous allowances from the back row of a lecture hall. Grandparents who live thousands of miles away can watch a child's first steps via livestreaming done smartphone-to-tablet.

But the digital revolution isn't solely responsible for the thickening inner rings. The explosion of American mobility also has made it much easier for us to maintain close relationships across substantial geographic separations.[5] Three generations ago, your best friend's decision to move to a nearby suburb might have made it impossible for you to maintain the same level of intimacy; today, keeping close requires nothing more than a quick ride down the interstate.

It doesn't end there. The sea change in the way Americans approach their careers—the growing sense that our professions are little more than a means to a comfortable retirement—has made close personal ties more important. This is not to suggest that previous generations weren't devoted to their families, or that industrial-era jobs were always the mother's milk of self-fulfillment.[6] But to the degree to which we've been reoriented to view our years of leisure in retirement as the reward for a lifetime of sacrifice—and that our sense of self-worth is less entwined with the way we make a living and more with how much we make—the role close ties play in our emotional lives has become that much more meaningful.[7]

To be sure, the suggestion that our inner-ring connections have been strengthened may seem counterintuitive. Our newfound focus on deepening our bonds with our closest family and friends has been obscured by the sense that the American family has fallen apart. Rising divorce rates and single-parenthood would seem to suggest that the traditional bonds of kith and kin have, if anything, begun to dissolve.[8]

But those flashier developments constitute only a piece of the puzzle. The extended mobility engendered by the Third Wave has made it more likely that Americans will want to be close to the people who naturally inhabit their inner rings. And so, the individuals we *choose* to make our most intimate—whether it's the people who filled out the inner-ring slots a couple generations ago or not—are, on the whole, getting more of our frequent and sustained attention.

While there's no perfect way to measure whether inner-ring relationships have been strengthened or weakened over time, the bits of evidence that exist have come to form a fairly convincing mosaic. Claude Fischer found in a recent study that, while small, the percentage of Americans who had at least weekly contact with their best friend had actually grown very modestly between the mid-1980s and the mid-2000s.[9] And in a study Fischer (in particular) has come to criticize, researchers using data from the General Social Survey, a sociological survey organized by researchers at the University of Chicago, argued that "in general, [American] core discussion networks in 2004 are more closely tied to each other, are more frequently accessed, and are longer-term relationships [than they were in 1985]. Even more than in 1985, the discussion networks we measured in 2004 are the closest of close ties."[10]

Evidence coming from inside family portraits reveals much the same picture. Conventional wisdom assumes that children are seeing less of their parents—that our propensity for longer working hours, combined with the stampede of women into the professional workforce, has depleted the time adults have to rear their children. But that supposition has been upended by underreported studies that suggest parents are actually spending more time with their kids than they were in the mid-1970s. The average number of weekly hours that mothers spent caring directly for their children grew from ten in 1965 to thirteen in 2000; among fathers, the number more than doubled from three to seven over the same thirty-five-year span.[11] As Fischer once explained to me, our perception is that families are eating at home less, but if the substitute is to go out for dinner, the net outcome may reveal that their time together has not diminished at all.[12]

By another standard, in fact, the problem isn't that American children are getting too *little* parenting—it's that they're getting *too much*. The term "helicopter parent" found its way into the popular lexicon because of concern that children are being micromanaged, sometimes well into their early adulthood.[13] The percentage of Americans between the ages of twenty-five and thirty-four living with their parents—quite high in the early postwar years when multigenerational households were more common—nearly doubled between 1980 and 2010, from 11 percent to more than 21 percent.[14] Maybe most important, 63 percent of those between the ages of eighteen and thirty-four know someone who has moved back in. Some of that has certainly been driven by the economic impact of the Great Recession. But even so, what's remarkable is that living at home through early adulthood has become a new norm of contemporary American life.[15]

Finally, even once kids are legitimately independent, ties between parents and children appear to have strengthened over time. According to a study done by the Pew Research Center, the percentage of adults who see or speak with a parent every day jumped from 32 to 42 between 1989 and 2005.[16] Maybe even more eye-popping, a survey of employers done by Michigan State researchers found that nearly a third of large companies had seen parents of recent college graduates involve themselves in the recruiting process—in many cases calling the prospective employers directly.[17]

The broad trend seems unmistakable. It may well have been that our grandparents, given the same opportunities, would have chosen to invest so much time and energy in their closest companions. It might be that different desires—maybe a more protracted need to be among like-minded peers, for example—would have compelled them to make the same selections we make today. We'll never know. But what's clear today is that the general constellation has changed and the inner rings have thickened.

No one doubts that there's a world of difference between our most and least intimate connections. But bonds formed between dear friends and near strangers can sometimes scratch the same itch. Indeed, if there's an alternative place in the constellation of rings where someone might find that same element of affirmation, it's the outer rings. One-dimensional relationships that connect individuals on nothing more than a single plane of mutual interest—those forged between political junkies, hobbyists, and sports fans, for example—can often cultivate the same kind of validation. And for that reason, Americans have become increasingly inclined to seek them out.

Love or hate President Obama; spend hours perfecting the art of crochet; devote the bulk of your free time to reading blogs about the Dallas Cowboys. If you can find someone who shares a similar passion, it can feel as if you're in the company of a kindred spirit. It's reassuring—self-affirming, in fact—to know that someone out there agrees with you implicitly, even if it's on something picayune. Finding a niche among like-minded contacts is a powerful draw, and our desire for approval has put its allure at a premium.

It's not hard to see why there's more opportunity to invest in outer-ring relationships today. After all, the great boon of the Chinatown Bus effect is that you can find your specific niche without all the *mishigas* that once separated people with similar interests. The millions of Dallas Cowboy fans scattered throughout the country can now connect via the Web in ways that were never before possible. So can fans of the Cincinnati Bengals—even if there aren't nearly so many of us. It's not that fans necessarily gather at sports bars, talking between plays about the state of local politics or their travails at work. Instead, information technology makes it incredibly easy to maintain one-dimensional friendships.

Given the limitations on our ability to track social capital, the most revealing evidence may not be in noting the explosion of new social media—as evidenced above, Facebook and Twitter are already fairly well-studied phenomena—but rather in surveying how important ideas are spread today versus the way things used to work. What is too often lost in our analysis of trending ideas is the way in which they reach an audience. And the best place to begin may be a look at what is inarguably the most consequential movement of the twentieth century, the campaign for racial equality.

Martin Luther King Jr., the civil rights movement's most iconic leader, did not become a national hero overnight. Rather, the grass-roots campaign he helped to spearhead grew powerful because members of the African-American clergy had, through the 1960s and before, developed a series of institutions that served as a foundation for change. It's not that African-Americans wouldn't have agitated for civil rights absent the bonds built by leaders in various cities and towns throughout the South. But the strength that empowered those on the front lines to withstand outside pressure over the long haul was harnessed not solely by the leadership's righteous ideals, but by the power of middle-ring relationships.

To put it another way: it wasn't just moving rhetoric or inspiring calls to action that propelled the nation out of the Jim Crow era. The civil rights movement was successful because the demand for equality spread through bonds that already existed within the community. King was a leader of the Southern Christian Leadership Conference, an organization of clergymen who were each held in high esteem by members of their congregations. But in addition to the moral sway the clergy had within their communities, the bonds forged among members of the SCLC itself—relationships that mark classic examples of middle-ring ties—served as a crucial foundation for the movement, even through hard times.

Some version of this story applies to the gamut of movements that pepper American history. Powerful ideas haven't spread on their own as much as they've traveled the connections forged by the institutions that constitute the middle rings. The abolitionists, the "know-nothings," the isolationists, the progressives, the John Birchers, the suffragettes—they all worked, to different effect, to shape the nation's history. But none emerged out of nowhere: each was incubated by connections forged between friends, neighbors, and familiar acquaintances.

That's not how things work anymore. More recently that "style" of movement has become almost antiquated. Far from harnessing the connections wrought by preexisting middle-ring relationships, the Tea Party and Occupy movements, two of the most prominent echoes of earlier campaigns for change, were fueled by messages sent through the outer rings. People offended by what they saw, respectively, as the stifling authority of Washington and the corrupting power of Wall Street found each other without nearly so much middle-ring brokering. Quite the opposite, the miracle of information technology—blogs and social networks, e-mails and

Twitter feeds—made it possible for individuals to find, connect, and organize ideological peers without knowing one another very well.

To be clear, every movement in American history has cultivated and mobilized people who might not otherwise have gotten engaged in the political process. Moreover, the ideas promoted by the Tea Partiers and Occupiers were filtered in some part through local clubs and civic organizations that inspired their members; fervor inevitably passed between friends who knew each other from class, from work, or just from around the neighborhood.

Nevertheless, what made both efforts influential was less their ability to mobilize new groups of people and more their capacity to connect far-flung individuals who already shared their same convictions. Where an outraged liberal college professor might have been able to do little more than write protest letters and angry journal articles in the 1970s, her counterpart thirty years later can connect instantaneously with a much wider audience. Where a conservative businessman might once have been limited to riling up members of his country club about the threat of bureaucratic overreach, today he can tap into a national, if not international, network of anguished libertarians.

That then points out one of the central appeals of impersonal relationships formed across a shared interest: a sense of belonging. However committed members of any flash-fire political movement are to their underlying ideals, they are also drawn in by the sense that they've found a niche. They've connected with people who, whether or not they live nearby, share a common affinity. This feature is not limited to the world of politics: people who are victims of the same disease, collectors of the same memorabilia, graduates of the same college, and denizens of the same profession can connect more readily than any generation before.

Maybe most magical, all the attributes that might make it impossible for people in the same niche to become inner- or middle-ring comrades can be glossed over through outer-ring connections.

Two people with nothing in common beyond a single point of interest can engage without worrying about other beliefs that might put them on opposite sides of a vast divide. A white Klansman from Kentucky may think a woman's place is standing over a stove. Nevertheless, he might unknowingly trade his rookie Stan Musial baseball card to a black woman from Oakland who owns a small business. And that's the point: outer-ring relationships sometimes pierce the prejudices that once balkanized American society, without necessarily addressing the underlying tension.

Barry Wellman has devised a term for our new capacity to seek out people much more specifically than before. He calls it "networked individualism."[18] We no longer have to join anything to find people who want to commiserate (or stick it out with a close friend who's become little more than an irritant).[19] Instead, when choosing where to invest our social capital, we can pick and choose more readily, and mix and match.

By most estimates, that is an almost unadulterated blessing. If life is short, better to spend what time we have with the people who offer us the most. In a world full of hassles, the last several decades have seen us shake off the burdensome obligations that stole precious minutes away from our dearest friends and most compatible acquaintances. There is, after all, little upside to traveling through a complicated set of Greyhound bus transfers when another motor coach service can get you from one point to another straight away.

But there's been a cost to the developments of the last several decades. Our search for affirmation—what MIT scholar Sherry Turkle has defined as a sort of communal narcissism—has compelled us to avoid relationships that expanded our intellectual horizons or drove conflict. Unless we enjoy it, we no longer have to maintain a close friendship with the woman who wants to haggle over politics. We no longer have to talk football with the guy rooting for our team's archrival. And life today doesn't just allow us to spend more time with the acquaintances who comprise our inner and outer rings; we can populate those categories with people who speak our language.[20] Never before have people who shared our concerns been so easily accessible, not only across the dinner table but around the globe.

Which brings us to the question of trade-offs. Besides the rings where we've chosen to invest more of our social capital, we also have to consider which acquaintances we've abandoned. Choosing among relationships is, some might say, a zero-sum game: while we've been empowered to invest additional capital in certain acquaintances, we've been compelled simultaneously to withdraw time and attention from others.

How then have the changes we've each made on an individual level begun to ripple across society as a whole? The trade-offs we're making individually—often without realizing it—are having major impacts on the whole landscape of American life. And that, as we'll see, is what we've most frequently failed to appreciate.

THE MISSING RINGS

*B*owling Alone, Robert Putnam's now classic exploration of what he termed "The Collapse and Revival of American Community," sparked a period of soul-searching through the mid- to late 1990s.[1] By laying out copious, frequently overwhelming research, Putnam's central thesis—that Americans were becoming estranged from one another—suggested in clear prose that American community was in a state of decline. Pundits across the political spectrum debated the cause and its implications, coming to a variety of different conclusions. President Clinton himself brought Putnam and a group of other scholars together at Camp David to discuss what might be done to rebuild communal trust.[2]

But *Bowling Alone*'s success wasn't driven solely by its call to action. The book was popular because its thesis rang true. From one perspective, American life at the turn of the twenty-first century was worthy of celebration: Clinton presided over the longest economic expansion in the nation's history, balanced the budget for the first time in a generation, and nurtured the development of the new, information-based economy. Moreover, a decade after the end of the Cold War, Washington's place atop the global hierarchy seemed entirely secure.

But despite America's inarguable climb up Maslow's hierarchy of needs, many people sensed dark clouds on the horizon, even if few could explain exactly why. A country that appeared at the time to be thriving seemed, by the same token, to be decaying from within. And *Bowling Alone* threw back the veil.

The country's underlying pessimism stemmed largely from the dramatic displays of conflict that emerged, throughout the 1990s, as fodder for outrageous newspaper headlines and vitriolic cable-television debates. The dialogue out of Washington had become consumed by what Clinton's allies termed "the politics of personal destruction," a particularly bitter manifestation of the culture wars that were dividing the American electorate.[3] Pitched political battles over abortion and gun rights, the separation of church and state, and a panoply of other proxies for deep-seated societal rifts had plunged the public discourse into a mud pit.

Ironically, by most standards the 1990s saw relief from many of the social ills that had previously gnawed at our sense of optimism: inflation, crime rates, drug use, and welfare rolls, each taken as a symbol of a coming demise during the 1970s and '80s, all fell to the point of vanishing from the nation's political consciousness during Clinton's eight-year tenure. Nevertheless, the equanimity of the 1950s—still fresh in the minds of most American adults—had failed to emerge amid economic rejuvenation. And so *Bowling Alone*'s central thesis highlighted something Americans could feel in their bones.

At the same time, Putnam's critics pointed to what they considered a fairly significant omission. Although his analysis had traced the decline of certain social conventions, it largely ignored the emergence of a new tool for personal interaction: information technology.[4] Even before the advent of Facebook and Twitter, LISTSERVs and e-newsletters had exploded through the World Wide Web. As a result, the critics charged, new communities were emerging to replace the hallowed institutions Putnam seemed so eager to reanimate.

Thinking back on that debate more than a decade later, it seems clear that *Bowling Alone*'s critics were right about one part of the story. As we saw in the preceding chapter, the communities that live online—the outer-ring connections that have become both more familiar and nearly omnipresent—have grown much more prolific. Combined with our new capacity (and propensity) to invest more social capital in the inner rings, we haven't become nearly as isolated as Putnam's analysis portended.

But *Bowling Alone* wasn't wrong. There's something qualitatively different about the connections that have emerged to replace the bowling leagues, PTA meetings, and dinner parties Putnam prized. Americans aren't isolated per se—one need only look at social media to see how new and exciting relationships are generated and maintained every day. But there's something distinct today about how we channel Tocqueville's "habits of the heart." And to understand the difference, we need to understand the trade-offs made when Americans decided to invest more heavily in the inner and outer rings.

Maybe the most compelling aspect of *Bowling Alone* was its breadth. Putnam didn't simply document the decline in what he called "social capital" (a term he used—in contrast to the definition used in this book—to approximate the gross total of how interconnected Americans were to one another). He offered example upon example showing that connections that were fairly commonplace during the 1950s had ebbed over the ensuing decades. Americans were less likely to vote, less likely to play bridge, less likely to volunteer, less likely to invite friends over for dinner, and, as the title indicates, less likely to join in organized activities such as bowling leagues. Putnam acknowledged that new sorts of relationships might have been forming online. But it is hard to read *Bowling Alone* without coming away convinced that something in America had gone seriously awry.

Putnam wasn't alone in sounding the alarm. Just a few years later, Theda Skocpol, one of Putnam's colleagues at Harvard, released a survey of American organizations revealing that Americans were joining different sorts of institutions than those they had just a few decades before. The groups that had thrived in the early postwar period—the Rotary Club, Kiwanis, Shriners, Elks, League of Women Voters, and volunteer fire companies—had dwindled over the decades. But that didn't mean Americans weren't joining. Those older associations had been replaced, she argued, both by professionally managed advocacy organizations (e.g., the National Association of Home Builders and NARAL, the abortion-rights lobby) and by more local organizations that met for a single purpose, such as agitating for a new community center.[5]

The implications of Skocpol's research went well beyond the realm of voluntary associations. Americans, it suggested, weren't simply spending more time and attention on certain more and less intimate connections; they were marshaling social capital away from the middle rings. The older associations had, by Skocpol's description, included "men or women of different occupational and class backgrounds," even while many were divided along racial and ethnic lines.[6] When men met regularly at a lodge, or when women gathered for a weekly chapter meeting, they were nurturing the sorts of familiar (but not intimate) bonds that would easily have fit Dunbar's definition of a "village." The associations that were prevalent in the earlier postwar period were born of the middle rings.

What replaced the Elks Club and the bowling leagues were more typically organs of the outer rings. Newer institutions tended to bring together individuals who, outside one point of contact, were less likely to be mutually familiar. In lieu of forming semiautonomous local chapters, national groups now more embraced a hub-and-spoke model, where organizers headquartered in Washington or elsewhere would reach out directly to members. The one-time supposition that members would attend a regularly scheduled tea was replaced by the request that members send donations designed to fund the work of professional staffers, who would then carry the banner.

Skocpol was alarmed by the picture her research revealed, but she acknowledged that the professional nonprofits that now dominate the world of nongovernmental organizations are almost certainly more effective in achieving certain discrete goals. Middle-ring relationships, after all, can be a headache, burning time and energy that might better be spent on advancing the cause. It's burdensome to keep a chapter moving—even beyond the cost of supplying coffee and doughnuts. Moreover, grudges between members can develop, leaving cliquish organizations mired in dysfunction.

And that's why the new breed of American association offers significant advantages to those agitating for change. Outer-ring connections are an ideal vehicle to harness the passion individuals have for a single concern. Neighbors who have never exchanged more than two words can join in the temporary service of ousting an incompetent school official. Adversaries on opposite sides of a picket line can lend their voices (and wallets) to the campaign for, say, marriage equality—even without realizing that they're contributing to the same cause.

For the purposes of our exploration of community, what's most important to acknowledge is that Skocpol was documenting a much broader shift. The new breed of organization that emerged wasn't built beside the old sort; the two types haven't managed to thrive in tandem. Rather, the new replaced the old: the outer rings have subsumed the middle. Because we all have a limited amount of time and attention, social capital invested in one ring generally requires divestment from another. And so, as we'll see, the shift that Skocpol noted within the sphere of voluntary associations signals a broader shift through the rest of American life.

Six years after *Bowling Alone* emerged as a national bestseller, Putnam's concerns about the state of American community were subject to another round of media attention when three sociologists released a study documenting a dramatic spike in social isolation.[7] The study, which prompted a *New York Times* article titled "The Lonely American Just Got a Bit Lonelier," compared similar, if not identical, questions asked of Americans between 1985 and 2004.[8] The authors found that the percentage of Americans who could boast at least one non-kin "confidant" had dropped from 63.9 to 47.1.[9] Nearly a quarter of Americans, they found, had no one to confide in at all. It was a striking conclusion—one that seemed to confirm Putnam's earlier concern that American community was in decline.

In the years that followed, other sociologists quibbled with the new study's methodology. They argued that the questions asked in 2004—about the stable of acquaintances with whom any individual would discuss an "important matter"—couldn't reasonably be tracked back to the wording used in 1985.[10] But the study's core findings have nevertheless been confirmed by other research.[11] A 2005 Georgetown University study, for example, found that 47 percent of Americans knew "none, almost none or a few" of their neighbors by name.[12] And two sociologists at the University of Washington, Avery Guest and Susan Wierzbicki, found a similar trend when looking at data between 1974 and 1996.[13]

Eventually, a sociologist now at Rutgers, Keith Hampton, took another look at the data. Even after scrubbing the methodology, the decline in community seemed palpable. By his calculations, more than a quarter of the respondents in 1985 had claimed to have a discussion network of five or more confidants. But by 2008, a mere 7 percent had a discussion network that large.[14] The percentage of respondents who reported having at least one non-kin confidant had fallen from 64 to 45 percent.[15] And the percentage claiming only one regular confidant had grown from less than 15 percent to nearly 35.[16]

Today, it's tempting to look at the sophisticated data that has emerged from the world of sociology and conclude that American community is falling away. And, indeed, for the same reasons that *Bowling Alone* rang true, data that confirms one of our basest fears about the state of American society—that future generations may be increasingly ostracized by one another—seems ominous. But when taken in combination with the reams of data detailed in the last chapter—statistics suggesting the degree to which Americans are investing more heavily in their inner- and outer-ring relationships—it's clear that something else is going on. Americans aren't being lost in a sea of social isolation. They're shifting their time and attention from one constellation of rings to another.

The great frustration, of course, is that it's nearly impossible to measure the gross amount of social capital that's been shifted away from the middle rings—or, at least it was until recently. But in 2012, sociologists Peter Marsden, dean of social sciences at Harvard, and Berkeley sociologist Sameer Srivastava, published what may be the most compelling evidence to date. Using data from the General Social Survey, they pieced together answers to questions focused on whom respondents had eaten dinner with over the previous month. What they found was fascinating.

Between the mid-1990s and 2008, the percentage of respondents who reported having eaten at least once with relatives increased from 52 to 59. The percentage reporting that they had eaten with friends outside their local neighborhood had also grown. But when Marsden and Srivastava dug into the data on how many Americans were spending at least one evening socializing with their neighbors—maybe the clearest proxy for a middle-ring relationship—the figure had fallen dramatically, from 44 percent in 1974 to 31 percent in 2008. The percentage who spent an evening at a bar or tavern fell from 19 percent in the mid-1970s to 14 percent after 2004. Maybe most tellingly, the proportion of Americans saying they never socialized with a neighbor grew from roughly 20 to 30 percent between the 1970s and the 2000s.[17]

Sociologist Andrew Cherlin came to a similar conclusion when noting how Americans had, over time, become more desirous of finding a "soul mate." He found data suggesting that as marriages had become more intimate over the course of the twentieth century—as the emotional connection between spouses became more important than whether a couple made good life partners—time and attention that would once have been invested in a wider net of friends and acquaintances was being transferred to "cocooning" spouses.[18]

In essence, an increasingly clear picture of a dramatic transformation emerges from these studies. American community isn't collapsing, as Robert Putnam feared in *Bowling Alone*. Nevertheless, it's evolving in remarkable ways. The distribution of social capital that was typical two generations ago—a moment in American history when we were heavily invested in middle-ring acquaintances—has given way. What limited time and energy Americans have today is devoted to our most intimate relationships and a set of much more one-dimensional connections. Along the way, the middle rings have become the missing rings.

While the sociological data paint the clearest picture, the shift of American social capital from the middle rings is also readily apparent in our everyday lives. Consider the evolution of how kids (or, specifically, adolescents) now play together. Admittedly, for as long as there have been video games, parents have been concerned about their effects on children. When Atari and Nintendo dominated the market during the 1980s concerns centered on the fear that staring at televisions screens would fry children's brains and strain their eyes. Those concerns still persist today.

But as much as the transition from pick-up games of basketball to indoor tournaments of Super Mario Brother marked a change in the rhythms of American adolescence, something important stayed the same: in between games or matches, kids still had to negotiate how to get along with each other. When they wanted a snack, they still had to battle over whether to microwave the leftover chicken nuggets or grab the spare string cheese. Moreover, in both instances, all-day tournaments fostered conversations on entirely unrelated topics: "I sure do hope I don't get Ms. Davis for homeroom next year—she's supposed to be wicked mean." "You're so lucky your parents are taking you to Disneyland over winter break—I have to go visit my aunt in New Hampshire."

Since the eighties, by contrast, the gaming industry has undergone a revolution. It's not just that the graphics have gotten more sophisticated or that the appeal has extended to older gamers. Rather, gaming—to use a term that's unintentionally ironic—has become social. Those engaged on their computers and tablets, let alone their Xboxes and Playstations, don't have to play with friends staring at the same screen; they can compete with anyone connected to the Internet, no matter where they're sitting, anywhere in the world. Look, for example, at World of Warcraft, a fantasy experience that offers gamers worldwide the chance to assume the identity of an avatar who exists in a fantasy online.[19] Having at one point reached a peak of twelve million subscribers, players interact with each other, fight monsters, coordinate efforts to complete fantasy challenges and, at times, compete with one another.[20] Not only do they no longer need to be in the same room—they don't even have to be on the same continent.

The upside to social gaming—in contrast to the primitive systems of a generation ago—is that players can develop real-world relationships through the software: a guy in Nebraska and a woman in Hong Kong can meet online, plot to storm a virtual castle, and, theoretically, shoot the breeze about what they've each read about in their local, online newspaper. Far from the isolating existence that many people likely associate with the stereotype of a teenager glued to a computer screen in his mother's basement, World of Warcraft has become the means to a much wider range of social interactions. Far from cut off, gamers are connecting. In fact, in some circumstances, players introduced online eventually visit with one another in real life.[21]

But inasmuch as it's worth celebrating those newfound outer-ring connections, we should acknowledge that whatever bonds the gamers are forming with their online buddies, they're giving up the middle-ring ties that once bound teenagers sitting in front of the living-room television. No one's learning how to share the leftover pizza. Friends who live miles apart aren't likely to commiserate about the need to clean up the decrepit park behind the middle school. It's unlikely that the guy in Nebraska will be able to lean on the woman in Hong Kong for help finding childcare when his wife leaves for a weeklong business trip. The tenor of the conversations between people playing the games has evolved as well.

What's most notable among the changes? With certain exceptions, these aren't the sorts of ties that span more than a single common interest.[22] In the case of World of Warcraft, players are tied frequently by their passion for fantasy and little more. Acquaintances aren't learning about one another in nearly the same depth, or across the same cultural chasms they would have bridged in person. They're not discussing the topics that would inevitably have come up across a bridge table, around a basketball court, over a cup of tea, or, indeed, at a Wednesday night bowling league.

Richard Ling, a sociologist at the University of Michigan,

focused on the other end of the spectrum: he conducted studies that suggested that mobile phones were drawing time and attention toward the inner rings.[23] As he explained: "While generally we must be open to both intimates and strangers when we interact in daily life, the mobile phone tips the balance in favor of the intimate sphere of friends and family."[24] That simply proves the same point from the other side. When it comes to the normal distribution of American social capital, the cost of our stampede to invest more heavily in the inner and outer rings has been borne by the relationships we once formed in the middle.

Released in 1986, the film *Stand by Me* is the story of four ordinary twelve-year-old kids on a wilderness adventure in the waning days of a 1950s-era summer. Based on a short story written by Stephen King, the film's plot is ostensibly driven by the foursome's search for a corpse in the woods. But the narrative's real subjects are the relationships between four youthful misfits brought together almost entirely through happenstance.[25] Gordie, the narrator, is an aspiring author who entertains the group with his imaginative stories. Chris, a stand-up guy from a family of ne'er-do-wells, is the crew's quiet and courageous leader. Teddy is the quirky victim of a physically abusive father. And Vern, the group's pudgy tagalong, offers comic relief.

In certain respects, the boys comprise the type of adolescent crew that has become an archetype in American history. The foursome is culled together from among the kids who lived nearby, bonded despite their differences. Even if a bit more intimate, theirs are quintessential examples of relationships forged through the middle rings. And that makes their circumstances an ideal jumping-off point for imagining whether the same four characters would have found each other in the circumstances of contemporary American community. Amid all the changes wrought by the last several decades, have the sorts of gangs that Gordie, Chris, Teddy, and Vern joined become relics of the past?

Admittedly, friendships are still forged among adolescent boys. But the landscape has inarguably changed. Today, just as we're less likely to shop along the local strip because we can order what we want online or travel to the mall or a big-box store that caters specifically to our demographic, we're less likely to befriend the kid sitting in the seat next to us because we can text our closest pals. We're less likely bump into a neighbor on the street because, in the growing suburbs, we tend to drive everywhere we go. A comic-book aficionado who loves Batman doesn't need to befriend the Superman fanatic down the street, because there's a whole world of Batman-lovers is just waiting to kibitz with her at the other end of a broadband connection.

At root, Gordie, Chris, Teddy, and Vern stuck together because, in the world of the early postwar period, none had a better option. Today, by contrast, the same four kids would more likely go their own ways. Instead of hanging out with whatever buddies each could find around the neighborhood, a kid like Gordie is more likely to spend his free time trading stories online with other aspiring writers. Maybe one of the guys would get sucked into a community of muscle-car fanatics. It's still possible that the old crew would have found their way to one another. But then again, many of the sorts of settings that brought them together—small towns— have been abandoned as Americans streamed into suburbs, which, as Bill Bishop argued so convincingly, are less likely to maintain the same sort of diversity.

Without getting too caught up in the fictional details, the broader truth of the story is readily apparent. The circumstances that once compelled Americans to develop the sort of familiar but less intimate relationships that were a staple of postwar American life have faded. Social capital spent on World of Warcraft or Facebook is time not spent outside talking with neighbors, shooting the breeze at a bar, or grabbing a burger with a colleague from work. And while there's nothing wrong with that per se, we ought not to be so naïve as to think that that those new relationships don't come at a cost.

Barry Wellman and his colleagues at the University of Toronto's Netlab have long argued that information technology, one of the major factors driving the new arrangement of American social capital, has had a less dramatic effect on the contours of our social lives than some might assume. They point out, for example, that we tend to e-mail with the same people we visit in real life.[26] But while there's no doubt that your best friend's pictures will show up on your Facebook feed, a lot of social networking use replaces time you might have spent on the middle rings. Studies bear that out: a 2009 study by the Pew Internet & American Life Project found that those who use sites like Facebook are generally in touch with a broader—and more diverse—set of acquaintances.[27]

Stanford sociologist Norman Nie has managed to quantify the same observation. He and several colleagues designed studies to explore how investments in certain types of relationships affected other categories. And what they concluded more than a decade ago was eye-opening: for every minute an individual spends on the Internet, the time he or she spends with friends is reduced by seven seconds, and time spent with colleagues by eleven.[28] Perhaps more jarring, the study found that for every e-mail sent or received, an individual lost a minute of time with his or her family.[29]

What's less clear is how those changes have affected the underlying architecture of American society. In earlier chapters I traced how the unique building block of our communities—the township—survived the changes that marked our nineteenth- and early twentieth-century transition from farm to factory. Although the Chicago School sociologists worried a century ago that the masses pouring into the nation's cities would destroy ties among neighbors, the township structure survived nevertheless.

But if the circumstances that brought together the boys from *Stand by Me* have faded, it may be time to ask that question again. Has the township survived the postwar period or, alternatively, have the Third Wave, the Chinatown Bus effect, the jump up Maslow's hierarchy of needs, and the search for affirmation opened the door for us to embrace something new?

10

EXIT TOCQUEVILLE

et's recall where we left off in our historical survey of
American community. What had seemed imminent during the early years of the twentieth century—namely, that
the massive migration from the wholesome countryside to the
gritty metropolis would leave Americans isolated and depraved—
had, just a few decades later, been proven wrong. As Jane Jacobs
revealed—and many academics later came to acknowledge—many
of the rhythms that had defined the Tocqevillian township had
survived despite the big shift. Indeed, cities thrived after the
Industrial Revolution in large part because the individual neighborhoods that subdivided urban America had embraced the same
basic social architecture that had been present in America's colonial villages and frontier towns.

But as the Second World War faded further into the rearview
mirror, America's cities faced yet another challenge. As the boomers embraced a spirit of rebelliousness and protest, the beam-
ing metropolises of the 1950s began to disassemble. Despite the
federal government's aggressive efforts to shore up the nation's
urban landscape (the Johnson administration's Model Cities ini-
tiative first among them), many Americans were left to wonder

whether Gotham and other large municipalities were breeding grounds for despair.

There was some déjà vu at work: the early twentieth century's fear of Dickensian urban turmoil mapped fairly well onto the Vietnam-era fear that ghettos were tinderboxes—a concern that came to a head when Newark and Detroit were set ablaze in the wake of Martin Luther King Jr.'s 1968 assassination.[1] In each case, a romanticized past seemed to be in decay: in the one instance, the small-town life of the 1800s; in the other, the vibrant middle-class lifestyle celebrated during the immediate postwar years. A half century after the Chicago School's concerns about urban life were disproven, a similar aura of fear swept through the national consciousness. Americans began to wonder anew whether cities were turning their residents into misanthropes.

Some observers weren't having it. Suspicious that the nation's despair might once again be misplaced, Claude Fischer decided in the 1970s to take a closer look at what distinguished cities from other parts of the country. A professor in the sociology department at Berkeley, he had easy access to a diverse set of communities throughout the Bay Area. And so he went into the field, pioneering new techniques to observe and report on the ways Americans interacted at the community level.

What Fischer found and later published in an award-winning book, *To Dwell Among Friends,* flew in the face of the conventional wisdom. City residents weren't isolated ne'er-do-wells, as many presumed. But, as he explained, they did tend to invest in different sorts of relationships than their counterparts in surrounding areas. Residents of small towns engaged more frequently in what Fischer termed "traditional" relationships—they were more apt to encompass family members, neighbors, and fellow congregants at church. In cities, by contrast, relationships were more "modern," meaning that urbanites were more often tied to work associates, club members, and friends. There seemed to be a tacit trade-off at work: people living in downtown San Francisco named a quarter fewer relatives among their network than those in semirural areas; on the flip side, only an eighth of city dwellers lived in a social world dominated by family, compared to a full half of those living further out.[2]

Fischer also discerned something else: those who lived in the bedroom communities surrounding cities—suburbanites, in essence—were the least likely to be involved in the traditional relationships of rural America. His broad conclusion: while it wasn't fair to say that community was in decline, how people in various types of neighborhoods connected to one another varied across disparate environments.[3] Different landscapes begat different flavors of community.

The explosive growth of the nation's suburbs, of course, is the big demographic story of the last several decades.[4] Between 1960 and 2000, the neighborhoods and towns that abut urban centers expanded to claim a larger share of the population than both urban and rural America combined.[5] We can infer that the transition from traditional social arrangements to the more modern alternatives has only accelerated since *To Dwell Among Friends* was first published. If cities are more modern than towns, and suburbs are more modern than cities, then America's embrace of "modern" community came well before the digital and mobile revolutions emerged several decades later.

That then suggests something truly profound: the social architecture that prevails in communities with thick middle rings differs from the sort that emerges when residents privilege both more and less intimate relationships. The township—a social structure dependent almost entirely on the strength of the middle rings—is fundamentally incompatible with the "modern" arrangements that have come into vogue. The way we invest our social capital today has compelled us to abandon the community architecture that previously defined the great bulk of American history. And that marks an unheralded, but crucial transformation.

————

Nothing illustrates the crumbling state of the American township better than a little-noticed shift in the definition of a familiar term. During the mid-2000s, two psychiatrists on the faculty of the Harvard Medical School, Jacqueline Olds and Richard Schwartz, noted that the definition of "neighborliness" had evolved dramatically over the course of several decades. In the early postwar period, being neighborly meant reaching out to the people who lived next door—taking a homemade cake to the family moving into the house across the street, offering to watch the kids in a pinch, saying hello at an annual block party, or inviting acquaintances to join a Wednesday night bowling league.

Over the years, however, the term came to denote almost exactly the opposite. Today, being "neighborly" means leaving those around you in peace. The neighborly family across the street refrains from playing loud music or leaving its garbage on the stoop. A neighborly homeowner avoids letting her house deteriorate and become a blight on the neighborhood. "Neighborly" neighbors avoid mentioning what they've overheard through the thin walls separating apartments. The sense of warmth once suggested by the term—a crucial ingredient for the sorts of the middle-ring relationships so important for township community—has been replaced by a kind of detachment.[6]

But the semantic change in neighborliness provides only the most superficial evidence of the township's decline. Robert Wuthnow noted in the 1990s that the places where Americans find meaning—the institutions that ground their sense of identity—have also evolved. As we've seen, Americans aren't nearly as invested in the missions of the membership associations that they choose to join today as their parents and grandparents were decades ago. It isn't just that the nature of those organizations had changed, as Theda Skocpol discovered. It's that each individual's emotional investment in each organization had ebbed.

In the 1950s, for example, a mother might have found satisfaction in the spirit of fellowship and charity that defined her Junior League chapter, and her husband might have taken pride in being a leader of the neighborhood watch. But as Americans increasingly have come to mark their involvement by sending checks to professional lobbying organizations like Planned Parenthood Action Fund or the AARP, their sense of personal responsibility has diminished; roles once filled by voluntary associations have become the government's responsibility.[7] Community policing, for example, the strategy of having officers become more intimately familiar with the people along their patrols, was promoted during the 1990s largely because the civic organizations that once served the same role had withered.

A similar shift is evident in the American workplace. The patterns that were predominant in the early postwar period—the industrial jobs that peaked during the 1940s and 1950s—facilitated casual acquaintances that are rarer today. The way that businesses have become specialized—farming out discrete responsibilities rather than housing a whole contingent of different sorts of employees—has eaten away at middle-ring relationships that might have existed between different kinds of employees. The interactions that might have flourished in the parking lot between an accountant and an engineer two generations ago don't happen because the accountants now work on one suburban campus and the engineers on another.

We need to qualify that: businesses like Dunder-Mifflin, the fictional paper company depicted in the long-running sitcom *The Office*, do still exist. Employees sitting in bays of cubicles, along rows of desks, or even in side-by-side offices are just as apt to have conversations by the watercooler, engage in casual banter in the break room, or bring Girl Scout cookie order forms to pass out among their colleagues. Those are still middle-ring relationships— and they reflect the sort of interactions that were common among colleagues at industrial mills in the 1950s.

But the patterns that once compelled mid-level company sales-men, factory floor clerks, and in-house counsels to sit together at the same table in a company cafeteria have ebbed over the years because fewer businesses house such diversified workforces within any single facility. When a small corporation has an antitrust con-cern, its chief executive is more likely to hire an outside firm with expertise in the subject than rely on a lawyer in the general coun-sel's office down the hall. Customer-service representatives are likely to be off-site as well. In the same way that community no longer serves as the connective tissue bringing Americans from different walks of life together, the propensity to separate different elements of the economy—to break down big, diverse corporations into more profitable and specialized parts—has tended to hack at the rhythms of townshipped life.[8]

And it doesn't end there. The number of subcontractors has exploded as people want to hire experts rather than jacks-of-all-trades.[9] In academia, generalists are increasingly rare, and schol-arly specialization has become the new norm.[10] The growth of the service economy has only served to drive the same trend, with firms likely to rent specialized services, often "consultants" assigned to a specific job, rather than bring experts on staff full-time.[11] Thus, businesses are harnessing the laws of competitive advantage: because work can easily be transferred from one office to another, and from one factory floor to another across the globe, those who do particular tasks best are doing those tasks exclusively.

In the early 1970s, my father did something crazy by today's standards: he hitchhiked around the world. He was in his mid-twenties, the economy was sluggish at home, and so he set off on a freighter across the Atlantic, became a chicken farmer on an Israeli kibbutz, and eventually made his way across the Khyber

Pass into Pakistan. For years, my sister and I were plied with stories from that journey, and with the tidbits of wisdom Dad had gathered at each stop along the way.

The legacy of that trip spurred the inevitable: like every kid who looks up to his father, I announced one night to my parents at some point in middle school that when I came of age, I too would hitchhike around the globe. But to my surprise, far from cheering my determination, my mother's face drained of color. "Oh, no you're not!" she exclaimed. "It's much too dangerous to hitchhike in today's world. It's different now than it was then."

A parent now myself, I understand where Mom (and Dad—he agreed) was coming from. But setting aside any parent's aversion to a child's risk-taking behavior, my mother's admonition seemed to rest on a dubious presumption. Was the world really more treacherous than it had been a generation or two before? My parents argued that hitchhiking had been a cultural norm back then, so it was safer to get into a stranger's car. But that was hardly a satisfying answer. And so, for years—at least until my junior year in college, when two weeks of traveling alone through Eastern Europe in the dead of winter convinced me to abandon the idea altogether—I harbored plans to set off on the journey despite their disapproval.

Years later, the questions I'd thrown back at my mother stuck with me: why had hitchhiking gone out of vogue? As it happened, the coauthors of the bestseller *Freakonomics*, Steven Levitt and Stephen Dubner, asked a very similar question in the fall of 2011. In the course of an investigation done for their radio program, they weren't able to uncover any good data on the subject. But they noted that what had been a rite of passage for many baby boomers was now seen as a sort of death wish for their children. And, like me, they wanted to know why.[12]

After some digging, the *Freakonomics* team emerged with two likely culprits. The first was that hitching had fallen victim to irrational fear. A slew of sensationalized 1970s-era movies about violent hitchers—films like *Texas Chainsaw Massacre*—and a sprinkling of real-life horror stories had convinced Americans that strangers looking for a ride were out for no good. Much like the fear of shark attacks—a danger so remote that no one can rationally fear being bitten, but simultaneously so horrific that many would-be swimmers are scared out of the water—hitchhiking got a bad rap. And so my parents' admonition, like those of parents around the country, seemed likely to have stemmed from that specious cultural meme.

Second, and more convincingly, the *Freakonomics* researchers argued that hitchhiking had become rarer because Americans had developed readier access to their own wheels. Armed with the ability to get around without depending on anyone else—between 1969 and 2009, the number of households with more than one car grew from three to six in ten, and drivers' licenses became nearly ubiquitous—fewer Americans were compelled to stick out their thumbs. In more mundane economic terms, as the cost of a personalized ride came down, the demand for its substitute—a ride in someone else's car—also declined.

What the *Freakonomics* team didn't discuss—and what may vindicate my mother's admonition most directly—is that something even more profound happened over the course of hitchhiking's decline. "Traditional" social architecture had imbued the average American with a certain familiarity with people from different walks of life. The norms perpetuated by the middle rings promoted a sense of assumed trust, if only because strangers weren't nearly so foreign. In the absence of townshipped life, it seemed much more likely that the guy with his thumb out—let alone the driver willing to provide a ride—was a weirdo. Indeed, *Bowling Alone*'s exposé of America's thinning connective tissue was designed to explain why social trust in the United States was nearing a low-water mark. As Putnam put it: "The best evidence suggests that social trust rose from the mid-1940s to the mid-1960s, peaking in 1964. . . . In the mid-1960s, however, this beneficent trend was reversed, initiating a long-term decline. . . . Most, if not all, of the decline in American social trust since the 1960s is attributable to generational succession. . . . At generation's end, a generation with a trust quotient of nearly 80 percent was being rapidly replaced by one with a trust quotient of barely half that."[13]

Putnam's research points to what may be the most underappreciated casualty of the township's decline: our fuller confidence in the goodwill of the average stranger. It's not just that we've lost the affinities that allow diamond dealers in Manhattan to inspect their jewelry with greater alacrity. It's not just that commuters without a car are less likely to catch a ride for free. It's that in the absence of the sorts of relationships we once had with people who were familiar, but not intimate—without friendly ties to people from other walks of life—we've become walled off.

That lines up well with Bill Bishop's argument in *The Big Sort*— that we live in monolithic communities. It also reinforces the observation that we not only live near people who share our worldview; the people next door have become strangers. Townships aren't just networks of social relationships—they offer each of us a window onto experiences beyond our own. As they've decayed, we've become more insular and suspicious. Absent a stronger bond with the roughly 150 people who might comprise our personal village, it's no wonder that it seems more dangerous to step into a stranger's car.

But it's not just that we've become less trusting in the absence of thick middle rings. Townships also bred a sort of mutual familiarity among people with very different backgrounds and worldviews. As in Toni Morrison's recollection of her life growing up in Lorain, Ohio, with people from all sorts of backgrounds trading recipes, it was through the mundane, middle-ring interactions of everyday life that Americans developed a better understanding of where their acquaintances were coming from. Townships served as the foundation for the American propensity to appreciate diversity—and in their absence, we've become both more ignorant and less sympathetic.

On a trip to Atlanta during my junior year of college, a friend took me to Mary Mac's Tea Room, an iconic Georgia restaurant serving traditional southern fare. Mary Mac's, I was told, had been a favorite of Jimmy Carter's. As a Jewish kid from Buffalo, I didn't want to miss it. The visit promised to be a cultural experience. Everything on the menu looked good. Fried Chicken. Country-Fried Steak. Chicken Pot Pie. Sweet Tea and Coca-Cola.

Then something caught my eye. In a corner of the menu, beneath the best-selling items that drew the crowds (and which are the archetypal staples of southern cuisine), I noted a dish I'd never seen offered before: "potlikker." The menu said that it was served with cornbread. When I waved the waitress over and asked her what it was, she was taken aback: "Honey, you never heard of that? I'm sure your mamma gave it to you when you were just a baby."

It was an awkward moment. My friend began to laugh, and I began to blush, insisting that I didn't know. The waitress beckoned some of the other servers over and giggled while repeating my question to the crew. Potlikker, they explained, is the liquid that is left in a pot after cooking down collard greens. It's a fairly standard dish in the South, and it's frequently fed to weaning babies.

In the spirit of adventure, I ordered a serving, much to the staff's amusement. And it didn't take long for me to realize that whatever potlikker was, it was an acquired taste. The ensuing grimace prompted gales of laughter from what was now my fairly sizable audience. True to Mary Mac's reputation, the rest of the meal was fantastic. But after we left I couldn't stop thinking about the waitress's quip. As novel as potlikker was to me, it seemed as though my ignorance had been equally perplexing to her.

Perhaps our mutual incredulity was excusable. After all, I was a white kid from New York who had come more than a thousand miles south to try something new. The waitstaff, which was overwhelmingly African-American, hadn't grown up in my community, let alone the same region of the country. The mismatch of our two experiences was, for the most part, understandable.

But the chasm that separated our mutual understanding is exactly what the missing rings might once have filled in. You needn't read Isabel Wilkerson's masterpiece on the Great Migration—the massive flow of African-Americans from the South into northern cities (like Buffalo) between 1915 and the 1970s—to realize that somewhere within a few miles of the home where I grew up, not far from Niagara Falls, were families that cooked greens as they had been taught by grandparents who had grown up below the Mason-Dixon line.[14] But I'd never met them—or if I had, I'd never developed the familiarity that would have exposed me to that part of their lives. The routines of my everyday life in the 1990s never compelled me to open that door.

And that suggests something more profound. The sorts of interactions that were once typical between Americans who were friendly but not intimate were a medium through which the norms in one pocket of society became accessible to those who lived nearby. Inner- and outer-ring relationships are generally centered on similarities: you're a member of the same family; you share the same love of vintage baseball cards. But relationships formed in the middle are not. And so, given the winnowing of the American township, the sort of mutual ignorance on display at Mary Mac's now exists, in many circumstances, among those who live next door to one another.

For as long as scholars have written about community, they've kvetched that things are headed down the tubes. It was that perpetual hand-wringing that caught NYU historian Thomas Bender's eye during the 1970s. In a little book published in 1978 that's become a classic among those investigating how Americans get along, he noted how generation upon generation of social scientists had taken turns predicting that the end of community was near. There was frequently a different reason—and often a reasonable rationale. From the Industrial Revolution through the dawn of the information age, successive scholars worried that the "habits of the heart" were fraying.[15]

Time and again, however, as Bender pointed out, the worriers had been proven wrong. America didn't devolve into a den of iniquity after industrialization. Small-town life didn't disappear in the twentieth century. What's more, life in the postwar American suburbs was studded with middle-ring connections. In *The Organization Man,* a book that sought to describe suburban life in the mid-1950s, the legions of Americans moving out of the nation's urban centers were almost entirely focused on their neighbors and the opinions of the popular crowd.[16]

But in the years since *The Organization Man* was written, American life has undergone a new litany of changes: the digital revolution, globalization, the transition to a service-oriented economy, the efficiencies of the Chinatown Bus effect, the ascent on Maslow's hierarchy of needs, and new ways to search for affirmation. Given that whole slew of factors, it's impossible not to ask: has the basic community building block that helped to spur Americans to independence finally been broken apart?

We need to be careful here, if only to honor Tom Bender's admonition that every generation claims that community is dying. It's entirely possible that townships, even if they're less apparent today, will eventually reemerge. But a broad conclusion is unmistakable: the shift in American social capital from the middle to the inner and outer rings has been profound. The evidence, while circumstantial, is overwhelming. As Stanford political scientist

Morris Fiorina, writing with Samuel Abrams of Sarah Lawrence College, declared in 2012, "Neighborhoods are not important centers of contemporary American life. Americans today do not know their neighbors very well, [and] do not talk to their neighbors very much."[17] The township, in essence, is dying.

This is not to suggest that the deterioration of our age-old method of organizing society is concomitant with the end of community. Indeed, I will argue that something else has emerged in its place. But before we analyze how America looks amid a society defined by thicker inner and outer rings, let's recall how monumental the transformation has been. As Alan Ehrenhalt wrote:

> In the 1990s, when many middle-class people are more likely to identify with a job, or a set of leisure interests, or with no entity at all larger than their own families, when courts have decided that geographical community is not a necessary component even of a political constituency, it is easy to forget that a neighborhood nearly everywhere in the 1950s was a tangible thing, a piece of ground, and physical marker in life.[18]

In an age when it is much easier to invest the bulk of your time and energy in the people you most want to seek out, there's little impetus to build a connection to someone less familiar. Townshipped community is dependent on the strength of middle-ring relationships. As the middle rings have faded, the sanctity of that building block—the explicitly local focus that James Madison, Alexis de Tocqueville, and Gordon Wood all identified as a central element of postcolonial American life—has begun to unravel. What remains, then, is the question of what will emerge in its place.

11

AND NOW FOR SOMETHING
COMPLETELY DIFFERENT

I have been almost entirely inactive on Facebook for quite some time now but I would just like to express my deep gratitude for what Facebook has done for me these past several days as I have been mourning the loss of my cat Napoleon. The ability to receive all of the kind words and thoughts and love from friends far and near, old and new, close and distant has been an incredible comfort. In the absence of any kind of formalized ritual for the passing of pets, this has really been the next best thing. This banging up against mortality has had me thinking about all sorts of things, among them, how this modern age with all of its convenience of mobility, means that we are often far away from "our people" and at times of crisis this is felt acutely. On the other hand, this modern age also allows us an instant connecting to great numbers of people at moments of need. I have heard from so many of you and every message, whether a brief public condolence or a thoughtful private note has helped me to feel a little less alone in this time of great sadness. So thank you. Really, truly. Thank you.

—Cassandra Bissell, my date to the 1996 Amherst Central High School prom, December 20, 2013, as posted on Facebook

It is one of the great unremarked ironies that *Bowling Alone* was released within months of another best seller, Thomas Friedman's *The Lexus and the Olive Tree*.[1] Now considered a quintessential exploration of "globalization," the *New York Times* columnist's turn-of-the-twenty-first-century exposé shined a spotlight on how new information technology, global supply chains, and huge multinational corporations have integrated Americans into a new post-Cold War economic system. Though no one has seemed to notice, Friedman's observation cut right at the heart of Putnam's central argument. If *Bowling Alone* was arguing that Americans were becoming more isolated, *The Lexus and the Olive Tree* contended that we were actually becoming more globally connected.

Putnam's and Friedman's books are rarely juxtaposed because their respective observations emerged from entirely different schools of literature. Putnam's work grew out of the fields of sociology and political science; Friedman was focused primarily on economics. But both books became standard-bearers for long-running trains of thought. *Bowling Alone*, like *The Lonely Crowd* and *Habits of the Heart* before it, was steeped in academic literature about the fragile state of American community. *The Lexus and the Olive Tree*, on the other hand, was designed to explain the transformation of the global economy in the aftermath of the Cold War.

Friedman's argument was grounded in a long history of social and economic scholarship. As far back as the 1970s, the Canadian philosopher Marshall McLuhan had predicted that geographic distances would be closed by new electronic media. The kinds of bonds once limited to local communities, the Canadian had argued, would eventually be shared across a much broader landscape.[2] The advances described in *The Lexus and the Olive Tree* make clear that McLuhan got a lot of the story right. As Friedman later wrote (in a book coauthored with Michael Mandelbaum), "in the span of a decade, people in Boston, Bangkok, and Bangalore, Mumbai, Manhattan and Moscow, all became virtual next-door neighbors."[3] Or, to use McLuhan's famous phrase, they had all become residents of the same "global village."[4]

It's quite a claim. After all, as Robin Dunbar's research into the lives of hunting and gathering societies made clear, relationships nurtured in villages—what I've identified as "middle-ring" relationships—aren't mere acquaintances. People who inhabit the same township know a fair amount about one another. Even if they aren't intimate friends, they're more familiar than strangers nodding to one another across the street. It was those relationships that Alexis de Tocqueville identified as a key feature of American exceptionalism during the 1830s. And more recently, they were what Charles Murray cited as a truly unique feature of American society:

> The first unparalleled aspect of American community life was the extent of its neighborliness. Neighborliness is not the same as hospitality. Many cultures have traditions of generous hospitality to strangers and guests. But widespread voluntary assistance among unrelated people who happen to live alongside one another has been rare. In the United States [however], it has been ubiquitous . . . keeping an eye on a house when its family is away, loaning a tool or the proverbial cup of sugar, taking care of a neighbor's children while the mother was running errands, or driving a neighbor to the doctor's office.[5]

What McLuhan predicted (and what Friedman later seemed to confirm) was that the sort of intimacy that had once been reserved for middle-ring contacts—to members of a local village or, say, within a city neighborhood—would eventually apply to a much wider circle of connections. Their view of modern life suggested that townships would simply expand to encompass many more contacts—that the miracle of modern technology would create a global village where we would all be able to connect with a much wider circle of friends.

But as Dunbar's research suggests, that's definitionally impossible. The cerebral cortex only allows us to keep an average of 150 middle-ring contacts at any given time; beyond that, we lose any true sense of familiarity. Much as we might want to maintain the same level of intimacy with a wider group of people, there is no way for townships to accommodate so many more acquaintances. And so as our time and attention has flowed out of the middle rings, a new social architecture, steeped in the largely one-dimensional contacts that populate the outer rings, has emerged to become the new, central building block of American community: the network.

This marks the apotheosis of all the upheavals described in earlier chapters. The host of changes to the landscape of American life and the rhythms of our everyday routines have combined not only to affect life at the margins, but to substitute networks of loosely connected contacts for traditional townships. It's not that Americans have consciously chosen to make the jump—it has happened organically. Townships emerged naturally from the bonds that define the middle rings; networks, by contrast, are born from farther-out connections.

I don't mean to argue that one social architecture is better than the other. It is, by any measure, a miracle of modern circuitry that anyone can follow the real-time Twitter feed of an academic who lives in Rio, or e-mail a farmer in sub-Saharan Africa. We are lucky to live in an age when we can access nearly any piece of information and connect with the vast majority of the world's population through a few clicks on our mobile phones. But the capacity to make an acquaintance is not a substitute for actually making the connection. The ability to e-mail someone doesn't make her a neighbor any more than it makes her a friend. It certainly doesn't suggest that we all live in the same "village."

The real question is what has been lost and what gained in the transition. More concisely: what are the implications? We tend to analyze momentous shifts in American life by sudden changes. But the first major shift in the nation's social architecture since the eighteenth century is a bird of an entirely different feather. It's not just that we're choosing to invest our time and attention in certain relationships rather than others. And it's not just that the central community building blocks of America's first two centuries have finally begun to dissolve. As we'll see, a whole new social structure has emerged, and with it a whole new set of challenges and opportunities.

The third section of this book is intended to untangle many of the implications—the trade-offs and dangers that have emerged with the triumph of networked community. But before we embark on that journey, it's worth noting what that claim is not meant to encompass.

First, it wouldn't be accurate to contend that villages, or townships, have suddenly become obsolete. There are plenty of places in America where neighbors still invite one another over for dinner, sponsor bridge tournaments, and bowl in leagues. The middle rings haven't disappeared entirely—they've just receded. As Charles Murray's spotlight on the chasm emerging between the middle and working classes suggests, further research on how individuals from different pockets (or strata) of society invest their time and attention may yield some fruitful conclusions.[6]

Second, I don't contend that social networks are a newfangled invention. As Columbia sociologist Herbert Gans, a scholar known for his incisive studies of postwar Levittowns, pointed out to me, even the most primitive hunters and gatherers developed networks outside immediate families and clans.[7] The human brain has long enabled individuals to work together to gather food and defend themselves from predators.[8] And although networked relationships have subsumed those that emerged in townships, more transactional relationships have existed throughout human history.

Finally, there is overlap between the various rings. It's no accident, for example, that conventionally outer-ring technologies frequently connect inner-ring contacts. It was that realization which prompted Facebook to purchase WhatsApp, a service that allows social networkers to home in on their more intimate friendships.[9] As noted above, the people we e-mail most frequently are usually individuals whom we also see in real life, suggesting that geographic proximity remains a potent predictor of whether people will actually connect.[10]

But none of those qualifications nullify my contention that the quality of the relationships we form has been affected dramatically by new norms of sociability. On the whole, Americans are investing less social capital in the relationships they maintain with the neighbor across the street, the waitress at the diner down the block, and the helpful clerk at the hardware store.[11] Time spent cocooned with nuclear-family members is time not spent with those who frequent the corner pub. Evenings spent trading online stock tips may preclude participation in a local softball league. And the fact that we can now keep in touch via e-mail with the favorite neighbor who moved to a new suburb means that we've got less time for the neighbor who purchased her old apartment.

Things are not entirely cut and dried. But the truth grounded in Dunbar's realization that humans only have so many slots to fill in their social constellations is that the choices we make individually have consequences for the broader social fabric. A society rich in middle-ring relationships can maintain the norms of township life. But one that's comparably richer in inner- and outer-ring relationships is more likely to be constructed around networks.[12]

———

What does this all mean for how we think about the state of American community? Hopefully, it moves us past the old, obsolete conversation about whether community is decaying or being reborn. As should now be clear, neither is the case—we're transitioning from one architecture to another.

There's always a temptation to wax nostalgic. But we have to be careful to recall both the good and the bad endemic to village life. Townships weren't just seedbeds for mutual understanding—they also cultivated the prejudice and division that has plagued American history. The Ku Klux Klan was as much a creature of the middle rings as any local bowling league, and the bands of neighbors who once kept African-Americans from moving onto the block were inevitably connected through familiar, if not intimate, connections. For that reason, it's not entirely clear whether abandoning the bonds that once kept neighborhoods together will signal a step forward in the fight for equality. Conflicting evidence has painted a fairly perplexing picture of the gaps that separate Americans category by category or demographic by demographic.

On the one hand, Americans elected Barack Obama to the presidency twice, suggesting that the out-and-out discrimination that was pervasive during the Jim Crow era is now beyond the pale. But at the same time, many African-American communities throughout the country remain mired in poverty and unemployment, often functionally separated from the mainstream of the nation's economy.[13] This harks back to the example I used earlier: a white supremacist today can sell a baseball card to an African-American woman via eBay without either knowing the other's identity. Is the economic integration that connects blacks and whites via the Internet a leap in the right direction, or a step back?

In exploring that question, the first and maybe most crucial piece of evidence is that Americans, of late, have become more tolerant on issues that historically bred division. Studies of one small town in Indiana found that between 1924 and 1999, the percent-age of residents who said that "Christianity is the one true religion and all peoples should be converted to it," dropped from 94 to 42 percent.[14] That's not only because fewer Americans are religious.[15] We're also less willing today to castigate those who hold a different view from our own. The shift largely lines up with what we saw earlier: Americans are more willing now to accept that other peo-ple are different—as long as they can find peers who affirm their personal worldview.

What's notable is that even as we've become more tolerant, we've kept our propensity to parse the nation's population by single identifying features—race, class, ethnicity, income, marital status, or other personal characteristics. Bill Bishop and Robert Cushing's research for *The Big Sort* revealed that Americans have, in fact, become more balkanized in this way. Minor distinc-tions in lifestyle choice are now upending the polyglot nature of many American neighborhoods. Those of us who prefer certain types of cars, architectural styles, particular modes of worship, and brands of political leadership are sorting ourselves into more homogenous communities. Suburbs that once comprised a whole range of people—different religions, professions, and ethnicities (if not races)—have become increasingly monolithic.

Moreover, Bishop discovered, our more perfectly sorted neigh-borhoods are less and less interconnected. When, for example, an Oxycodone epidemic ran through a section of eastern Kentucky, Federal Express chose to suspend deliveries of prescriptions for fear that trucks might be attacked by groups of addicts.[16] But the crisis in that corner of the state was hardly noticed elsewhere, because Harlan County was so dissociated from the communi-ties nearby. Outer-ring connections almost certainly knew what was happening: the executives at FedEx's headquarters in Mem-phis, for example, must have been aware of the service disruption, not to mention people scattered around the world who needed to get medication into certain corners of Appalachia. But they were functionally distinct: the people who might only have found out through middle-ring connections—through conversations at the barber shop or while waiting for some dry cleaning—seemed largely to have been left in the dark.

It's not just that individual communities are becoming more monolithic: a networked society doesn't bring people with different experiences into contact with one another. Natural rhythms once put Americans from different stations in touch at the store, on the street, in the newspaper, even at church. Until fairly recently, the cross section of people who lived near one another passed the same billboards, watched the same televisions shows, and listened to the same radio stations. And so, whatever divided them—issues of race or ethnicity, political creed or religious affiliation—they were more familiar, if only perfunctorily, with the way other people approached the world.

To an underappreciated degree, that's no longer the case. Networks allow us to interact more exclusively with people who share our sensibilities on any given topic—even if the roster differs dramatically from subject to subject. A Republican activist who loves to crochet can blog happily with progressive knitting enthusiasts without ever discussing the upcoming elections. While in a township the two might have given one another the cold shoulder or, more hopefully, might have engaged in a productive exchange of ideas, their outer-ring interactions breed no real sense of mutual understanding outside the yarn.

Unfortunately, our newfound tolerance has come on the cheap. Admittedly, townshipped life sometimes bred prejudice. But today, however enlightened we've become, we're choosing to interact with acquaintances without knowing anything about their background. Studies of Facebook have shown, for example, that friends typically agree with one another 67 percent of the time on issues that divide the country evenly. But people assume between 9 and 12 percent more of their friends agree than really do.[17] The transformation of American community has enabled us all to be more tolerant without having to confront the sort of conflicts that fueled bigotry in previous eras. We can "be ourselves," without needing to interact in any substantive way with people who might not approve of the choices we've made in other aspects of our lives.

If the transition to networked community has been a mixed blessing for the nation's cultural cleavages, the effect it's having on the ties in local neighborhoods is even less clear. After all, much as the data laid out in *Bowling Alone* pointed to the dissolution of American community, it's not as if Americans have become entirely isolated in their homes. We still live in places where neighbors interact—even if those relationships are less meaningful or deep. And that distinction is important because, as it turns out, the issue of whether a neighborhood is classically "vital" turns less on how intimate the neighbors are with one another and more on how well they can band together to solve ordinary problems.

Community vitality was recently the subject of a groundbreaking study led by Robert Sampson, a sociologist at Harvard. What he uncovered after looking at a range of data compiled over time about neighborhoods in Chicago was counterintuitive: aggregate measures of whether individuals are connected to one another don't necessarily line up with other indicators of neighborhood health. Gangs, after all, are laden heavily with social interactions, and members are often even more closely tied than the members of a church choir. Rather, the issue that seems to determine whether a community functions well is what Sampson terms "collective efficacy," the prolific capacity for neighbors to work together when they have interests in common.

It's not that Sampson's research concluded that neighborhoods got better as they became more functionally disconnected; he wasn't celebrating a lack of intimacy. Rather, his contention was that a neighborhood's success is determined more directly by the confidence an individual resident has in his or her ability to fix a problem. The question is not whether two neighbors are likely to know one another by name, but whether they both understand how to get a traffic light installed at a dangerous intersection, or how to ensure an incompetent teacher is fired from the local elementary school. The key to successful neighborhoods is community trust more than neighborly warmth.

This is not to say that participation in formal organizations works at cross-purposes with collective efficacy. Civil society, as nonprofits are sometimes called collectively, can be invaluable to the vitality of a neighborhood. But, as Sampson's research indicates, it's actually more important that community norms—even if they're established among strangers—maintain a standard of safety and decorum. Disapproving looks from the couple sitting on a park bench, or the good example set by the woman who keeps up her front lawn, have a more powerful effect on a community's civic health than neighborly ties. And in that, Sampson's argument echoes James Q. Wilson and George Kelling's "broken windows" theory, introduced in the early 1980s, which suggested that the implicit sign of disorder sent by an unrepaired pane of glass has the potential to set off a wave of criminality.[18]

This points to an auspicious element of networked community. If vitality doesn't go hand in hand with the middle rings, then a society full of vibrant networks—even if they're made up of hermits—might well signal an important step forward. Even if residents aren't becoming members of local clubs, don't know their neighbors by name, or aren't hosting bridge tournaments on the weekend, they can still maintain healthy neighborhoods. Our willingness to chip in to construct a wheelchair ramp for a local kid offers more direct evidence of whether a neighborhood will endure more or less crime.[19]

The good news is that even as individual membership has declined since 1970, collective efficacy has remained stable—and that's a crucial and heart-warming revelation. Community trust, it turns out, can flourish without a townshipped arrangement. Neighbors who know each other only tangentially can be active on the same LISTSERVs. Emotionally cold communities can project a certain air of civility. People who are entirely consumed by their work or enveloped in networks disconnected from the surrounding neighborhood can still live in places that are classically vital. In short, the utility of townshipped community can still be tapped, if not bolstered, in a networked society.

It's been well over two centuries since the American Revolution, and more than 180 years since Alexis de Tocqueville wrote the most enduring exposé of the new world's exceptional qualities. Looking back, what may be most remarkable about the legacy of America's independence is the durability of the township. Indeed, inasmuch as the desire to break away from King George was driven by the fact that Americans had adopted a different social architecture, those same social building blocks endured through the upheavals of the nineteenth century and most of the twentieth century.

Suddenly, that foundational element of American society—the bedrock beneath American exceptionalism—appears to have cracked. It's not that we haven't noticed various elements of the change; it's just that we've never put them together in a way that revealed the outlines of the broader effect. Robert Putnam wasn't wrong that Americans had, over the course of the postwar period, become less social in the ways that previous generations had interacted with one another. And though few noticed *The Lexus and the Olive Tree*'s apparent conflict with *Bowling Alone*, Thomas Friedman wasn't misguided in arguing that globalization was bringing individuals across the world into closer and more dynamic contact. Putnam and Friedman were exploring different aspects of what was really the same phenomenon.

The reason why the separate pieces of the puzzle haven't been put together before is that it's not obvious why township society and networked society can't exist in harmony, one enhancing the other. Why should we have to choose between the bowling league and the Facebook feed, or between texting with our best friends from high school and developing a new crew in college? Radio didn't eviscerate the newspaper business, and television didn't render the radio obsolete. Just as networks of contacts have always existed, townships have persisted as networks have become preeminent.

Nevertheless, as each successive invention inevitably changes the landscape on the margin, the factors that have defined the last several decades have set off an earthquake. As Robin Dunbar's studies indicate, there's a trade-off to be had when we invest social capital: time spent on one set of relationships is time that cannot be spent on another. And so it's not that townships and networks don't coexist, or that one has ever entirely eclipsed the other. But we've hit a tipping point, and the foundational building block that governed American life through the whole of our independence has been replaced with something else.

The change hasn't been good or bad per se. There are advantages and drawbacks to both ways of organizing society. Maybe more important, the benefits offered by each—the warmth and familiarity of townships and, alternatively, the speed and efficiency of networks—make different sorts of demands on a society's support systems and institutions. Townships are good at some things, and lousy at others—as is also true of networks.

As we'll see next, the broad sense that America is adrift—that rhythms of life that buoyed our rise on the global stage have begun to decay—is not driven by some overarching truth about the end of the American Century. At root, it emerges from the fact that institutions geared for a townshipped era are now operating in a networked age. The systems we now depend on to drive economic growth, steer the ship of state, and support those in need were all designed to work in conjunction with a society structured like the colonial villages, frontier towns, urban neighborhoods, and vibrant suburbs of the early postwar period. Now that we've broken free of that structure, we're finding that yesterday's institutions aren't equipped to keep up.

On the one hand, that's discouraging. It augurs that what's happening in America today isn't cyclical; it won't work itself out. It suggests that simply reinforcing flailing institutions that have worked for decades, or tinkering at reforms around the edges, won't fix our problems.

But on the other hand, the idea that our problems stem from an epic mismatch between the rhythms of contemporary life and a series of institutions designed for an earlier age should encourage optimism. It's not that America is simply unwinding, as some have argued.[20] Rather, we're at a turning point. If we take a fresh look at what a networked society does and doesn't do well, we can map out a plan to develop institutions that compensate for what we now lack.

Part 3

===

America
Explained

=====

VALUABLE
INEFFICIENCY

For centuries—until its eradication in the late 1970s—the scourge of smallpox terrorized societies around the globe. Sometimes referred to as the "speckled monster," the disfiguring disease infected nearly half a million Europeans each year right through the eighteenth century. Roughly half of those afflicted lost their lives, and a third of the survivors lost their sight. The psychological fear of infection alone took a toll. Sir Jeffrey Amherst, a commander of British forces during the French and Indian War, considered infecting the residents of hostile Native American villages just to soften them up in advance of an attack.[1]

But much as smallpox struck terror in people before a vaccine was available, certain quirks of the disease were commonly known. For example, contemporary wisdom determined that survivors could not be infected again, so in many cases they were asked to care for the stricken. Moreover, even before the emergence of a vaccine, doctors concocted a process they termed "variolation," injecting the pus from a smallpox victim into a healthy human with the hope that he or she would contract a milder form of the disease. The risks were real: 2 to 3 percent of those subjected to variolation perished in the process. But to many people, the benefits seemed worth the risk. George Washington, for example, ordered that his troops be variolated after a smallpox epidemic undermined American efforts to conquer Quebec during the Revolutionary War.

A few years earlier, a teenage medical student in England had visited a sick dairymaid near Bristol. When Edward Jenner suggested to his patient that she might have smallpox, the dairymaid replied "I shall never have smallpox for I have had cowpox," expressing the widespread belief—then unproven within the scientific community—that victims of a fairly mild disease common among people who handled cattle were immune to the more serious smallpox. The remark spurred Jenner to spend the next several years exploring possible connections between the two illnesses.

Eventually, and after several risky experiments, Jenner concluded that the dairymaid's supposition was not only correct, but that purposefully infecting individuals with cowpox would inoculate them from the disease's more serious counterpart. And over the next half century, what Jenner termed "vaccination" (from the Latin root, *vaccinia*, used to denote cowpox) replaced variolation as the common prophylactic against the speckled monster.

For several decades, the story ended there.[2] But then, by happenstance, in the spring of 1879 a French scientist named Louis Pasteur was experimenting with chicken cholera. Having prepared several cholera cultures for injection into a batch of fowl, he turned to a separate research project—a distraction that lasted the entire summer. The following fall, when he injected a series of chickens with the months-old cholera cultures, something odd happened: rather than die, as most fowl did when exposed to the disease, these chickens fell ill and then recovered. Pasteur concluded that the old cultures had spoiled. He prepared a fresh set, and bought a new set of chickens.

What happened next has become legend: as Arthur Koestler, who retold the story in his 1964 text on the roots of creativity, explained, when Pasteur injected both the new and old groups of chickens with the *fresh* batch of cholera, only the *new* chickens showed symptoms of the disease. The chickens that had been exposed to the spoiled batch beforehand were unaffected. Realizing at once that the spoiled cultures had done for the *old* chickens what cowpox had done for inoculated humans, his face brightened, and, an eyewitness reported, he exclaimed to those in the laboratory: "Don't you see that these animals have been *vaccinated*!"[3]

Pasteur's exclamation marks one of the great moments in the history of modern medicine. In realizing that exposure to a less potent form of a disease-inducing germ could inoculate an individual from contracting the full-blown illness, the French scientist's laboratory work saved future generations from a range of illnesses. The vaccines that we take for granted today—from polio to hepatitis, from measles to mumps—all stem, in one form or another, from Pasteur's apparent "aha!" moment.

What's important to note is that Pasteur's epiphany didn't just materialize out of the blue. His breakthrough was midwifed by his familiarity with Jenner's previous work. The broad concept of vaccination—Pasteur's sudden insight—was made possible by the application of an old idea to a new set of circumstances. He had taken a step into what the author Steven Johnson recently called the "adjacent possible."[4] By piecing together the bits of information available to him at the moment of invention, Pasteur moved one step up the chain of knowledge. His new thinking stood on a foundation provided by Jenner's research, just as Jenner's "aha!" moment had been prompted by the dairymaid's common wisdom.

That example, as Koestler wrote, reveals the essence of the creative process. Our common perception that ideas come to people almost accidentally—that genius is fleeting and miraculous—misses a truth about nearly all intellectual breakthroughs: they are the products of existing ideas being put together in a new way.[5] As Koestler put it:

The creative act is not an act of creation in the sense of the Old
Testament. It does not create something out of nothing; it uncov-
ers, selects, re-shuffles, combines, synthesizes already existing
facts, ideas, faculties, skills. The more familiar the parts, the more
striking the new whole. Man's knowledge of the changes of the
tides and the phases of the moon is as old as his observation that
apples fall to earth in the ripeness of time. Yet the combination of
these and other equally familiar data in Newton's theory of grav-
ity changed mankind's outlook on the world.[6]

The same process applies to the great inventions of the last few
years—even though we may be inclined to give credit to the apparent genius of one person. The iPhone didn't emerge sui generis out
of Steve Jobs's head. No team at Apple could have invented such a
device in 1975, if only because the constituent ideas that merged to
place a graphically integrated handheld device into the adjacent
possible hadn't yet been invented. A whole series of individual
ideas—mobile phones, graphical interfaces, satellite connectivity—
had to be blended and perfected simply to conceive of a phone like
the one Apple eventually created. It's not taking anything away
from Jobs's genius as a manager or Apple's ingenuity as a firm to
argue that their ideas flowed from separate "parent" work done
beforehand.

The fact is that creativity is born when existing ideas are combined in a new way. Intellectual breakthroughs are often generated when someone intensely focused on a single field is suddenly
thrust into another. We imagine that, as Thomas Edison once
argued, genius is "of inspiration one percent, of perspiration
ninety-nine."[7] But in reality, invention is most frequently sparked
by combining thoughts across wildly different frames of reference. Consider, for example, at how an unlikely pair discovered
the genetic structure of life.

By the 1940s, scientists had grown fairly certain that the information passed from one generation to the next was dispatched by some cellular mechanism. But they were still perplexed by the process that fueled heredity—they did not understand how genes were structured or how specific traits were passed down from parents to their children. Aware that unlocking that mystery would be a signal scientific achievement of the twentieth century, several leading scientists set out to uncover the truth.

Most, embracing Thomas Edison's axiom, worked feverishly in in their own laboratories to find life's underlying architecture. Erwin Chargaff, a Columbia University biochemist, focused on finding the constituent building blocks of genetics. At Cal Tech, Nobel laureate Linus Pauling, a leading light in the world of physical chemistry, developed a theory that the genetic code was structured as a triple helix. In London, a biophysicist named Rosalind Franklin, convinced that experimental data held the key, was using X-ray diffraction to build a data set large enough, she hoped, to decipher the underlying code.

Trained in entirely different fields, James Watson, who had studied bacterial genetics, and Francis Crick, who had earned a degree as a physicist, were not thought to be mavens of laboratory work. But the two young men shared the rather unconventional notion that discoveries flowed less from the mind-numbing research and more from the process of splicing together bits of information. Less encumbered by the myopia of a single scientific discipline, they felt free to play with ideas originating independently from the worlds of biology, chemistry, and physics.

By most accounts, it was that freedom to borrow and steal from other disciplines that gave them a leg up. While the others spent long hours trying to build more comprehensive data sets, Watson and Crick were engaged in free-flowing conversations on walks through the park. While their counterparts were boring down more heavily into their respective fields of expertise, Watson and Crick were batting different concepts back and forth across a wider range of subjects. They pondered how the individual nucleic acids bonded. How were they sequenced? Slowly, by splicing the information available to them—much of it garnered from evidence published by their competition—their conversations led them to decipher the code: genes were structured in a double helix, a biological language now known as DNA.

Watson and Crick's triumph illustrates the underlying foundation of creative thinking. Trapped in their own intellectual stovepipes, the world's leading biochemists, physical chemists, and biophysicists had been unable to fit the individual pieces of evidence together into a comprehensible whole. The breadth of Watson and Crick's exposure rather than the depth of their expertise propelled them to victory. As Richard Ogle once explained, "The most fundamental characteristic of the imagination is its ability to let us *free ourselves from the grip of present reality*. . . . This characteristic enables us to construct and play with alternative ways of seeing, understanding and acting in the world that allow something new, interesting, and useful to emerge."[8]

Koestler's insight that "all decisive events in the history of scientific thought can be described in terms of mental cross-fertilization between different disciplines" has been witnessed time and again in the history of human innovation.[9] Our impression that Gutenberg invented the printing press masks his real genius: the ingenuity to merge several preexisting technologies—movable type, ink, and paper—into a new device that could spread ideas.[10] Velcro was invented by a Swiss engineer who noticed the way cockleburs had attached to his pants and dog after a walk in the wilderness. Militarized tanks were thought up by Ernest Swinton after he caught sight of a Holt Caterpillar tractor, and imagined how its durability might be an advantage on the battlefield. Levi Strauss constructed the first pair of jeans from the discarded canvas used to make sails near the harbor in San Francisco.[11]

More recently, author and entrepreneur Frans Johansson coined a new phrase to define intellectual cross-fertilization: citing the family that built Florence into a bastion of scholarly revolution during the High Renaissance, he coined the term the "Medici effect." It's an apt comparison because the Medici served as patrons to an astonishing array of artists and thinkers, forming a beehive of talent that compared notes and shared ideas generation upon generation. Florence's place at the center of several overlapping fields of inquiry made it a hotbed of new thinking.

Analyzing the successes of the Brain Science program at Brown University, Johansson determined that the same principles of creativity had applied. By coalescing a group of experts in fields ranging from mathematics, medicine, neuroscience, and computer science, the university had developed an intellectual petri dish primed to incubate bold new thinking. In explaining how Brown's researchers had developed a system that allowed a monkey to move the cursor on a computer game with its mind, Johansson wrote that the "incredible breakthrough was a result of different people from different fields coming together to find a place for their ideas to meet, collide, and build on each other."[12]

That suggests something else: the Medici effect needn't be predicated entirely on happenstance. In fact, the groundwork for innovative thinking can be jerry-rigged. No one can guarantee that any particular constellation of intellects will generate a major breakthrough. But it's certainly possible—if not plausible—to set parameters that are more likely to incubate collaboration. By putting people from different stovepipes in close proximity, we can create a petri dish of potential. And, as recent research reveals, businesses that embrace cross-disciplinary collaboration are, in many circumstances, more likely to succeed in the long run.[13]

For those engaged in creative capitalism, that's a fairly intuitive proposition. Decades ago, and even before he became the company's chairman, Mervin Kelly realized that keeping Bell Labs at the vanguard of technological progress required designing a research campus that compelled constructive teamwork. He feared that engineers working on new technologies at the company's campus in Murray Hill, New Jersey, would be sequestered in their own teams without access to the wisdom from experiments being done in the wings nearby. When charged with laying out a new campus, he embraced a design that forced employees to mix it up. Long hallways were constructed so that scientists bumped into each other on the way to the bathroom. Researchers learned from the technicians working on the front lines. The results were spectacular: over several decades, Bell Labs invented transistors, solar cells, lasers, and the operating system Unix, among a bevy of other products, staking an unquestioned claim as one of the most dynamic centers of twentieth-century innovation.[14]

The same insight drove subsequent generations of entrepreneurs. When Steve Jobs was debating the design of the new Pixar studio he planned to construct on the site of an old Del Monte fruit cannery in California, designers debated how to shape the new campus. As Walter Isaacson explained in his biography of the Apple cofounder, plans were made to construct "a traditional Hollywood studio, with separate buildings for various projects and bungalows for development teams." But then he changed his mind, based on a theory that creativity was enhanced when a physical environment "encourage[d] random encounters . . . and unplanned collaborations." He said:

> Creativity comes from spontaneous meetings, from random discussions. You run into someone, you ask what they're doing, you say "Wow," and soon you're cooking up all sorts of ideas. . . . So

we designed the building to make people get out of their offices and mingle in the central atrium with people they might not otherwise see [in part by decreeing that there would be only a few centrally located bathrooms].[15]

The Medici effect has been borne out in academic studies as well. Research by University of Chicago sociologist Ronald Burt found that there's a direct connection between the diversity of an employee's exposure to different viewpoints and her propensity to come up with useful new ideas. Burt's studies of several major corporations, Raytheon among them, led him to conclude that "managers with networks that span structural holes tend to receive more positive performance evaluations, faster promotions, higher compensation, and participate in more successful teams."[16] Or, as he put succinctly: "People whose networks span structural holes are at higher risk for having good ideas."[17]

We should be careful here: it's not just that two people with disparate but compatible ideas pass in the hall, or stand behind one another waiting for coffee: they need to be in touch and have the opportunity to explore in detail what their counterparts are saying. As noted by Brown professor Richard Locke, who has been researching the genesis of innovation for decades, new ideas are bred when there's enough familiarity among colleagues with different ideas that they actually dive into one another's work.[18]

In essence, dynamism results from trust—a fact confirmed in Northwestern University sociologist Brian Uzzi's study of the most commercially successful Broadway musicals. The hits weren't the ones created by groups who had teamed up before, or who had been brought together entirely anew. The most successful shows came from teams that spliced familiar partners together with new blood. Success comes from compiling a group that includes a degree of both novelty and confidence, dynamism and familiarity.[19]

———

Jane Jacobs is unquestionably best known for the argument that framed *The Death and Life of Great American Cities*—namely, that neighborhoods, properly crafted, maintain an organic quality of their own. But Jacobs's second book, *The Economy of Cities*, made a different claim—one that focused more squarely on the issue of creativity. Less than a decade after Arthur Koestler published his treatise on the foundations of innovation, Jacobs came to the remarkable conclusion that the process later termed the Medici effect was, in many cases, a phenomenon of everyday routines. Having spent hours watching the patterns of life from the stoop of her Greenwich Village brownstone, she discerned that the sorts of interactions that incubate new ideas are suffused through the chance encounters of a well-functioning neighborhood.

The Economy of Cities compared the two leading industrial centers of northern England—Birmingham, which in the years following the peak of Britain's industrialization had flourished, and nearby Manchester, which had declined. The crucial distinction, Jacobs concluded, had everything to do with the nature of the businesses that defined each metropolis: Manchester's behemoth manufacturing plants had replaced the winding city streets where smaller firms had once been set in close proximity; Birmingham had retained a critical mass of smaller shops and storefronts.

Jacobs acknowledged that the larger textile plants in Manchester were more efficient. But, she argued, Birmingham had persevered through the textile industry's decline exactly because it had spurned the impulse to cut slack out of its system. However much waste went into maintaining a slew of smaller, sometimes redundant businesses along Birmingham's streets, the diversity had allowed it to adapt to the changing tides of Britain's national economy. In the end, Birmingham had benefited by adhering to a less efficient production model.

To Jacobs, that suggested something profound: while the inevitable collision of different ideas between small firms may make them less efficient on a day-to-day basis, it allows them to thrive over the long haul. In other words, while the Medici effect flourished in Birmingham at the cost of productivity, it had been bulldozed in Manchester. Whatever edge Manchester had gained through economies of scale, Birmingham's vitality emerged from the dynamism of a nimbler spirit of commerce.[20]

Jacobs went on to trace similar dichotomies through contemporary history. She noted, for example, that there would have been no reason, before New York emerged as the nation's commercial capital, to expect the Big Apple to become more commercially powerful than Jersey City, which was situated just across the Hudson. Both cities sat at the mouth of the same river connecting them to the Erie Canal. Moreover, New Jersey was on the American mainland, making it much easier to reach the vast market of customers living at all points west. The Garden State's expanse offered another selling point: in the largely undeveloped areas farther from the Hudson, a spate of chemical companies chose to set up plants near one another and then build a regional infrastructure unencumbered by the conflicting patterns, schedules, and needs of businesses operating in other sectors of the economy. It appeared more efficient to grow in Jersey.

New York had no such advantage, if only because there was no way to avoid the mishmash of overlapping firms and industries. Trucks full of textiles would inevitably get caught behind tourist buses, which themselves would be stuck behind cabs. It was often impossible for booming businesses to expand where they were. Everything was more difficult—and invariably more expensive. At first glance, it seems obvious that business would eventually cross the Hudson in favor of the Garden State.

As we all know, that's not what happened. New York City has thrived—it has resurrected itself even after periods of epic decay—because, in an echo of Birmingham, the rhythms of life and commerce in the Big Apple support long-term adaptability. Businesses glean advantages when they are sited near firms engaged in other sorts of commerce. Proprietors from disconnected industries bump into one another while traversing the narrow island grid. In Jacobs's view, the same chaos that often proved wasteful also incubated new ideas.[21] And in that context, Jacobs coined a term that may be the best description of the Medici effect: "valuable inefficiency."

Jacobs was arguing that the dynamic Arthur Koestler had identified as the key ingredient to innovative ideas at an individual level—and that Frans Johansson would later apply at the level of an individual business—also applied to the geography of a local neighborhood. She contended that new thinking was generally pollinated when experts from entirely divergent fields collided through the everyday interactions of cosmopolitan routines.[22] And so, much as we frequently assume that innovation emerges out of some combination of dumb luck, above-average education, and innate intelligence, there's another factor at work as well: community.

But what structure of community is most likely to incubate new ideas? Or, to put it differently, which sorts of acquaintances are more likely, as Ronald Burt said, to put individuals at the "greatest risk" of having good ideas?

In an effort to answer that question, Mark Granovetter, who is now a professor at Stanford, published a paper in 1973 that contained one of the most enduring phrases of twentieth-century sociology: "the strength of weak ties."[23] When it comes both to career advancement and, more importantly, to the spread of innovative concepts, Granovetter argued that the connections we maintain with our close contacts are not nearly as important as the breadth of our extended networks. Economic dynamism, in essence, emerges less in the cliques that watch Monday Night Football together than in the longer list of contacts we each maintain in our virtual rolodexes. You don't hear about a job opening from your best friend, but from the guy you played racquetball with a few months back. You don't hear about a big new idea from the woman who works in your pod, but from a college friend who dropped in for lunch while driving through town.

Over the past forty years, Granovetter's thesis has been widely embraced. But as we've established, not all weak ties are created equal. Some of the contacts we make outside our most intimate friends and family are closer than others (middle- and outer-ring acquaintances might both be considered "weak ties"). Some are forged among those who are connected across a single point of interest but have no real sense of the other's identity. Others are formed between members of basketball leagues who, despite working in disparate fields, talk shop when walking to pick-up games at the local YMCA.

Moreover, it's not obvious that weak ties will spur the Medici effect, if only because the two individuals involved in a "weak" relationship may be mirror images with nothing much new to share. An unemployed twenty-seven-year-old computer engineer in Palo Alto might be well served by an extensive network of friends in the software industry—but is that sort of homogenous network more or less productive when he's looking for a big new idea?

Undoubtedly there are good ideas to be had when smart people working in the same field share ideas readily. Indeed, McGill psychologist Kevin Dunbar found when studying the annals of microbiology that breakthroughs emerged most frequently when researchers sitting next to one another engaged in serious discussions about their experiments.[24] But on the other hand, it seems possible that the Medici effect is actually driven less by cultivating interactions between like-minded people and more by whether it bridges some intellectual chasm.

It was in looking at the plight of America's rust belt that my friend Sean Safford revealed just how powerfully the architecture of weak ties could affect a region's economic dynamism. Having grown up, like me, just outside Buffalo, Safford set off to investigate why certain manufacturing regions had managed to be reborn after the nation's industrial sector had begun to ebb, while others had languished. In the spirit of Jane Jacobs, he compared two places that represented, in similar fashion, broadly divergent experiences: Allentown, Pennsylvania, and Youngstown, Ohio.

Both cities, Safford determined, had through the postwar years emerged as blue-collar, industrial powerhouses. Moreover—and maybe most important—they had both been defined by similarly high quotients of what James Coleman, and later Robert Putnam, had defined as social capital. But that's where the similarities seemed to end. When each city's core industrial foundation began to decay in the 1970s and 1980s—as Allentown and Youngstown's steel mills, brake-assembly plants, and other factories fell on hard times—the cities headed in different directions.[25]

Allentown claimed the happier of the two stories. The factory town made the subject of a Billy Joel song avoided the perils that might have befallen a city competing with cheaper steel plants overseas. Instead, and however reluctantly, Allentowners embraced the challenge of hitching the Lehigh Valley's regional destiny to alternative high-tech and service-oriented jobs. And the success of those efforts is revealed by the statistics: in Allentown, the number of jobs centered on the old industries of steel, automobiles, textiles, apparel, and cement fell from 77 to 28 percent in the three decades that followed the 1970s, even as overall employment grew. That marks a praiseworthy adaptation: the Lehigh Valley found a way to thrive by moving workers into other sorts of manufacturing jobs and other economic sectors altogether.

Youngstown, by contrast, took a different tack. Perhaps because there didn't seem be any better option, the residents of eastern Ohio adopted a defensive posture, hoping to ride out the storm. They figured that efforts to make local industries more efficient—

combined with some protective tariffs imposed by the government in Washington—might enable Youngstowners to hold onto their old routines. But in the end, they couldn't withstand the barrage: the city's employment rolls diminished even as the percentage that worked in industry—more than four out of every five workers—remained roughly even, suggesting that no new economic engine was replacing what had been lost.[26] In a nutshell, Safford concluded that Allentown had managed to surf the Third Wave, while Youngstown had been caught in the undertow.

The great curiosity was that the two cities had appeared to exist in roughly the same sociological environment—one that seemed to characterize nearly every town in America's industrial heartland. Distinctions between the two included the differing rhythms of the industries in each region and the proximity of Ohio and Pennsylvania to other commercial centers. But Safford wondered whether there wasn't a sociological element to the story. And so he took a closer look.

What he discovered was that the structures of the relationships that defined life in each city were entirely different. Driven largely by quirks in the way the region had developed, Youngstown was communally stovepiped: it wasn't that the residents of any given neighborhood ostracized those who lived "across the tracks"; rather, the folks who lived in any given neighborhood worked in the same factories, voted for the same politicians, frequented the same bars, and contributed to the same charities. There was an extraordinary degree of overlap in each frame of life, and there were few outliers.

Allentown, by contrast, had a very different social architecture. The Lehigh Valley was home to a wider range of corporate interests, a broader diversity of ethnicities, and a more expansive cohort of competing colleges. As a result, eastern Pennsylvanians were exposed to a much more diversified set of acquaintances. Neighbors attended a variety of different colleges and worked in different mills. They were congregants at different churches and regulars at different bars. So the average citizen wasn't nearly so ensconced in any single bubble of connections.

The stage that had set the Medici effect to work in Allentown was absent in Youngstown. And, though Safford never used Johansson's term, that best accounted for the two cities' divergent fates. As the postwar economy had given way to a new postindustrial landscape, the residents of eastern Ohio were without the social resources to adapt. Allentown, by contrast, was alive with cross-cutting relationships, giving residents—or, at least many of them—the wherewithal to transition into a new industry and a new career.[27]

Years earlier, Safford's mentor, Richard Locke, had noticed a similar split when researching how Italy's two major car companies, Fiat and Alfa Romeo, had responded to pressure to rein in production costs during the 1970s and 1980s. As Locke explained:

> Since Fiat is located in Turin, a highly polarized, one-company town lacking a vibrant associational infrastructure, information-sharing and cooperation between moderate groups within both the company and the local union movement proved fleeting. . . . As a result, disagreements over the company's restructuring efforts escalated into an all-out struggle between the local unions and the company and resulted in massive layoffs, the decimation of the local union movement, and major social dislocation, especially among laid-off automobile workers.
>
> Alfa, on the other hand, is situated in Milan, a more cosmopolitan city packed with many well-organized interest groups and secondary associations. These organizations facilitated information sharing and cooperation between labor and management at Alfa and thus supported negotiation between these two parties over the massive changes under way at the firm.[28]

The point isn't that the number of connections—"social capital" by James Coleman's definition—determines the economic dynamism of any certain town, although it can certainly have an effect. It's not even that a specific distribution of a region's time and attention can reasonably be understood to be the magic bullet. Rather, whom you know has a bearing on whether you're at risk for a having an innovative idea. The rhythms of everyday life may spur individuals to keep to themselves, to stay within the confines of those who share their experiences or, alternatively, to live within a swirl of different ideas and challenged assumptions. The Medici effect's full blossom depends largely on the latter.

The outstanding question, then, is how the transformation of American community will affect the dynamism of the nation's economy over the long term. Our hope has to be that the networks that have become the building blocks of American life will make more typical the sorts of cross-cutting interactions that propelled Watson and Crick, Bell Labs and Apple, New York City and Allentown. In the best-case scenario, the outer-ring relationships that have thickened would generate the balance of societal trust and novelty that's so crucial to the broader project of innovation.

Unfortunately, the evidence to date hasn't borne that theory out. By several estimates, American innovation has slowed of late, as massive investments in fields like green energy and pharmaceuticals have failed to produce the return that investments in information technology generated just a few decades ago.[29] (Some of that analysis, we should note, predates the new development of "fracking.") George Mason University economist Tyler Cowen recently argued that innovation in the United States has actually stagnated, noting that we've picked the low-hanging fruit of technologies produced by previous generations and are burning through the competitive advantages those breakthroughs bestowed on today's

economy.[30] Peter Thiel, a cofounder of PayPal and a powerful figure in the world of venture capital, has sounded a similar alarm,
arguing that whatever advances Silicon Valley has spurred of late
have been cancelled out by America's failure to make progress on
other technological and scientific fronts.[31]

No fair assessment can blame the stagnation of American innovation entirely on the structure of American community. The
Medici effect—as evidenced by Pasteur's discovery of vaccinations
alone—is not born only through the sort of cross-cutting relationships found in townships; it can also be driven by efforts within
any one field to braid new ideas together. Indeed, there's a compelling argument to be made that the key to innovation in the
future will be expanding the universe of people working in a single
pocket of research to a form a cluster of experts around specialized
challenges.

But we shouldn't dismiss the role played by the disappearance of the middle rings. The new model of innovation inherent
to networked community is different, in at least one fundamental
respect, from the archetype that has long served as a foundation
of American ingenuity. In townshipped communities, a variety of
challenges and worldviews were discussed through the course of
chance meetings and during the coffee breaks at organized events.
They were the fodder for the back-and-forth at the corner bar, and
they were the bridge between people from entirely different walks
of life.

It's not that people involved in networked community don't
pass anyone on the street; it's not that they don't drink with pals
as frequently as previous generations. It's just that the chance that
those interactions will germinate new ideas is much less likely
now because a greater bulk of their interactions are with closer
and more distant acquaintances. American community is coming
to look more like Youngstown and less like Allentown. And that's

thrown a wrench into the organic innovation that once was inherent in the structure of ordinary American communities.

Some people will counter the suggestion that the transformation of American community has changed the way we drive innovation by arguing that networks have always been a key to American ingenuity. It's a reasonable argument. There are, without a doubt, parallels between the centers of creativity at the turns of the twentieth and twenty-first centuries. Detroit was a bustling hub of engineering know-how in the early 1900s, attracting a critical mass of mechanics and engineers in much the same way Silicon Valley has become a beacon for present day techies.[32] In both places, those interested in the same problems rubbed elbows at the same restaurants, and traded ideas over cups of coffee and bottles of beer.

But that analogy misses a crucial distinction. Detroit emerged as the center of the automobile industry almost by accident: the confluence of existing experts in shipbuilding, engine design, and carriage manufacturing—each predating the nascent automobile industry—made Michigan a hotbed for innovation because mavens of different fields were congregated there. That's not the model at work in the Bay Area, where engineers and programmers have congregated because of their similar interests. It's not that one model is better than the other—but they're different, and the shift marks a new model of growth, both for good and for bad.

It's worth noting that there's movement afoot to return to the model of innovation through diversity, as evidenced by the pull of what Richard Florida has termed the "creative class."[33] The big suburban campuses that defined the exodus of businesses from urban areas—the sprawling, isolated facilities that were in vogue during the 1970s and 1980s in particular—are being abandoned by firms eager to capture the vitality of urban America. The so-called Platinum Mile in Westchester County, a stretch of highway north of Manhattan that was once dotted with big corporate office parks, has seen its vacancy rate rise to nearly 20 percent as firms have migrated back into New York City.[34] And UBS, the financial giant that moved its offices out of Manhattan for Stamford, Connecticut, in 1996 has since considered a move back.[35]

It seems clear that two central tensions define the way American community life bears on economic innovation. The first is the balance between efficiency and collaboration. The environments that, through most of the twentieth century, were at the greatest risk of incubating new ideas were, to paraphrase Jane Jacobs, valuably inefficient. The random intersection of individuals from different pockets of society spurred big new ideas—even when they appeared to waste resources. Regions focused too exclusively on efficiency may have been able to produce more with less, but were eventually overcome by an insufficient capacity to adapt to new circumstances.

More pertinent today is a tension between the old sort of innovation native to American townships and the new sort generated by networks. In both cases the Medici effect can be a powerful force. Yes, there's no guarantee that a town that incubates various interests will drive new ideas. Nevertheless, it seems less likely that networks of individuals ensconced in conversations on topics with which they agree will yield as many big breakthroughs. And that marks our central challenge.

No one can claim credibly that Americans are intellectually isolated today, even if we are caught in what Eli Pariser once termed "filter bubbles."[36] What remains to be seen—and what ought to worry anyone looking at the future of economic growth—is whether the new arena for the Medici effect will, in the end, prove as effective as the old. The manner in which Americans organized themselves—what Tocqueville saw as such a crucial element of

American exceptionalism—had an altogether underappreciated effect on the growth and dynamism of the American economy. And so when it comes to innovation, abandoning that underlying feature will present both danger and opportunity throughout the remainder of the twenty-first century.

13

THE ROOTS OF
DELIBERATION

When rioting broke out in Brazil during the spring of 2013, it caught much of the world by surprise. Conventional wisdom had long held that South America's most populous nation had made significant strides in bridging the gap from poverty, integrating itself into the thriving global economy. After a decade of steady growth and an explosion of development, FIFA, international soccer's governing body, had chosen Brazil to host the 2014 World Cup, and the International Olympic Committee had awarded Rio de Janeiro the 2016 Summer Games. It seemed to many analysts as if Brazil was well on its way.

But those living in the poorer quarters of Brazil's teeming cities—and many struggling to maintain their place in the emerging middle class—hadn't gotten the memo. To them, it seemed more as though the country's newfound prosperity was being squandered on frivolous amenities for those already well off. Brazilians climbing out of poverty felt as if they weren't getting the support they were entitled to from the government. And when bus fares were raised at the same time cranes were hovering over World Cup stadium sites, a wave of protests followed. To those who had been so taken with Brazil's rapid development, the upheaval came as something of a shock. That then spurred many to ask a more far-reaching question: amid explosive economic growth, how should a society address its underlying inequalities?

Brazil's dilemma in 2013 was what some might consider a high-class problem: the country wasn't squeezing the last drops out of an economic lemon as much as it was trying to figure out how to distribute its newfound bounty.[1] More frequently, societies caught up in turmoil aren't so lucky, faced with the challenge of addressing an unwinding economy or a global downturn. And that points to one of the most foundational questions facing scholars of any age: why, when beset by similar crises, do some societies fail while others succeed?

In an attempt to address that eternal question, Peter Blair Henry, a Jamaican-born economist at the Stanford Business School (now dean of New York University's business school), began to delve a little deeper into the narratives emerging from the developing world. Many of the islands dotting the ethereal light blue water between Brazil and the United States had inherited similar backgrounds but achieved entirely disparate outcomes. Why, Henry asked in a paper co-written with Conrad Miller in 2008, had his native Jamaica devolved into an international basket case while Barbados, Jamaica's Caribbean neighbor, developed into an economic tiger?

The comparison was apt, if only because the two island nations had emerged from the same broad circumstances. Both had been colonized by the British during the seventeenth century, and both had been settled in large part by slaves brought from Africa to work on sugar plantations. Both had escaped from the heavy hand of colonial power during the 1960s, and upon winning their independence, both had chosen to maintain a British-style parliamentary democracy, private-property rights, and the traditions of common law.

The similarities ended there. After their respective emancipations, Barbados had enjoyed a relatively steady rate of growth and a rising standard of living. Jamaica, on the other hand, struggled with high unemployment and runaway inflation. Measured in 2002, nearly forty years after their independence, Barbados's per capita gross domestic product had outpaced Jamaica's by a factor of three, and the gap between the two nations' per capita incomes had expanded by a factor of five. While Jamaica had struggled for nearly two decades to recover from the oil crisis of 1973, the Barbadian economy had bounced back readily.

Henry's first supposition was that institutional differences explained the divergence. So he and Miller traced how choices made by the two nations' economic policy makers had affected each society's reaction to a monetary crisis during the early 1990s. Their research revealed that their central banks had made, respectively, different choices in facing the challenge, and that those choices had long-term effects.[2]

But beneath the stories of discrete decisions made at the top of each country's economic establishment were underlying realities that contributed to the divergent decisions. The bankers, after all, hadn't acted in a vacuum; they were each perched atop societies driven by very different social dynamics. As a team of reporters at National Public Radio's *This American Life* and *Planet Money* discovered in reporting a story inspired by Henry's research, the community architecture across the two islands differed starkly.[3]

The reporters decided to explore the relationship between social frameworks and economic outcomes. Faced in the early 1990s with circumstances that threatened to force both nations to devalue their currencies—a move that would have chilled foreign investment—the labor and business communities in Barbados forged a sweeping compromise: the unions agreed to drastic wage cuts, while employers narrowed their profit margins, enduring short-term pain in order to avoid long-term stagnation. In doing so, Barbados laid the foundation for future growth.

In a similar crisis, the Jamaicans proved unable to reach any substantive compromise. The animosity harbored by small-business owners frequently shaken down by the police reflected a corrupt political culture. Distrust and recrimination made the prospect of any Barbadian-style compromise remote. As a result, Jamaica was unable to avoid the pressure to devalue its currency, upending the prospects for future investment.

The difference, the Planet Money team concluded, had been driven as much by distinctions in the two countries' social architecture as anything else. In the much smaller Barbados, business owners and laborers hadn't always been on the same side of political conflict—but they had always been in touch. Their routines were intertwined in ways entirely foreign to the rhythms of life in Jamaica. As a result, a deal was within the realm of possibility: labor was willing to accept lower wages without fear of reprisal from the rank and file, while small businesses were willing to agree to lower profit margins without abandoning the interests of individual entrepreneurs. The government could embrace the compromise without facing severe political recrimination.[4]

Of course, as Henry and Miller noted, each nation's central institutions had played an important role. Had Jamaica's banking community behaved like its counterparts in Barbados (which had chosen *not* to devalue its currency), the two countries' economic fates might not have diverged. But what also seems clear is that the rhythms of life in the two countries played a role in separating their fortunes. The ties between citizens on the street laid the foundation for decisions later made by each nation's leaders.

The United States hasn't reached the level of dysfunction that paralyzes Jamaica. But judging from the exasperation Americans now feel about Washington's ongoing failure to tackle the nation's big challenges—the tendency of Congress to let issues come to the breaking point before piecing together a temporary solution—it seems we may be headed in that direction. Faith in the capacity of government to lead has fallen to a record low.[5] And it's not clear to anyone—save those who pray for the return of what they think would be "real" leadership—what might be done to turn things around.

Explanations for the gridlock abound. Many on the left blame recalcitrance within the conservative movement—Republicans, they claim, cave in too frequently to the irresponsible demands of Tea Party activists.[6] Others cite the nefarious influence of the filibuster, which allows a minority of senators to block substantive bills supported by the broad majority.[7] Some argue that gerrymandering—the manipulation of legislative districts to guarantee the outcome of an election—has polarized the House of Representatives.

But while Democrats fault Republicans and conservatives blame progressives, most of the country is simply fed up. A recent *New York Times*/CBS News poll found that 72 percent of Americans believe that the country is off on the wrong track.[8] While a majority of Americans believed that "the government is really run for the benefit of all people" in 1987, the figure has since plummeted.[9] During the government shutdown of 2013, 70 percent of Americans disapproved of the way the Republican Congress was handling budget negotiations and 61 percent disapproved of their Democratic counterparts.[10] So the nation's despair isn't directed at any single party or institution; it extends across the aisle.

If Americans from across the political spectrum can agree on anything, then, it's that Washington can't get out of its own way. Something has changed to preclude the collegiality of earlier eras. As PBS interviewer Charlie Rose often points out in conversations with the nation's leading thinkers, Washington now seems fundamentally incapable of arriving at optimal solutions. Too often, Congress is compelled simply to kick the can down the road.

Worse still, beneath the veneer of frustration is the sense that something more nefarious is corrupting the system. Nostalgia suggests that previous generations were more inclined to put the public interest above their own parochial concerns. It's as if a self-interested fever has spread through the governing class. Whether that's true or not, there's certainly veracity in the suggestion that something has changed. The question is: what threw the American system so far out of whack?

The merry-go-round of culpability often begins with the suggestion that "special interests" have co-opted the government's concern for ordinary Americans. The burden of campaign fundraising—the collective costs of running for federal office rose more than ten times between 1974 and 2010—have compelled politicians to accept donations that appear, by most estimates, to be high-class bribery.[11] The growing army of lobbyists who have become expert in manipulating the system with strategically placed political patronage, many claim, wields an influence that drowns out the voices of individual citizens.[12]

The effect, the conventional story goes, has been to drive the nation's politicians to ideological extremes. After all, to the degree that lobbyists aren't working to erect boondoggles like the infamous Alaskan "bridge to nowhere," they're likely using their considerable influence to enforce the interests of big money donors with an agenda of their own.[13] Candidates who depend on donations from the conservative Club for Growth can't afford, in many cases, to vote to raise taxes on the very wealthy—even if they've concluded, deep down, that it's the responsible thing to do. Democrats invariably feel similar pressures from more progressive groups.

If the power of special interest–driven lobbyists hasn't forced politicians to eschew bipartisan collaboration, many argue, then gerrymandering certainly has. Sophisticated technology now allows party hacks to invert the system: by manipulating the borders of legislative districts, bosses can often guarantee election outcomes. In 2002, a full 91 percent of congressional incumbents defeated their opponents by 10 percentage points or more.[14] And to the extent that gerrymandering isn't as pervasive or determinative as some claim, Bill Bishop has revealed that Americans, separate from efforts to redraw district boundaries, have gerrymandered themselves by migrating into politically homogenous communities.[15]

The proliferation of news outlets has only exacerbated the very same trend. Politicians, after all, are in the business of saying what their audiences want, and in much the same way that their policy agendas are radicalized by gerrymandered districts, the audiences who watch Fox News and MSNBC demand ideological purity. A Republican who says something outlandishly conservative on Fox News is less likely to suffer the wrath of a moderate constituency—let alone one on the left. The same is true of a progressive on MSNBC. So members of both parties have yet another good reason to move away from the political center.

The effect has been unmistakable. Academic researchers have found that between the Congress sworn in with Jimmy Carter and the Congress that sat for the third and fourth years of George W. Bush's administration, the percentage of moderates dropped from 30 to 8, while the percent who were "strong" conservatives or liberals grew from 27 to 57.[16] According to data compiled by political scientists Keith Poole and Howard Rosenthal, two-fifths of the Senate's Republicans and a third of House GOPers could be considered moderates as late as the early 1990s; by 2012, that label could be fairly attributed to only a tenth of Republican senators, and an even smaller slice in the House. Among progressives through roughly the same period, moderates dropped from 35 to 12 percent of the House Democratic caucus, and from 27 to 15 percent in the Senate.[17]

It's not just in Washington: the same sort of polarization has spread across the country. The 2012 election resulted in a sea

change in state capitals throughout the nation: because one party
or the other was so dominant, half of state legislatures were subject to veto-proof majorities—almost double the number from four
years earlier. All but three states were subject to one-party control.[18] As the Associated Press reported:

> Democrats in California gained their first supermajorities since
> 1883 in both the Assembly and the Senate. Republicans captured
> total control of the North Carolina Capitol for the first time in
> more than a century. The GOP set a 147-year high mark in the
> Tennessee statehouse and won two-thirds majorities in the Mis-
> souri Legislature for the first time since the Civil War. Republi-
> cans also gained or expanded supermajorities in places such as
> Indiana, Oklahoma and—if one independent caucuses with the
> GOP—Georgia. Democrats gained a supermajority in Illinois
> and built upon their dominance in places such as Rhode Island
> and Massachusetts.[19]

Which pulls us to the other side of the dysfunctional ledger: not
only has the nation's political scene been polarized over the last
several decades, but our leaders seem to have discovered an affinity for "my way or the highway" politics. In the Senate, for example, members have little if any compunction about stymieing the
policy-making process.[20] Between 1955 and 1961, the Senate only
took up a single vote to break a filibuster—a reflection of how sel-
dom senators were willing to employ dilatory tactics. But between
2009 and 2010, there were eighty-four such votes.[21] By another
tally, less than a tenth of the important legislative bills considered
by the Senate faced obstruction in the 1960s—but nearly three-
fourths are subject to filibuster threats today.[22]

In the House, similar efforts to steamroll the opposition have
been reflected in changes to the decrees that govern legislative
debate. The Speaker and his deputies, who craft the rules that

determine when and if any amendments can be made to a bill being considered on the House floor, have more frequently chosen to shut down members of the opposition. During the first two years of the Clinton administration, nearly half the rules were "open"—members of the minority were free to offer amendments. But the Congress that came into office with Barack Obama permitted only a single open rule. Over the intervening period, the percentage of closed rules, which restrict the opportunity to offer amendments, shot up by a quarter.[23]

All of the divisive elements listed above feed off one another. Candidates from gerrymandered districts pander to certain news outlets, and special interests enforce a member's ideological purity. Politicians learn that the key to getting anything done in the House or Senate is to be rigid—that the surest route to influence is their unflagging support of the House leadership's restrictive rules. Zealotry garners each member more media attention and additional special-interest money, inducing them to become more intransigent (or "principled," depending on your point of view). As this merry-go-round continues, it drags down with it the public's confidence that Washington has the capacity, or the gumption, to get anything done.

There's just one problem with the conventional wisdom: none of the purported causes of the government's contemporary dysfunction are new. That's not to suggest that Washington isn't more polarized than ever before, or that the dynamics that compel bipartisan collaboration haven't eroded over the last several years. But the litany of menaces we often blame were all present in eras when the gridlock wasn't so pervasive. Certainly there are differences in scale—but the distinction holds: the policy-making process muddled through in earlier eras despite the same pernicious influences. Why have things only recently gotten so bad?

Lobbyists aren't new to Washington—the term was coined (quite possibly apocryphally) during the nineteenth-century administration of Ulysses S. Grant.[24] And while they've been vilified as a group, the special interests that are most powerful in Washington frequently lobby for a legitimate cause: the AARP, for example, represents the interests of older Americans, as the VFW does veterans. Moreover, these so-called special interests—whose demands need to be weighed against broader public concern—are often manifestations of the same affinity for voluntary associations that Tocqueville celebrated in the 1830s.

Money isn't new to the political process either—even if there's more of it today. Historian Robert Caro's *Master of the Senate* demonstrated how powerfully campaign contributions shaped the purportedly halcyon days of the 1950s and 1960s: Lyndon Johnson used his influence on the donations made by oil interests in Texas to wield power over his colleagues.[25] Even earlier, Pierre du Pont was so exasperated by Woodrow Wilson's decision to establish an inheritance tax during the First World War that he donated $92,500 to Charles Evans Hughes's presidential campaign in 1916—a sizable donation even without adjusting for inflation.[26]

Which brings us to redistricting. Information technology has certainly made it easier to pinpoint how one city block votes versus another, and so the specific lines separating districts can be manipulated with greater precision. But improvements on the margins of data analysis hardly represent a revolution. Politicians have been manipulating the borders of their districts since the dawn of the Republic. For every crazy-looking diagram of a district crafted to guarantee an electoral outcome in the next election, a political historian can easily find a map just as crazy from decades or centuries before.

Have cable networks and blogs fostered a more partisan media? A historical lens reveals that the polarized press we have today is a throwback to an earlier era. Fox News and MSNBC may signify a turn away from the ethos of the Walter Cronkite era, when balance was the watchword of the mainstream press. But through most of the nineteenth and early twentieth centuries, Americans got their news through highly partisan newspapers, many owned by media barons such as Joseph Pulitzer and William Randolph Hearst. For example, many historians believe—although it is quite possibly apocryphal—that the Spanish-American War was pursued largely because of public sentiment manipulated by "yellow journalists."[27]

Finally, has the filibuster, almost by itself, ruined American democracy? Without question, senators have increased their use of procedural tools to stymie legislation. As never before, there's a sense than every substantive bill will be filibustered, so any proposed bill needs the support of a supermajority of senators. But it is not the result of some new rule—in truth, with the exception of a change made in November 2013 to protect certain presidential nominations from endless scrutiny, the rules of the Senate have remained relatively stable. And so the real change has been a declining compunction among senators to hold policies hostage even in the face of broad-based support.[28]

At root is a central mystery: if the institutions we blame for Washington's gridlock were present in earlier eras, why have things now gone off the rails? If the common excuses for today's dysfunctional politics don't explain the more present gridlock, what's changed? The answer, like the explanation for the decline of economic innovation, lies in the disappearance of the middle rings.

On a certain level, Washington's devolution can be traced to a change in the rhythms of life inside the capital Beltway. As experts at the Bipartisan Policy Center have argued, the routines of political life have evolved over the last two decades, leaving members of the political class strangers to one another, and as such, incapable of forging compromise.[29] In an earlier era, politicians moved their families to the Washington suburbs and became enmeshed in the oft-vilified Georgetown cocktail circuit. Today, far from enrolling their children in the capital's tony private schools, many refuse even to sign a lease in Washington, sleeping in their offices and rushing to the airport as soon as votes are done for the week. Whatever time they do pass on Capitol Hill, they spend dialing for dollars largely in cubicles across the street from their official offices.

But the dysfunction isn't only a function of what's happened between the politicians—it's also a reflection of how the architecture of American community has changed. If politicians, slippery as they can be, are adept at understanding what will and won't appeal to their constituents, we have to wonder whether the American electorate has disrupted the collaborative spirit in Washington. After all, if there were a political advantage to be had by reaching across the aisle, politicians would likely grab it.

Bill Bishop was among the first to make a connection between sociological change and political gridlock. Noting the absence of any proof that gerrymandering had played a significant role in making districts more monolithic (there's no reasonable way, for example, to shape a district around San Francisco that isn't wildly progressive), he traced gridlock to the more recent tendency of Americans to sort themselves into communities of common interest.[30] In the absence of having neighbors with cross-cutting political views, politicians had become trapped by the staid mindsets of various constituencies.

But it's not just that. After all, not only have we chosen to live in more ideologically monolithic communities, but the reshuffling of American social capital has deprived us, in nearly every facet, of the capacity to imagine the world through other eyes. In a townshipped community, there were disagreements among those who lived near one another, ate in adjoining booths, drank on adjacent stools, and played in the same softball tournaments. Everyone on

Spring Street might have voted for Adlai Stevenson in 1952, but they could not avoid Eisenhower voters in the course of a typical day-to-day routine.

Today, if you don't know your neighbors—if you've transferred social capital away from the middle rings—your political frame of reference is limited both to the people you love most and the legions who, through outer-ring networks, share your point of view. If you're a progressive, you've "liked" progressive groups on Facebook that then ply you with facts and arguments. If you're a conservative, you get an e-mail each week from the Heritage Foundation with updates on their newly released studies and talking points. Absent the fundamental ability to understand those on the other side of a cultural or political divide, it's almost impossible to stomach the possibility that "our" representative in Washington might be the one collaborating with people who represent a different flavor of constituent.

The sorts of conversation endemic to townshipped community often seem inappropriate in more contemporary circumstances. Middle-ring contacts are more likely to bicker about political issues—one fellow might think the local congressman a stuffed shirt, while another is convinced he's a beacon of sanity. No matter whether these two emerge with any sort of mutual understanding— whether or not a schoolteacher manages to convince a dry cleaner to support the local school budget—the course of everyday conversation made it more difficult to view the proposal itself as an abomination. Partisans were once more inclined to disagree in an agreeable way. And in turn, they were less inclined to vilify representatives in Washington in instances where they disagreed, even if they supported the opposition.

The change, then, isn't that Americans today are necessarily more polarized, or are less inclined in the routines of their everyday lives to believe in compromise. It's that those on the other side of any given issue now are not only wrong, they're almost alien.

You can't say, "that's a crazy position to take, but I understand why Jack thinks that" if you don't know Jack, or don't know what Jack's take is. Without the firsthand exposure gained from passing conversations, it's much easier to castigate the other side—whether your position has hardened or not.[31]

Charles Murray, who explored how different classes of Americans have become more alien to one another, found another problem: "As the new upper class increasingly consists of people who were born into the upper-middle-class bubble, the danger increases that the people who have so much influence on the course of the nation have little direct experience with the lives of ordinary Americans, and make their judgments about what's good for other people based on their own highly atypical lives."[32]

What we too often miss is how the new style of political engagement has filtered up to members of Congress. It's not just that their constituencies are more monolithic, that they're more desperate for campaign contributions, or that they're paralyzed by the burdensome demands of special interests. It's that they know compromising isn't seen as a demonstration of virtue; it's evidence of apostasy. Among their constituents, moderation is seen as fealty to an objectionable agenda. It suggests a lack of character or a dearth of principle.

In essence, the spirit of collaboration that allowed politicians in Washington to tackle big challenges wasn't organic to the nation's political system. It was built from the ground up. The dynamics that once allowed the political leadership of Barbados to overcome the barriers to collaboration—the dynamics that defined the townships Alexis de Tocqueville described in the 1830s—have been disrupted. The ascendance of networks as the building blocks of American community has driven the nation's politics to resemble Jamaica's. Senators haven't become more inclined to filibuster today because they're less concerned about the public interest. Their intransigence reflects the public's new appetite.

In the mid-1990s, a Stanford professor named James Fishkin, frustrated by what he saw as a growing crisis of confidence in western democracy, began to wonder whether there wasn't a proactive way to reanimate public discourse. Having simultaneously noticed many of the same trends that Robert Putnam described in *Bowling Alone,* he wondered whether efforts to bring participants together to discuss and solve big public policy challenges might show the way to broad consensus. Maybe promoting deliberation would reinvigorate democracy. And so he set about to test that proposition using a process he came to term "deliberative polling."

To begin each exercise, Fishkin would survey a mass of voters on some discrete subject, and then cull from that universe a representative sample who would be invited to attend a conference. When they had gathered, he would divide them up into smaller groups, each comprising voters from a range of viewpoints and backgrounds. Each group would be asked to deliberate over several possible solutions to a common challenge—how best to solve an energy crisis, for example, or how to close a budget deficit. Usually the participants would be provided with extensive briefing materials, a moderator to keep the discussion focused, and an opportunity to pose questions to a range of experts. At the end of their deliberation, Fishkin would poll the group again to see whether their views had evolved.[33]

In June 2011, Fishkin conducted a deliberative poll among roughly four hundred citizens from across California. Broken into small groups, the participants had opportunities to ask questions of expert panels, moderated by PBS's Judy Woodruff. While disagreements didn't melt away over the course of the weekend, remarkably enough, participants did, in fact, change their opinions on some of the weightiest issues, offering some constructive guidance to policy makers eager to follow public sentiment.[34]

The results of the dozens of deliberative polls taken between

1995 and 2004 together revealed a similar pattern. Nearly three-quarters of the time, before-and-after surveys showed major changes in position among participants.[35] The process wasn't a panacea; differences of opinion, or distinctions that spanned divisions of race, class, or background didn't evaporate after a day's worth of conversation. But individuals who had taken polar positions on issues of public policy—many of whom had a pernicious view of individuals who held an opposing view—were often stripped of their venom. Fishkin submitted that the intractable problems that faced society might well be solved if citizens were simply provided an adequate forum to hash through possible solutions.

There are substantial distinctions between deliberative polling and typical middle-ring conversations. Casual interactions at Starbucks, for example, aren't likely to include experts on any given issue (unless, of course, the participants take to googling on their iPads). But, to some degree, Fishkin's experiments artificially re-created the sort of cross-cutting exchanges that are present organically in townshipped community. The small group discussions at his conferences mimic exchanges that were once the hallmark of barbershops, taverns, bridge games, and bowling leagues of eras past. Deliberative polls replicated the lost patterns of a previous age.

Fishkin's work returns us to the issue that was a focus of *Bowling Alone*: social trust. In the absence of thick middle rings—as we chose to spend more time with more and less intimate acquaintances—our faith in institutions has declined. We may presume that the institutions have changed, not the voting public. In some cases that's true. But more often, the reality is actually the other way around.

Traditionally, we imagine that the through lines that connect democracy and community runs primarily in one direction: public policy is designed, after all, to affect the workings of our local neighborhoods. For that reason, we focus on what policy makers can do to steer American community life—what sorts of legislation have the potential to breathe new life into civil society. Those on the right, reflecting Robert Nisbet's treatise from the 1950s, *The Quest for Community,* often wonder whether government bureaucracies aren't undermining bonds that might otherwise flourish between family, friends, and neighbors.[36] Those on the left wonder whether additional investments—new resources devoted to education, infrastructure, and community programming—might empower the residents of impoverished neighborhoods to thrive despite trying circumstances. But a closer look shows that the influence appear to flow both ways.

When he published *The Radicalism of the American Revolution* in 1993, Gordon Wood looked beyond the explicitly political narrative that defines our understanding of the struggle for independence. George Washington and his peers were unquestionably driven by a desire to free themselves from the tentacles of British monarchy. But that wasn't the whole story: they were also driven to adapt the nation's political framework to the social architecture beneath it. The township architecture of community that had begun to emerge near the end of the eighteenth century couldn't abide the incumbent system of British rule. And so the Constitution that was written several years after the Revolution was designed to accommodate townshipped community.

We may not be on the verge of a revolution today, but we face a similar conundrum. Our political system isn't in rhythm with the networked community that replaced the American township. That's not to suggest we should abandon the Constitution: there is a way for American government to adjust. But we ought not to minimize the challenge. In his revelatory work exposing how Facebook and Google are obviating the cross-cutting interactions in American life (a full 30 percent of Americans get news from Facebook), Eli Pariser put it well: "Ultimately, democracy works only if we citizens are capable of thinking beyond our narrow self-interest. But to do so, we need a shared view of the world we cohabit. We need to come into contact with other people's lives and needs and desires."[37]

Pariser was focused on technology, but the principle applies across the American experience. Our dwindling faith in American government is apparent in our own front yards. Three factors will determine whether we'll be able to adapt. The first is the extent to which networks continue to subsume townships. The second (as evidenced by the results of deliberative polling) is how capable we are of establishing patterns in networked society that reflect the benefit of townshipped familiarity. And the third is our capacity to re-form the political system to fit twenty-first-century community.

We don't know how things will turn out. Already, efforts are being made to develop technologies that might alleviate neighborly alienation, allowing people who live near one another to use social networks to build bonds.[38] If the federal government can't break the current gridlock, it's likely that local government and nonprofits will emerge to fill the void. So we need not be despondent. But if America is to thrive in the decades to come, recalibrating the relationships between democracy and community will be one of our most trying challenges.[39]

THE GIANT
SUCKING SOUND

The transformation of American community has affected other aspects of our lives as well, a fact made evident when, in early October 2006, the city where I spent the bulk of my childhood was hit by a freak two-foot snow squall. Normally, most Buffalonians wouldn't have blinked an eye. The area is famously accustomed to wintery weather. But because the storm passed through in the autumn, the trees hadn't yet shed their leaves. As snow accumulated on the foliage, the weight felled limbs that had survived decades of blizzards. Power lines were downed throughout the region and the electricity was out for over a week. Many roads were too choked with debris for electrical crews to pass for repairs.

For most area residents, the disruption wasn't much more than temporary. Kids celebrated a few extra days off from school. Adults caught up on crossword puzzles by candlelight. And most families survived just fine by heating up cans of Campbell's soup on their gas stoves.

But when the authorities went door to door to check in on each family, they discovered one slice of the population caught in more perilous straits. In houses and apartments all across town were elderly citizens, frightened, confused, frail, hungry, and entirely alone. One by one, the police scooped them up, whisked them to generator-powered facilities like hospitals and nursing homes. Once there, they were generally provided a cot and some warm food. But eventually, the trickle developed into a barrage, and soon, western New York's health-care institutions were nearly overwhelmed.

It was, for many, a Katrina moment: a natural disaster unveiled a portion of the community that had, to that point, been invisible to other slices of the population. Worse, the region's care providers realized that this was the type of client profile set to expand as the baby boomers moved into their retirement years. The October storm revealed that much as we assume that people who make it to their ninetieth birthday will have found their way into an old folks' home, many elderly Americans remain independent well past frailty. And for many who bypass institutionalization, one fallen tree limb may be all that stands between them and a life-threatening crisis.

That's not to suggest old people should be forced automatically into assisted-living facilities. One of the great miracles of the recent decades is that we've developed the capacity, through medical and public health advances, to keep many of them from having to give up their independence. But that boon has come at a cost. The sheer volume of vulnerability made apparent in western New York illustrated the degree to which, as more Americans manage to live to old age, we'll either need to finance a dramatic expansion of expensive institutions like hospitals, nursing homes, and assisted-living facilities, or build out our capacity to keep them at home.

Contemporary policy makers are now coming face to face with that very challenge. When, in the early 1990s, Independent presidential candidate Ross Perot was arguing that that the North American Free Trade Agreement would send American jobs to Mexico, he famously suggested that he could hear "a giant sucking sound" coming from south of the border. His assertion, of course, was belied by the more than twenty million new American jobs created during the Clinton administration.[1] But the iconic phrase lives on, and actually applies more appropriately to a more recent question: what can be done to stem the massive, ongoing transfer of wealth from younger Americans to their parents and grandparents?

It's a challenge that hangs over nearly every serious debate in Washington. America is on the hook to provide more support to its older citizens than it is currently capable of bankrolling. The claims retirees are slated to make on Social Security and Medicare—programs designed explicitly to cover the elderly—are likely to outpace the collective generosity of their children. And our economic growth is anemic in large part because we haven't figured out a way to ensure that our social safety net will remain solvent.

If health-care costs weren't exploding—if they hadn't grown from a mere 5 percent to a full 17 percent of the nation's GDP over the last half century—the political gridlock discussed in the preceding chapter might be less concerning.[2] But the federal government now spends four times as much on elderly people as it does on Americans younger than eighteen.[3] And the percentage of Americans over the age of sixty-five is expected to grow by roughly half between 2010 and 2030.[4] The giant sucking sound, it seems, is only going to get louder.

The question is why—and two conventional narratives have come to frame the answer. The first is largely demographic: as the baby boomers age out of the workforce, the number of workers paying into the system won't keep pace with those drawing benefits out. In contrast to their parents, the cohort born in the early postwar years will likely be remembered as the generation who ate their children's lunch.[5]

Second, many people argue that the unsustainable growth of entitlement programs has been driven by a health-care delivery system run amok. Despite the fact that the United States spends a much higher proportion of its GDP on health care, our outcomes lag behind other developed countries. We pay for health care on the basis of volume rather than quality, a fact made evident by our tendency to reward doctors and hospitals for the number of procedures they do, rather than the consistency of the outcomes.[6] Meanwhile, according to the World Health Organization, we rank fortieth in life expectancy.[7]

But while those two factors get all the press, there's a third issue at play—one that most Americans would likely celebrate. Health-care costs are being driven up by the fact that, on the whole, Americans don't die young anymore. Over the last several decades, the rate of death from acute medical conditions, infectious diseases, malnutrition, and workplace accidents has been stemmed by miraculous advances in medicine and public health. And, by almost any standard, that's fantastic news.

The flip side of that coin, however, is that as fewer people are taken in their younger years by the comparatively affordable ailments that used to kill us, more of us are living to face the scourge of chronic conditions. The onset of Alzheimer's disease and debilitating osteoporosis generally comes only after an individual is well into his or her retirement. As we've come to live longer, that different breed of challenge has begun to claim a greater proportion of our health-care dollar, and those costs are only expected to grow. As Jonathan Rauch recent wrote in *The Atlantic*: "Seniors with five or more chronic conditions account for less than a fourth of Medicare's beneficiaries but more than two-thirds of its spending—and they are the fastest growing segment of the Medicare population."[8]

Take the case of Alzheimer's disease. The burden of caring for Americans with dementia has already eclipsed the expense of caring for those afflicted by cancer or heart disease, and things are only slated to get worse. As of 2012, 3.8 million American age seventy-one or older suffered from dementia; by 2040, that population is slated to grow to 9.1 million. As a result, the aggregate cost of caring for them is expected to grow by 80 percent over the same span of time.[9]

Unfortunately, the nation's social safety net hasn't adjusted to the new landscape. Like the Pentagon during Vietnam, it seems as if the world of medicine is fighting the last war. Institutions constructed to address the challenges of a population that died much younger have been caught flat-footed when asked to care for the nation's burgeoning population of old people. Emergency rooms are equipped to handle patients undergoing heart attacks, not those found wandering the street in confusion; nursing homes are primarily geared for elderly people who are thoroughly incapacitated, not those suffering from a handful of ongoing ailments. And as a result, we're trying to drink soup with a knife: we're spending billions of dollars to treat Americans suffering from chronic conditions with measures designed to face down acute crises. That turns out not only to be bad for the patients—it's unnecessarily costly as well.

Acknowledging that the giant sucking sound results largely from what most Americans consider to be a miracle—namely, the fact that we've conquered so many of the things which once killed us off at younger ages—isn't meant to diminish other factors, like our fee-for-service model of delivery. But it is to suggest that we've missed a big part of the story. We tend to view health-care spending through the prism of medicine: how much do we need to spend on doctors, hospitals, and nursing homes to give Americans the treatments they demand? But the issue isn't medicine so much as it's care. And care isn't delivered exclusively by doctors and nurses—it's provided by community as well.

Surprising as it may be to younger Americans, the health-care infrastructure we take for granted today—hospitals, nursing homes, pharmacies, and other facilities—is the product of developments that began well after the turn of the twentieth century. Before the New Deal thrust the government to the forefront of a movement to provide a wider safety net, the bulk of that responsibility fell on communities, employers, and benevolent associations. The burden that subsequent generations have laid on entitlement programs like Medicare and Medicaid marked more of a revolution in the broader context of American history, and a dramatic break from what existed before.

During the Industrial Revolution and the Gilded Age, Americans were much more dependent on their inner- and middle-ring relationships to guarantee they would be looked after in illness or poverty. Those who grew frail were frequently at the mercy of their family, friends, and neighbors. And so older Americans tended to view their estates not only as assets, but also as leverage to ensure that their children would, indeed, provide care in their infirmity— or else get written out of the will.[10]

It wasn't just families that bore the brunt. Through the early twentieth century, community organizations played a more central role in caring for those unable to take care of themselves. As Theda Skocpol has documented, the turn of the twentieth century marked the peak of voluntary associations, a phenomenon fueled by the fact that no public institutions were available to handle the challenges facing a nation streaming from farm to factory.[11] Lewis Mumford, in an effort to explain how community was structured in the teeming cities of the Gilded Age, noted that private nonprofits were at the center of each neighborhood's capacity to care: "In every industrial center remedial agencies from soup kitchens to building and loan associations, from social settlements to employment bureaus, have been endeavoring to supply, partly from private means, the necessary facilities for living and enjoyment that were left out in the growth and expansion of the industrial town."[12]

Absent the sort of care provided by family members, neighbors, and charities, there was, for most Americans, no safety net. But for the largely private efforts to help those in need, members of earlier generations were left to suffer in squalor—and many did. It's not that Americans lacked the means necessary to access hospitals and nursing homes but that, in many cases, there were no such facilities to speak of. The institutions that Americans would be likely to turn to today—government agencies, city-run shelters, public insurance programs—weren't around. In their absence, communities did the best they could.

The point is that through most of American history—certainly during the decades that predated the construction of our contemporary social safety net—Americans more rarely thought to look to government bureaucracies for help. The meal a neighboring family provided to a destitute widow wasn't designed to augment the food she purchased with food stamps—it was frequently the only meal she would get. The education provided at the local settlement house wasn't meant to supplement options provided through the GI Bill—it was the only way for many in the tenements to better their education. The few dollars paid to a doctor who came to see a sick child weren't reimbursed by Medicare—they were paid out of the family till.

The norms of reciprocity—the ties that bound generation to generation and neighbor to neighbor—weren't a panacea. In many cases, those in need were provided spotty care, if any at all. But that architecture of care was very different from the one that prevails today. It lacked the benevolent hand of government. Bonds cultivated in township community were a lifeline to generations of Americans in need. In the absence of care provided through the middle rings, many Americans would have gone almost entirely without.

Looking back, we tend to think of the Great Depression as a dark anomaly in the nation's history. But the 1930s also saw a sea change in the way Americans conceived of the country's social safety net.

In 1990, historian Lizabeth Cohen published *Making a New Deal*, a remarkable account of the wide-ranging effects that rippled out from America's experience in the decade preceding the Second World War.[13] During the Hoover Administration, many of the country's private social service agencies had gone belly-up; at the same time, businesses that had for generations been a care-giving backstop were forced to pare down their employee benefits and siphon off their charitable giving. Many of the people struggling to make it began to look elsewhere for help.

Arguments abound even today about whether the New Deal really solved the nation's cataclysmic troubles: while the Roosevelt administration's defenders remain convinced that the alphabet soup of new programs restoked the country's economic engine, detractors now argue that the mobilization efforts made in preparation for World War II were the real salve. But wherever you come down in that debate, what can't be disputed is that FDR's White House tenure signaled a broad transformation in the nation's sense of how to solve a big problem. Faith in big bureaucracies reached its zenith in the wake of the New Deal and the war, propelling the nation into what would later be derisively termed the "era of big government."[14] To a degree many may not appreciate today, our social safety network is the legacy of that era.

It's become second nature for many to assume that institutional care—a nursing-home bed or an assisted-living facility—will be available when our parents are no longer able to live independently at home. But those sorts of facilities were established in large part because Washington financed their creation. To be sure, hospitals and benevolent homes may have existed before the 1930s, and we should be careful not to assume that every caring institution today is wholly dependent on state sponsorship. But on a host of levels—National Institutes of Health funding for new treatments, Medicare funding for doctor visits, Medicaid funding for nursing-home care—the foundation for today's health-care infrastructure was laid in Washington. Even the advances in public health—the fortification of foods and the purification of water—were frequently done at the behest of government regulators.

The emergence of that new social safety net represented a massive shift in the way care was provided. Suddenly, not only could those in need depend on their inner- and middle-ring connections; the impersonal networks that held agencies, hospitals, bureaucracies, and health-care networks together—namely, outer-ring ties—augmented the care that had prevailed for generations. The combination sparked a modern miracle. The remarkable improvements in our quality and length of life were largely an outgrowth of the new social safety net.

But over time that new crutch exacted a cost. As Robert Nisbet argued decades ago, government bureaucracies have, in many ways, supplanted the primary role that communities once played in guaranteeing care from neighbor to neighbor.[15] Beyond augmenting what existed before, the new infrastructure assumed, in many cases, the role played by acquaintances. Hospital wards and the whole panoply of services that could be provided centrally within a single building diminished demand for the sorts of services that had once been provided, generously, by neighbors and friends. The expectation that your friends from the Rotary Club might help your family out if you lost your job faded when unemployment insurance emerged to provide relief.

In an echo of the crisis mentality wrought by the Depression, we've been caught flat-footed once again today: having let the supports that existed in the middle rings lapse, fear that we may lose the services provided by outer-ring institutions—a specter driven by their exorbitant cost—has sparked the sense that we may no longer have the wherewithal to support those in need. The shift is illustrated starkly by the transformation of the way younger generations prepare for retirement—a period that now, given our longer life expectancies, requires significantly more savings. In 1980, 80 percent of those working at medium- and large-scale businesses had "defined benefit" pensions that guaranteed a monthly payout as a percent of their salary for the rest of a retiree's life. By 2009, that figure had dropped to 32 percent. In their place, many employers now offer their staff members "defined contribution" plans such as 401(k)s, which set aside a much more limited pot of money to cover a retiree's expenses.[16] But the new style of pension can run out.

The switch from defined benefit to defined contribution has been a boon to management, which has been freed from obligations that many companies would never be able to fulfill. It was, in large part, pension obligations that brought the Big Three automakers to their knees during the early part of the Obama administration.[17] But the shift has been a blow to workers who, even when taking advantage of the new alternatives, are unable to fill the gap between what they've saved and what they need. In 2011, more than half of all American workers said they had less than $25,000 in their bank accounts, and the average baby boomer had saved only enough to draw down roughly $6,000 annually for living expenses.[18] Moreover, public pension funds, which cover more than a tenth of American employees, will need as much as $2 trillion dollars extra to cover what they are scheduled to owe.[19]

Taken together, what's emerged is an epic mismatch. A system whose foundation was laid during and after the Great Depression, designed largely for an industrial economy full of workers who retired in their fifties and died in their sixties and seventies, isn't properly calibrated to the new realities of American life. We're saving less than we need and drawing down more than we have: a worker earning the average salary today will contribute only a third of what he or she is likely to take out of Medicare alone.[20] So it looks now as if the giant sucking sound is going to get us—at least without some drastic changes made in the near term.

There's a silver lining to the story. Just as Americans realized during the Great Depression that we didn't have to continue providing care using the old system, we don't now have to continue depending on the model we've inherited. It would be one thing if the costs of caring for an aging population were entirely fixed—but they're not. Our burden is being driven largely by the fact that it's too expensive to care for those suffering through chronic conditions with a system designed to address acute illness. And so rather than ask how our existing infrastructure can be made to handle the new demands of an aging population, we need to think about what sort of infrastructure is most appropriate to provide the care Americans are going to require in the years to come.

Any comprehensive effort to answer that question needs first to take into account several underlying conditions. The current health-care system will never be dismantled. We'll never return to the era of care-free zones made vivid on Robert Kennedy's famous 1968 tour of the impoverished pockets of Appalachia. And committees of bureaucrats—"death panels" as Sarah Palin once dubbed them—will never decide who will live and who will die.[21] There may be, over time, a cultural change to embrace quality of life over quantity. But the idea that a ninety-five-year-old grandmother will ever be denied a life-saving operation, or that a seriously ill child will not be allowed to undergo a life-saving procedure because a bureaucrat says it's too expensive is simply not plausible.

Those unthinkable options aside, however, we may be close to better and less expensive ways of providing for those who need help as they age. No one doubts that it's prohibitively expensive to treat moderately serious victims of dementia with the ham-handed tools of hospitals and nursing homes. You can't "treat and release" someone suffering from Alzheimer's disease the way you might the victim of a heart attack. Similarly, you can't patch up emphysema the way you might remove a cancerous tumor. But in too many cases today those institutional remedies remain the only options available: you either send confused elderly people back home from the hospital into an environment that isn't safe for them, or institutionalize them in a facility where they don't want to live, are provided with services they don't need, and their freedom is needlessly restricted—and those costs are borne largely by the taxpayers.

The result is that people living independently with chronic disease (including mental illness) are cycling in and out of hospitals and nursing homes, driving up entitlement costs without necessarily receiving the sort of care they deserve.[22] Consider what happens when someone notices that Grandma, who still lives by herself, has become dangerously weak from anemia or is bruised from a fall. All too often, she's taken to the emergency room, where she's patched up, given a new medication, or told to get a walker. But when she's sent back home, her circumstances haven't changed a bit. She's confused by self-medication. She's still eating a diet lacking in protein. Almost inevitably, she takes yet another trip to the emergency room, where once again she's patched up and sent home.

At first glance, you'd think Grandma, who is no longer entirely capable of taking care of herself, would be best placed in a nursing home. But we need to be careful about jumping to conclusions: there's a broad spectrum of care between isolation and institutionalization. There are ways to make homes safer, to retrofit staircases and toilets, to connect frail people with tailored supports, and to provide services to patients living independently. Unfortunately, in the contemporary world of medicine the choices are all too often between outpatient visits (on the one hand) and out-and-out life inside a full-time residence (on the other). What we need is to find a middle ground that offers not just the medical care that's emerged over the course of the last several decades, but the sort of personal care that was a hallmark of townshipped community.

What stands in the way of our capacity to provide a dynamic alternative to institutional care? It's not lack of demand. Instead, in most communities, the decay of the middle rings has left a near total absence of the vibrant familiarity that would allow existing care providers—social service agencies, Meals on Wheels, physical therapists—to piece together the capacity to keep Grandma at home. If systems were in place to ensure that elderly Americans were eating well, taking the right medications, avoiding the frayed corners of old rugs, bathing regularly, and keeping their finances straight, millions of institutionalized Americans could be returned to life in their communities. If the patterns of care that existed earlier in American history still prevailed—or, more specifically, if they hadn't been shunted aside over the last several decades—we wouldn't be so burdened by our dependence on expensive institutional care.

Let's be clear: the missing element of care is something different from our conventional perception of "home health care"—a service that amounts, in many cases, to an overworked nurse arriving periodically to administer a shot. Rather, for many who might otherwise be institutionalized, independence requires an augmented version of what existed in spades years ago: the neighbor who mows the lawn, the relative who brings a meal, the church parishioner who flattens a bump in the carpet. We need service providers to fill in the gaps that have been left vacant by the absence of townshipped community.

What's more, we've never been better equipped to keep those with conditions more independent. We now have scooters and walkers, special beds and custom toilets, new ways to monitor vital signs, and much more sophisticated ways to access and combine the information in real time. For all the recent advances in social networking, very little has been done to connect the people and organizations that might, properly scaled, serve as the foundation for a new system of nonmedical care. And the efficiencies of our new capacity to harness information technology offer a window onto what could be another major transformation.

The question is whether we can reverse-engineer the magic of township relationships into connections among the nation's care providers. Today, in all too many cases, those in need are given help through a hub-and-spoke system: each is directly connected to the "patient," but few are rarely, if ever, connected to one another. While that kind of system might have worked well during an earlier era, it stifles the efficiencies and innovations that might be harnessed by ensuring familiarity among those who are serving the same population. And we've now got a bevy of tools to coordinate them with unprecedented efficiency.

What if, for example, a grocery delivery service were connected to Meals on Wheels, and both were connected to the company that launders sheets, and all were connected to the maid service—and all of that information, as well as blood tests and anecdotal reports from family members, were put online for a social worker to monitor? What if a doctor could incorporate that data into recommendations for how to treat an illness or a chronic condition? And what would the dire warnings about the skyrocketing costs of health care look like if that sort of system emerged as a central part of the nation's social safety net? Suddenly, the choice Grandma (or her family) faced about keeping her at home wouldn't be so stark. If we could work out the privacy concerns—no small task—the burdensome cost of institutional care wouldn't weigh nearly so heavily on an imcumbent social safety net that, in the final analysis, isn't appropriate for the challenges of the twenty-first century.

————

The giant sucking sound certainly isn't the only challenge Americans will have to face down in the decades to come. Indeed the growing cost of health care marks only one of several overarching problems we'll need to address. But the task we face in shoring up our social safety net offers a window onto a wider-ranging mismatch. The institutions that worked effectively when set atop a foundation of townshipped community aren't always adequate in a new environment. In an era defined by networked community, we will have to embrace a reform agenda that incubates solutions that fill the gaps that have emerged in the absence of thick middle rings.

That's not a modest mandate. But there's hope to be found in the fact that the United States has been compelled to made big adjustments before. As mentioned above, up through the Great Depression, a great bulk of personal care was generally provided through family, neighbors, and friends—the inner and middle rings. Then, through the so-called era of big government, many of those responsibilities shifted to the outer rings—to bureaucracies created by the infrastructure built up through the New Deal and LBJ's Great Society.

Today, the changing architecture of American community is exacerbating the demographic challenge that might have been addressed more expeditiously if the middle rings were still abundant. The growing costs of health care won't be easy to stem, though the health-care reforms the Obama administration enacted during the president's first term in office—even beyond those which expanded access to insurance—will likely play a big role in shaping the future. Nevertheless, the debates that so frequently dominate the world of politics—namely, those revolving around proposals to raise taxes or cut benefits—can't be allowed to drown out discussions of more wholesale reinvention.

That's not to suggest we dismantle the institutions that grew over the course of the twentieth century. Americans will not abide a circumstance where Americans in need of urgent care are denied access for lack of funds. But rather than bicker endlessly about how to balance the books, we need to think creatively about how the transformation of American community has exacerbated the crisis, and how adjusting our institutions to our new social architecture can play a crucial role in shaping a long-term solution.

THE MARSHMALLOW TEST

A s we've seen, there's very little to be gained by arguing over whether the transformation of American community is good or bad. The shift has happened and we need to adjust. The last chapter argued that the institutions that seem so feckless today will have to adapt to the new rhythms of American life. But maybe we shouldn't just leave it at that. Maybe there's something more we can do.

The first part of this book traced how an upheaval in the structure of American community has shifted the intersection of motive and opportunity—our social architecture has evolved because what we desire has changed and the universe of what we can have has expanded. Today, the bulk of our effort to improve life in America is directed at the latter half of the equation: what can we do—what bill can Congress pass or what program can business sponsor—to provide Americans with opportunities to strengthen ties that bind them to their neighbors. And some of the most heralded campaigns to reinvigorate the spirit of community offer a great deal of promise.

The movement to establish universal national service, for example, aims to bring Americans from different pockets of society together in a common cause. Organizations like City Year, which served as the model for AmeriCorps, have made a down payment on the idea that every American should contribute a portion of his or her life to the common good. Volunteers are encouraged to develop the sorts of bonds that might once have formed organically among classmates, church parishioners, or co-workers from across the tracks. There's a reason that President Clinton cites the establishment of AmeriCorps among his proudest achievements, and that the Clinton Foundation today remains committed to expanding the opportunity to serve.

But efforts to augment the chance to give back mark only one possible strategy. We need also to consider what might be done on the other side of the equation—to affect American motives. The townshipped communities of earlier eras, as David Riesman argued more than sixty years ago, were the product of an American population defined by a certain social character. Is there something we might do to mold the nation's citizenry to build more familiar connections to a wider range of acquaintances?

Before answering that question, we need to determine whether, in fact, compelling Americans to rebuild village-oriented relationships is even a worthy goal. After all, if the transformation of American community is a fait accompli, there might not be much value in trying to thwart the erosion of the middle rings. But the issue isn't whether we can turn back the sands of time; it's whether, individually, Americans will develop the wherewithal to bridge the gaps that now separate individuals with disparate worldviews. It may be that the prolific connections between neighbors and colleagues that existed in generations past will never be restored—but that doesn't mean that individuals shouldn't have the capacity to build familiar connections with acquaintances who espouse divergent points of view.

The real question is whether there's something that would give Americans the nerve to break out of their cocoons. Is there a way to mold our social character that would compel us to reach beyond our comfort zones? Fortunately—at least for those who believe that good things happen when people with disparate worldviews get to know one another—the answer to that question is yes. Beyond the sorts of institutional reforms suggested in the last chapter, there's a strategy available that might well induce future generations to rebuild the bridges that have disappeared.

During the 1960s, Walter Mischel, a psychology professor then on the faculty at Stanford, conceived of a revolutionary experiment designed to measure an individual's capacity for self-control.[1] Conducting what is now known as the "marshmallow test," he placed a four-year-old and a researcher in a room with an edible treat set on a plate between them. At the outset, the researcher would explain that she needed to run an errand, but would return soon. She would then make clear that during her absence the four-year-old could ring a bell, which would call the researcher back, at which point the child would receive permission to eat the treat. However, if the child waited for the researcher to return without sounding the bell, the child would be given a second treat along with permission to eat both.[2]

What Mischel was bent on measuring was how capable any individual child was of stifling his or her impulse to indulge immediately—and the results spanned the gamut. Some kids rang the bell the moment the researcher left the room. Others held out. The strategies the strong-willed kids employed to resist temptation were remarkable. Some covered the marshmallow up with a napkin, while others sang songs. What was on display, Mischel concluded, were the various strategies that humans of all ages use to delay gratification—strategies that, among adults, tend to be masked by other behaviors.[3]

Even more illuminating was what happened next. Curious about how early childhood self-control corresponded to an individual's behavior in adolescence, Mischel contacted the same kids who had taken the first marshmallow tests roughly a decade later. What he found was that those who had been able to withstand the impulse to eat the first marshmallow were, by most measures, more successful than those who had gobbled it down.[4] Those who had given in to temptation had "lower S.A.T. scores, higher body mass indexes, problems with drugs and trouble paying attention."[5] As Mischel and his fellow researchers later argued, "The seconds of time preschool children were willing to delay for a preferred outcome predicted their cognitive and social competence and coping as adolescents."[6]

That result suggested something else: the attribute measured by the marshmallow test is, as psychologist Joachim de Posada once told a TED conference, "the most important factor for success."[7] Reams of subsequent studies, often ignored in the midst of our polarized debate over education policy, have supported that supposition. It's virtually undeniable today that what academics have labeled "noncognitive skills" are the most influential determinants of lifetime achievement.[8]

The most convincing evidence of the connection between impulse control and long-term success has been documented by Terrie Moffit, a Duke University professor who, with a group of colleagues, spent decades keeping tabs on roughly one thousand subjects born in Dunedin, a city in southern New Zealand.[9] What Moffit concluded, looking at her subjects after they had turned thirty-two, was that those who had displayed only a limited capacity to withstand emotional impulses at a young age were much more likely to have developed problems as adults: decades on, they were more likely to be overweight, to have contracted a sexually transmitted disease, to be alcoholics, and to abuse drugs. And maybe more interesting, after disaggregating the data, Moffit and her colleagues were able to determine that the trends held even when controlling for social class and IQ.[10]

The correlations didn't end there. Only 11 percent of the Dunedin subjects who as children had scored in the top fifth for self-control subsequently suffered from multiple health problems, compared to 27 percent among those in the bottom fifth. Only 10 percent at the top could later be considered "low income," compared to nearly a third of those at the bottom. Among those who had children, single parenthood was endemic only among those who hadn't scored well. And maybe most glaring, only 13 percent of those at the top had been convicted of a crime, compared to 43 percent of those at the bottom.[11]

Other scholars have uncovered similar sorts of results. One study that disaggregated thirty-two separate personality variables—self-esteem and energy level among them—determined that, in the end, self-discipline was the most accurate in predicting college GPA.[12] Others argued that self-discipline is twice as powerful as IQ in predicting an eighth-grade student's grades.[13] As explained by Paul Tough, the *New York Times Magazine* and *New Yorker* writer who has become a beacon for this whole field of research, the factor that now appears to be the most powerful determinant of an individual's success is his or her ability to control impulses, stay focused, avoid distractions, manage emotions, and control thoughts. "Psychologists call them personality traits, [but] the rest of us sometimes think of them as character."[14]

Inspired broadly by Walter Mischel's earlier work on the marshmallow test and keyed generally to the concern that contemporary American education fails students too frequently, a field of research has more recently emerged to explore the causes and effects of self-control. Frequently tied to the mission many educators have to break the cycle of urban poverty, a small coterie of scholars has tried to answer the question whether impulse control might explain why certain individuals are able to escape the traps of dysfunction while others are not.

At the vanguard of the campaign to determine whether "grit"

holds the key to boosting the potential of underprivileged students is Angela Duckworth, a professor at the University of Pennsylvania who developed a "grit scale."[15] After years of research, Duckworth was able to determine that additional grit not only lined up with lifelong success, it correlated with an individual's proficiency in specific tasks. Working in conjunction with administrators at West Point, she found that that undergraduates who scored nearer the top of her grit scale were more likely to maintain high GPAs even than those who had done better on the SATs (which, broadly defined, is more commensurate with a measure of IQ).[16] Moreover, the traditional measure of an undergraduate's aptitude as a soldier—a grade known colloquially as the "Whole Candidate Score"—was less reliable than his or her grit score in predicting whether the soldier would survive "Beast Barracks," the toughest part of a cadet's training.[17]

How this notion of "character" connects to the challenge of maintaining the different sorts of relationships may not be immediately apparent. But we can infer from the evidence that grit plays an integral role in determining how we invest our time and attention. Those who aren't able to withstand the impulse to lash out at a disagreeable acquaintance are unlikely to bond in any depth with someone who has a different worldview, if only because they're unlikely to be able to stifle the impulse to lash out or talk back. And so, if the challenges that arise from the shift from townships to networks have been driven by our diminishing capacity to harness the strength of America's diversity, enhancing our noncognitive skills offers the best hope we might have to encourage the formation of friendly but unintimate connections.

People mean well when they tell a kid to "dream big" or "reach for the stars." We all hope that children avoid the sad fate of counting themselves out before they have a chance to make it big. The ubiquitous refrain that you can "be who you want to be" is meant at its core to convince students that their gender, race, or background shouldn't prevent them from striving to achieve. But it also suggests that no barrier is too steep to overcome. Kids bereft of hope might never try.

Unfortunately, the problem among adolescents of all backgrounds isn't that they lack a mental image of the life that they'd like to live. Even among the most privileged, one thing standing in their way is a lack of wherewithal. The problem isn't that they've failed to dream big; rather, it's that they lack the gumption required to jump through the hoops that would get them from point A to point B. The path to anything worth having is dotted with scores of first marshmallows, and those most apt to achieve their dreams are those most capable of setting aside temptation.

Self-control by itself isn't always determinative. The grittiest student at a failing school may never be able to overcome—and that, of course, is why efforts to improve American education are so important. But what should also be apparent is that many of the steps between a kid and her dream are buttressed by successful relationships. Becoming a star on the team, to say nothing of emerging as a powerful politician, requires the capacity to get along with people who have different ideas and difficult personalities. It demands the ability to set anger or frustration aside in the name of a more important mission. Success, in essence, is born from the ability to maintain the types of relationships that once suffused the middle rings, and those sorts of ties are predicated on self-control.

It's no secret that different sorts of ties demand disparate competencies. Our most intimate connections require love, compassion, attention, and time. Transactional ties, by contrast, depend on a certain degree of mutual concurrence, lest they be thrown over for more agreeable alternatives. What neither demands—or, at least, what neither requires in the best of circumstances—is grit.

Marriage can be a struggle; kids aren't always easy to handle. But at the end of the day, the elements that tie us to our most and least intimate connections—commitment on the one hand and convenience on the other—can subsume the impulse we all have to eat the marshmallow. If your kids are driving you nuts, you love them anyway. If a Facebook acquaintance starts spouting racist malarkey, you can engage someone else.

The relationships that fall in between, by contrast, need to be grounded in self-control. The ties you maintain with the annoying office comptroller who controls your department's budget and with the irritating parent who has offered to give your son a ride home from camp demand a modicum of grit. What happens when a casual friend forgets the appointment you made to meet for coffee? What happens when the dry-cleaning clerk makes a disparaging remark about your favorite baseball player? If the goal is to maintain a friendship, earn a promotion, or simply keep cool in line, you can't eat the marshmallow.

A new national bounty of grit can't solve all our problems. The Medici effect explored in chapter 12, so intertwined with the process of innovation, depends on the specific dynamics of a given community. But grit forms the foundation; self-control allows an individual to harness the potential of creative collaboration. It is self-discipline that allows people to maintain relationships with acquaintances who don't share their point of view. And so a community that weaves diverse neighbors together without self-control is more likely to disintegrate.

This is not a situation where, as in *Field of Dreams,* "if you build it, [they] will come."[18] Figuring out a way to augment American grit will not magically reconstitute the middle-ring-rich communities of generations past. Nevertheless a grittier America would, at least, make it more likely that we'd each connect with a wider range of neighbors. We'd have greater wherewithal to maintain the dynamism of previous eras. And so we have to ask: What can be done to imbue future generations with the propensity to delay gratification? What might we do to compel our children not to forsake the sort of relationships that, for decades, fueled American ingenuity, collaboration, and mutual concern?

Late in the fall of 1993, my high school biology teacher presented a lesson on the complicated molecular process by which cells generate energy. It's not that I remember the Krebs cycle because it was riveting—my eyes had glazed over well before our forty-five-minute period had come to an end. But as the bell rang, the class received what we considered shocking news: Mr. Gresens announced that, rather than quiz us the following week with a multiple-choice test, he planned simply to supply us with a blank sheet of paper. From there, he explained to a stunned room, we would each be required to re-create, from memory, a diagram of the Krebs cycle in its entirety.

Even before he had retreated to his office with a wry grin, cries of anguish suffused the classroom. Textbooks were slammed. Many of us dejectedly packed up our overstuffed backpacks while cursing the pointlessness of high school. Of all the ridiculousness we'd already been forced to endure, this seemed particularly egregious. Few of us were headed for careers in biology, so why should we all have to fill our heads with such useless information? To a group of angst-ridden teenagers, memorizing the details of some obscure molecular process captured the essence of what was wrong with American education.

Many of us went home and whined about the indignity over dinner, even before kvetching on the phone to our friends. But then we did what Mr. Gresens surely had predicted: we went up to our rooms, closed the door, turned down the radio, and got about the businesses of transcribing the Krebs cycle over and over until, after dozens of attempts, we'd committed the thing to memory. It was

painful, and for most of us there wasn't even a marshmallow waiting as a reward. But when, a week later, we handed in our formerly
blank sheets of paper, most of us aced the test, equipped almost
preternaturally to complain about whatever came next.

Nearly two decades later, I couldn't hope to re-create the Krebs
cycle on paper. In fact, I had trouble deciphering its Wikipedia
entry when preparing to write these paragraphs. Just as we had
all predicted at the time, few of us have ever used the information we crammed into our brains that week to any useful purpose
(though one of us became a biology teacher). Now, Mr. Gresens
may have hoped that some of us would be inspired by the beauty
of molecular science. But the content we were required to commit
to memory wasn't entirely the point. Beyond the subject matter,
the act of memorizing served to accomplish something much more
rudimentary: we learned during those hours in our rooms the skill
of focusing our minds.

That old-school method of teaching—a teacher simply present-
ing information that students are expected to imbibe—has more
recently been replaced by a different method of instruction. As if
responding to the criticism of our whining at the time, education is
geared now to teach kids "how" to think rather than plying them
with information they are not likely to put to any use. Concentration on learning styles and the art of collaboration has replaced
rote memorization. By most measures, that makes intuitive sense:
to compete in the globalized economy of the twenty-first century,
the issue isn't whether you know the intricacies of any biological
process so much as that you have the mental acuity to solve complex problems in groups.

But for all the advantages of the new teaching methods, it's hard
not to wonder whether recent reforms have scuttled the grit derived
from the tedium of the Krebs cycle. Surely, the jobs of tomorrow
will require a different set of skills from those of the mid-1900s—
technological literacy, the capacity to understand markets and to

adapt to changing situations. But new ideas are still the province of some combination of deep thought and collaboration—both of which require an ability to forgo the marshmallow. Our transition away from the lesson plans that required students to conquer their boredom may in the end be doing future generations a disservice.

Our challenge isn't to find a way back to the old style of teaching, much as I honor Mr. Gresens for spurring me to overcome lousier impulses. There's real value in the educational techniques gleaned over the decades. But we have to wonder whether there are things that could be included more proactively in our school curricula to prompt a grittier America. And fortunately, we're in the midst of an educational revolution that sheds light on that very challenge.

Galvanized by the research derived from the marshmallow test, a field of research has emerged more recently on the causes and effects of delayed gratification. Some scholars have come to wonder whether impulse control might offer insights into why certain individuals are able to escape dysfunction while others are mired in counterproductive patterns. At the vanguard of the campaign to instill more grit in students are widely acclaimed efforts like Geoffrey Canada's Harlem Children's Zone (HCZ), and charter-school organizations led by the likes of the "Knowledge Is Power Program" (KIPP) in cities throughout the United States.

In his book *Whatever It Takes,* Paul Tough traced the HCZ's efforts to inculcate certain tenets of middle-class America—patterns of behavior that are normal for a white kid growing up in the suburbs—into the rhythms of inner-city life. At root was Canada's supposition that the approach many middle-class parents take to raising their children—showering them with affection, encouraging them to be inquisitive, being sensitive to their concerns and responsive to their opinions—differed dramatically from the emphasis on obedience and respect prevalent in urban areas.[19] Could those different patterns of parenting be contributing in an important way to middle-class students' long-term success?

This has been the key question for those looking to shake up a status quo of failure. In looking, for example, at which inner-city high-school graduates made it through college and which dropped out, David Levin, one of the founders of the KIPP network of charter schools, noticed:

> The students who persisted in college were not necessarily the ones who had excelled academically at KIPP; they were the ones with exceptional character strengths, like optimism and persistence and social intelligence. They were the ones who were able to recover from a bad grade and resolve to do better next time; to bounce back from a fight with their parents; to resist the urge to go out to the movies and instead stay home and study instead; to persuade professors to give them extra help after class.[20]

What Canada, Levin, and other educators have come to focus on is what sort of culture and curriculum can best equip kids with the power of self-discipline.[21] What can be done, either at the outset or later in children's development, to give them the ability to withstand an emotional hijacking?

James Heckman, a Nobel laureate who has become a leading figure in the movement for educational reform, has argued that brain chemistry is a key component, and that studies done on rodents may offer a window onto what happens among human children.[22] A study done by Michael Meaney, a neurologist at McGill, determined that the offspring of rat mothers who had spent more time licking and grooming their pups were better equipped to deal with stress later in life. Those who had been cuddled more frequently were better at finding their way through mazes, and lived longer. Humans and rats are very different creatures—but there may be lessons we can draw from Meaney's experiments. Research among human subjects has discerned that the stimulation kids receive from their caregivers actually changes the way the synapses work in their brains, and that the most effective interventions are done very early in life.[23]

Moreover, as revealed famously in a long-term study of the Perry Preschool Project, which served a group of children drawn from similar circumstances in Ypsilanti, Michigan, interventions from professionals early in life can have long-term effects on an adult's capacity for self-discipline. The study provided one group of three- and four-year-olds with two years of daily preschool programming and a weekly afternoon hour-and-a-half visit from the teacher; another similar group, provided no similar service, served as a control. The researchers kept track of individuals from both groups until they were forty, and then published the remarkable results.[24]

What they concluded was that those students who completed the program scored higher on achievement tests through the age of fourteen and were more literate when measured at nineteen and twenty-seven. They were less likely to be held back in school, less than half as likely to need special education, and significantly more likely to graduate from high school. They were four times more likely to be employed and twice as likely to avoid the dole. They were less prone to crime and delinquency, and females were less likely to get pregnant in their teenage years.[25]

Something very important is at work here. Unlike intelligence, which is largely immutable from birth, grit, it seems, is a quality that can be augmented by outside influences. And while the Perry Preschool program makes clear that interventions made at an early age may be the most effective, it appears that noncognitive skills can be developed even after students have reached adolescence, as the KIPP, Harlem Children's Zone, and other programs have proven. In essence, we've not only figured out a trait that helps determine success in life—we've actually figured out how to imbue grit in children who might not otherwise develop it. That's not just good news for those who might otherwise have given up on public education. It suggests that a key barrier to cultivating a new era of thick middle rings may be overcome.

There's a lot we still don't understand. How much can grit be augmented as someone ages? Does the teaching style Mr. Gresens employed in my ninth-grade classroom have the potential to raise the lifelong level of impulse control? What seems clear, however, is that the discussions we typically have around the issues of education policy too often drown out another question: what exactly is it that we're trying to teach our children? We want every graduate to read and write. We want them to be intellectually stimulated and to be well versed in the fields of science, technology, engineering, and math. But above all, we should want them to be resilient; we need them to be able to focus in spite of temptation.

In the end, we need to provide Americans not only with the opportunity but also with the wherewithal to develop the types of relationships that once defined the middle rings. That's not a prescription to restore townshipped community; it's a strategy to fill some of the holes left untended during a networked era. America's social character will be a crucial determinant of our national trajectory, and today, it seems, we're fortunate to be on the cusp of uncovering the tools required to provide future generations with the blessing of self-control.

Conclusion
=====

THE CRISIS OF AMERICAN EXCEPTIONALISM

Beneath the barrage of depressing headlines in the nation's newspapers today lurks a more ominous question: is America in decline? In a recent *Time* magazine poll, more than 80 percent of Americans expressed a belief that the last several years had seen the United States take a step back.[1] The oft-repeated promise of the American Dream—that the future will be better than the past, and that the next generation will have it better than those who came before—now seems increasingly far-fetched.

It's not difficult to understand why. As one analyst recently pointed out, not since the Great Depression has median income fallen so steadily for so long.[2] And the economic effects of our fall from grace correspond to a familiar litany of disheartening indicators: among the globe's thirty-five most advanced economies, the United States ranks thirty-fourth in child poverty. We rank twenty-eighth when it comes to four-year-olds in preschool, and fourteenth in the percentage of young adults with post-secondary degrees. Our obesity rate is ten times that of Japan, and we've fallen behind most of Europe in measures of social mobility. At the same time, we've put a larger percentage of citizens behind bars than many of the world's most repressive regimes.[3]

The list just goes on and on. The median net worth of middle-income families fell from nearly $130,000 to less than $95,000 between 2001 and 2010, when adjusted for inflation.[4] The average family lost 0.6 percent annually of its income in real dollars over roughly the same period—the first time that real income and wealth fell over the course of a decade since the Second World War.[5] Between 1970 and 2012, America's debt-to-GDP ratio more than doubled from 28 to 62 percent.[6] Between 1965 and 2012, public debt almost doubled from 38 to 74 percent of America's GDP—and it's slated to grow to 90 percent in the 2020s and to nearly 250 percent in the 2040s.[7]

The litany of depressing statistics and accompanying vignettes—plant closings, corporate scandals, tuition hikes, and the like—has done nothing but heighten the concern that our competition will define the future.[8] Developing countries around the world—China first among them—appear poised to eat our lunch. Climate change threatens to force us to choose between affordable energy and environmental protection. The specter of terrorism imperils our commitment to civil liberties. Taking all these concerns as a whole, it's no wonder so many of us think that the United States will soon fade into the annals of history.

Worse still, it's not clear what might propel us out of the morass. Beyond the ingenuity of Silicon Valley and the more recent discovery of domestic natural gas reserves, we're rarely treated to good news on the economic front. The social safety net seems frayed and wildly out of balance. Between 1999 and 2012, the proportion of Americans who believed that "most people who want to get ahead can make it if they are willing to work hard" fell from 74 to 63 percent.[9] In 2008, a majority of middle-class Americans believed that their children's standard of living would be better than their own; by 2012, a plurality believed it would be the same or worse.[10]

The barrage of discontent has begun to define the nation's psyche. Between 1987 and 2012, the share of Americans who endorsed the statement "I don't believe there are any real limits to growth in this country today" dropped from 67 to 51 percent, while those who disagreed grew from 28 to 45 percent.[11] Maybe most notable, the government appears gridlocked and incapable of reaching any consensus about how to jump-start an American renaissance, revealing a paralysis that has led many to question whether the elements that Tocqueville believed responsible for America's exceptional qualities have finally run their course.[12]

Tocqueville, of course, had identified a series of features unique to the American experience, each of which contributed to the nation's dynamism and resilience: our propensity to join voluntary organizations; the "superiority" of American women; and our more attentive focus to purely commercial interests, among many others.[13] That intellectual frame—identifying which among America's attributes have come under the most strain—has informed three distinct views that now prevail about America's future prospects.

The first view, typically championed by those on the right, suggests that our story is rooted almost exclusively in checks on the power of government. As members of the Tea Party frequently argue, government overreach is today at the root of our problems, undermining the very spirit of liberty. When asked about how to right the ship, they prescribe a drastic retrenchment of the federal bureaucracy, believing that free-market solutions are better equipped to address the nation's big problems.

The second view, espoused more often by those in the center and on the left, is that the uniqueness of the American story has been driven by the nation's propensity to invest in the future. Even in the depths of the Civil War, President Lincoln committed the federal government to establish both an intercontinental railroad and a national network of land-grant colleges. Amid dilapidated infrastructure and woefully deficient test scores, adherents of this view argue today for a broad new wave of public investment.

Unfortunately, members of these two schools all too frequently fall victim to what *New York Times* columnist David Brooks has termed "the No. 1 political fantasy in America today, which . . . is the fantasy that the other party will not exist. It is the fantasy that you are about win a 1932-style victory that will render your opponents powerless."[14] Even for those not squarely in one camp or the other—those who see merit in proposals made on both sides of the aisle—the temptation is to blame the persistent and self-defeating inability of the nation's leaders to compromise. In his recent book, for example, *Time* editor-at-large Fareed Zakaria argued that "a 'can-do' country is now saddled with a 'do-nothing' political process, designed for partisan battle rather than problem solving. By every measure—the growth of special interests, lobbies, pork-barrel spending—the political process has become far more partisan and ineffective over the last three decades."[15]

Zakaria's argument points to the conclusion made by adherents of the third school—that the die is cast. This view—that the very features that once set us apart have been so thoroughly disseminated to countries across the globe that America is now just one among many—may be best epitomized by Harvard and Oxford professor Niall Ferguson's book *Civilization*. The West's commitments to "competition, science, property rights, medicine, the consumer society, and the work ethic" have been incorporated into the cultures and economies of nations now poised to compete on a level playing field.[16] Lacking any real competitive advantage, the United States has begun its painful descent back to earth.

There are, undoubtedly, varying degrees of wisdom among the disparate views of American decline. Most Americans, for example, have been frustrated at one time or another by the sometimes wasteful machinations of our government. Nevertheless, in many cases, the most fervent opponents of state largesse are among those most dependent on entitlements like Social Security and Medicare. Moreover, it's hard to see how making vulnerable populations more vulnerable would jump-start the nation's renewal.[17] Indeed, recent evidence suggests that "austerity"—as many derisively refer to the Tea Party's recommendation of drastic federal cutbacks— failed when tried by David Cameron's government in the United Kingdom.[18] And so the hope that we might cut our way to prosperity appears more by fervor than logic.

By the same token, anyone who has flown into one of the dilapidated airports that serve America's premier cities—LaGuardia in New York is a prime example—has likely come away convinced that paltry public infrastructure is at the root of the problem. The disparity is particularly harrowing for anyone who has recently returned from China, where many of the airports gleam.[19] The United States devotes only 2 percent of its annual GDP to infrastructure investment—less than half of what Europe spends, and a mere sixth of China's equivalent investment.[20] Nevertheless, it's not entirely clear how we would finance an explosion of new building: though some dispute whether the nation's budget is really in such dire need of rebalance, a country whose deficit is out of control seems a lousy candidate for the next New Deal.[21]

No one can doubt that many of the institutions that were once uniquely American—or, at least, creatures of the West—have recently been adopted elsewhere around the world. It's been more than two decades since Francis Fukuyama published *The End of History*, arguing that free-market democracy had finally vanquished its competitors as the prescription for societal success.[22] Whether or not you bought into Fukuyama's thesis—even if you believe, as some do, that history has "returned"—what's undeniable is that many of the rhythms that propelled American preeminence have been adopted elsewhere. Nevertheless, compelling as the declinists' explanation may be, it suggests that American society is just another iPhone, blessed by nothing more that a better menu of apps. That's hardly a convincing way to understand why America has had such a remarkable run over the last two centuries.

Near the end of his career, having spent much of his life wrestling with this topic, the eminent political sociologist Seymour Martin Lipset argued that American exceptionalism wasn't due simply to the fact that the country's citizens were more committed to civil liberties or public investments than their counterparts in other nations. Nor, in Lipset's mind, had the United States been propelled by a unique set of political or social institutions. Rather, by Lipset's estimation, America's exceptional story had been driven by the country's good luck in avoiding the impenetrable social divisions that plague most other societies around the globe. Because the United States hadn't been cleft nearly so deeply along the lines of tribe, caste, religion, ethnicity, and class, Americans had managed to maintain an unparalleled spirit of dynamism and resilience.[23]

Lipset wasn't blind to the fact that America hadn't always lived up to its reputation as a "melting pot." The institution of slavery and the legacy of Jim Crow make plain the fact that prejudice and discrimination are woven into the fabric of the nation's history. But inasmuch as the background of individuals preordains their role in most societies—to the extent that the circumstances of their birth determine whom they might know later in life, where they might live, or what they might do—the proverbial door has, for most of our history, been opened a few degrees wider. And to Lipset's view, it was that feature, beyond any other, that fueled America's rise to the top of the global food chain.[24]

It would be easy to ascribe the facility with which Americans have pierced defining social barriers to a series of historical quirks.

We are, after all, a nation of immigrants, and it might be expected that each successive wave of newcomers would feel compelled to welcome the next. As Jon Stewart playfully pointed out on a 2012 episode of *The Daily Show*, American history is rife with successive waves quickly, if haltingly, incorporated into the broader American story.[25] The Bill of Rights, moreover, is imbued with a commitment to individual liberty, an ethos that often serves to prevent one group from being subjugated by another. Even the words enshrined on the Statue of Liberty—"Give me your tired, your poor, Your huddled masses yearning to breathe free"—speak to a celebration of diversity that's fairly unique to the United States.[26]

But beneath it all, our history of broad inclusion is not rooted in some blithe paean to the generosity of the American spirit. Rather, like the foundation for America's economic ingenuity and political accommodation, our commitment to melding new and different people together was forged in the rhythms of everyday life. Townshipped community was an unparalleled gateway to assimilation because neighbors weren't able to avoid one another; quite the opposite, they were frequently compelled to become codependent. The very essence of American exceptionalism was born from the architecture of American community.

It's impossible to overstate how important our unique sociology has been to the nation's dynamism. In the United States, our "little platoons," Edmund Burke's term for the contacts who comprised the core of any individual's social universe (that is, middle rings) were organized around the diversity of people who lived nearby— the people who comprised the local township.[27] In Europe, by contrast, the networks of people who shared the same class or language or profession were more likely to define any individual's contacts. And so America's exceptional capacity to metabolize the infusion of new ideas, new cultures, and new populations wasn't derived by some ephemeral commitment to inclusion—it results from a specific feature of our social architecture.

I don't mean to suggest that American history is defined exclusively by rags-to-riches stories. For every Andrew Carnegie, there have been millions who were born and died in squalor, and thousands who have lived in luxurious circumstances they did not themselves earn. But even more than economic mobility, America has been unique in its social fluidity. Even with all the blatant counter-examples, through most of the twentieth century, Americans were relatively unencumbered by division. Amid all the tensions that existed between different pockets of society, life in the United States provided citizens with an unusual degree of access and exposure.

There are at least two additional things of note about the connection between American community and American exceptionalism. The first is that big, disruptive changes almost always stir existential angst among the chattering American public. It was just two decades ago when, as the Cold War came to a close, we worried that Japan might usurp our role on the global stage. Three decades before that, in the wake of Sputnik, many worried that the Soviet Union might claim the mantle of postwar global domination. In the late 1970s, a New York University historian wrote that scholars of every American generation have worried aloud that some new development threatened to incite the end of American community. And yet, at least to that point, Americans had not become as isolated as any had feared.[28]

Nevertheless, if, as I've argued above, something more drastic has happened—if the basic building blocks that survived the nineteenth and the bulk of the twentieth centuries have finally been subsumed by a new system of networks—we need to take notice. To the degree that townships remained preeminent through the upheavals of First Wave (agricultural) and Second Wave (industrial) society, the middle rings served as the foundation. So, as the middle rings have become the missing rings, tomorrow's chal-

lenges will need to be metabolized through an entirely new constellation of societal strengths and weaknesses.

Let's be clear: it's not that townships themselves are magical, or that the middle rings are themselves hallowed. Rather,
our exceptional rise to the top of the global pyramid has been
driven by the fact that the institutions of American society were
built to accommodate, exploit, and strengthen the community
architecture on which they were built. Our federal system, with
its checks and balances, divided powers, bicameral legislature,
and judicial review, among other elements, was built explicitly
to govern a society structured, as Tocqueville noted, from the
township up.

That points to something that is too often lost in our attempts
to decipher the state of our union. The American system of government doesn't contain some secret sauce cooked up to guarantee
growth and social harmony. The architecture of our constitutional
system didn't, by itself, propel the United States from a ragtag set
of colonies into the most powerful nation on earth. Rather, the
structure of our national charter fundamentally complemented
the architecture of colonial American community.[29] It marked a
rare case in human history when a country's governing apparatus
was almost perfectly calibrated to the society beneath.

But now that balance has come undone. Institutions so pervasive that they've faded into the background of our collective
consciousness—the nature of our social safety net, the structure of
our educational system, the core contract between employer and
employee, and so on—were all erected atop a community architecture that, while not obsolete, no longer coincides with reality.
The calibration that kept America humming for more than two
centuries is suddenly out of whack. Our society is coming face to
face with what I earlier called the epic mismatch: the institutions
that frame American society no longer line up with the routines of
our daily lives.

For most of us, that realization should be a source of both great fear and hope. It suggests, at least from the perspective of public policy, that the approaches we once used to construct solutions to nationwide challenges may no longer apply. *The Unwinding*, George Packer's 2013 narrative exposé of how our institutions have decayed in the decades since the late 1970s, tapped into our quiet but pervasive fear that everything is falling apart. Exploring the toxic brew of complacency, greed, and moral turpitude that have come to define contemporary American life, Packer issued a general indictment. And by making his argument not only through statistics but also through the life stories of several individuals, he articulated what many Americans feel: as a society, we're in the midst of a long, slow descent.

The good news is that while Packer told one important part of the story, he overlooked the quiet but radical transformation unveiled in the pages of this book. Yesterday's institutions aren't unwinding because we're no longer as committed as we once were to the American Dream; if anything, Packer's stories are evidence that many Americans themselves are as hardworking and resilient as ever. Rather, it feels as though things are falling apart because institutions built for township society don't work without the middle rings. The networked society that's emerged is still searching for ways to exploit the advantages of stronger inner- and outer-ring ties. We're not unwinding as much as we're evolving—but the reforms required to revive the spirit of American exceptionalism are lagging behind the shift.

Look, for example, at the challenge wrought by our newfound need to finance an explosion of retirees. Progressives long to return to a regime of defined benefit pensions—the retirement system that guaranteed a certain income for life. As many conservatives argue, that sort of retirement system is no longer feasible. Too many businesses fail, and too many employees jump too frequently from job to job, field to field, and city to city to expect that any individual firm will cover the costs of retirees' needs once they've left the workforce.[30] In many cases, that leaves us in a stalemate: one group wants to return to the way things used to be, and the other offers solutions that may not address the underlying problem.

What we need to do is move past the old debate and imagine how a more reasonable twenty-first-century pension system can be built to match the new American career. What's the best way to help Americans finance their golden years in a society driven by global competition, increased efficiency, a burgeoning service sector, and the proliferation of new networks? Rather than try to build from our existing infrastructure (a hybrid of public programs and private pensions), we should develop a system that enhances the ability of employees to jump from one position to another in search of more dynamic and exciting opportunities. The prospect that we might be able to create new institutions, rather than shore up those geared to complement an earlier reality, should be the fount of hope for the future. The new structure of American society might, in the end, rekindle our dynamism.

It's probably right for us to mourn what we've lost, as Packer and countless others have done. There were blessed elements of past eras that are unlikely ever to return. But the alchemy of connections in the new patterns of contemporary American life may well spark the same vitality captured by the last two American centuries. Maybe, with a few adjustments, the transformation of the last few decades augurs a brighter future than would ever have been possible under the old regime.

There are reasons to be optimistic. Tempting though it is to presume that networked community will extinguish the sort of crosscutting connections that were unavoidable in villages, towns, and neighborhoods, networks may turn out to be even more dynamic.

The revolution in technology, combined with the modern aversion to bigotry, could reanimate the elements that fueled American exceptionalism through the early postwar period. As the Pew Research Center's Lee Rainie, working with Barry Wellman, wrote in 2012:

> Small densely knit groups like families, villages, and small organizations have receded in recent generations. A different social order has emerged around social networks that are more diverse, and less overlapping than those previous groups. The *networked* operating system gives people new ways to solve problems and meet social needs. It offers more freedom to individuals than people experienced in the past because now they have more room to maneuver and more capacity to act on their own.[31]

The great hope is that connections made across better-integrated disciplines—doctors and scientists kibitzing through mobile devices, across social networks, in real time—will spark even more creativity than that generated in townshipped society. To hear the deans of exciting new industries—venture capitalists surveying the landscape in Silicon Valley, researchers enveloped in projects designed to discover the true nature of dark matter, journalists on missions to uncover elements of the political process shrouded in mystery—it's hard not to be confident.

At the same time, however, a balanced look at the potential dynamism born in outer-ring relationships will cause many to hedge their bets. Some of the same studies documenting the extent to which racial and ethnic separations have eroded have simultaneously found other corrosive sorts of divisions that have emerged in their stead. A study comparing American social networks in 1985 and 2004 concluded that while society was less segregated by race, there was less mixing among Americans of different ages and with different levels of education. Claude Fischer and Mike Hout, in their analysis of twentieth-century sociological change, found that divisions along lines of class and education have actually deepened.[32] And as we've seen, Charles Murray's *Coming Apart* highlighted the widening chasm between the cultural patterns of working- and middle-class America.

Those conflicting trends may be best illustrated by a look at what's happened in American religious life. Turn on a broadcast of one of the nation's megachurches—a service of Joel Osteen's Lakewood Church in Houston, for example—and there's no mistaking the fact that Americans of all races are worshiping, at least in some circumstances, under the same roof. That signals incredible progress from the era when Martin Luther King Jr. pointed out that "the most segregated hour of Christian America is 11 o'clock on Sunday morning."[33]

But that doesn't mean we've been woven into a uniform tapestry. Whatever progress we've made on racial segregation, we've largely replaced with other de facto discrimination. As University of Chicago Divinity School Dean Martin Marty explained to Bill Bishop for *The Big Sort*:

> I've always argued that what society needs are town meeting places where people with very different commitments can meet and interact. Churches have been that. If you're a Methodist and you move to Des Moines, Iowa, and you get to the nearest Methodist church, thirty or forty years ago, you would have an open encounter. People who were pro-Bush or pro-Kerry would talk. Fertilization would go on. Now it simply doesn't happen.

We have to wonder, as we invest more heavily in inner- and outer-ring relationships, whether the opportunities to be in touch with a broader spectrum of contacts will compensate for the attrition of the middle-ring bonds that were once built between acquaintances. Will a networked society manage the same magical diffusion and collision of ideas bound up in previous eras?

In his book *Loose Connections*, Robert Wuthnow included a vignette about a middle-aged man who had taken great pride in joining his local volunteer fire company. Frank Purelli works hard to make a living, loves his family, and is, through his service as a first responder, deeply invested in his neighbors' well-being. Then he considers quitting. It's not that he wants to hang up his boots; his years of service have been a real source of personal pride and joy. But in the end, he concludes, it's become too difficult to afford the sacrifice. His wife works a full-time job, and he has two small children to help raise. Time with the guys at the firehouse is time he's not lending a hand at home.[35]

By some accounts, Purelli's story is just another example of the decline of voluntary associations. If only Americans today were more like the ones that Tocqueville celebrated in the 1830s— unusually engaged, committed to their collective well-being, and willing, if not eager, to sacrifice in the name of the collective good. But for the loss of the nation's long history of mutual concern, many have argued, it might not feel as if America were declining, or at least unwinding.[36]

True as that may be—indeed, fire services, mirroring changes across the spectrum of American life, have become increasingly professionalized, obviating the demand for volunteers—Purelli's story also offers a window onto the transformation of American community.[37] Volunteer firehouses still exist today, just as there are still vestiges of communities imbued with the old patterns of township life. But over the last several decades, our newfound capacity to reinvest our social capital in our most and least intimate relationships has impelled us to abandon those in between.[38]

In the preface to *That Used to Be Us,* Thomas Friedman described the way his childhood had framed his worldview:

> To this day, my best friends are still those kids I grew up with in St. Louis Park, and I still carry around a mental image—no doubt idealized—of Minnesota that anchors and informs a lot of my political choices. No matter where I go—London, Beirut, Jerusalem, Washington, Beijing, or Bangalore—I'm always looking to rediscover that land of ten thousand lakes where politics actually worked to make people's lives better, not pull them apart.[39]

What so many of us have missed—what I misunderstood in the years after my family moved from Cincinnati to Buffalo—is that the world of Friedman's childhood, like my father's, is gone. Friedman is still looking for the patterns of community that have been disrupted by the developments he has done so much to explain. The same influences that have worked to flatten the globe, putting us in closer touch with acquaintances around the world, have made strangers of the people next door.

That's not to wax poetic about some lost spirit of American community. Much as I might have liked, in my childhood, to have been woven into the same tapestry of connections that defined my parents' early years, that alone is no reason to worry about the state of American community. At root is a much wider concern. It's time for us to grapple with the question of how upheavals in the routines of our everyday lives are affecting the nation's long-term trajectory. Rather than remain dejected, we need to focus our attention on how the new building blocks of American society can be harnessed to maintain the American Dream.

In the end, the issue is not whether to embrace change—we don't have a choice. Rather, our challenge is to adjust the institutions that frame our lives to the new networked architecture that has emerged. How can we harness far-flung networks of the digital age to tackle challenges of the twenty-first century? How we respond to that call to action will shape the sort of world our children inherit. The decisions we make today may well determine whether the long legacy of American exceptionalism can survive. Decline, after all, is only inevitable if we're unable to adapt the institutions of yesterday to the routines of tomorrow.

Acknowledgments

Nearly a decade in the making, this book grew from the germ of an idea to a series of wide-ranging conversations, to a seemingly endless period of research, to an article in *National Affairs*, and finally to a full-length work of nonfiction. I owe a debt of gratitude to an expansive list of co-conspirators, each of whom has helped to bring the project to fruition.

First, I'd like to thank the Clintons and my colleagues at the Clinton Foundation. This project was pursued independently from my role as a senior Fellow at the foundation—indeed, it began before I became a foundation employee—and *The Vanishing Neighbor* does not purport to speak for the foundation or the Clintons themselves. But there's little doubt that the president and secretary's legacy of public service—to say nothing of the foundation's ongoing work—has been driven by a focus on helping societies around the globe address many of the issues identified here. It remains an honor to help the foundation continue in that mission today.

Before and during my tenure at the foundation, my thinking has been shaped independently by dozens of conversations with academics, journalists, colleagues, and peers. The ideas presented in the preceding chapters are suffused with their insights and inspiration. Any errors are my own, but I would feel remiss in failing to acknowledge those who took the time to hear my analysis, offer some of their own, voice their disagreements, and deepen my understanding of what's really happened to American community.

Among those deserving of special notice are Matt Bai, Victoria Bassetti, Robert Bellah, Thomas Bender, Matt Bennett, Bill Bishop, Cassandra Bissell, Sir Courtney Blackman, Jonathan Bowles, John Bridgeland, Alan Brinkley, Andrew Cherlin, Lizabeth Cohen, Matthew Desmond, E. J. Dionne, Robin Dunbar, Claude Fischer, James Fishkin, Tom Freedman, Al From, Geoffrey Gagnon, Bill Galston, Herbert Gans. Geoff Garin, Dan Gerstein, Geoffrey Godbey, Kristen Gong, Mark Granovetter, Jason Grumet, Liz Halloran, Keith Hampton, Froma Harrop, Doug Hartmann, Risa Heller, Peter Blair Henry, Mike Hout, Daniel Hruschka, James Davison Hunter, Jim Kessler, Joel Kotkin, Daniel Kurtz-Phelan, Richard Locke, Elaine Kamarck, John Kelly, Neil MacBride, Peter Marsden, Will Marshall, Andres Martinez, Tony Marx, Mike McCurry, Conor McKay, Charles Murray, Jeffrey Nussbaum, Kevin O'Connor, Holly Page, Sasha Polakow-Suransky, Robert Putnam, Bruce Reed, Sean Safford, Reihan Salam, Robert Sampson, Lorin Scher, Robert Schlesinger, David Shipley, David Shribman, Fred Siegel, Alice Siu, Jeffrey Solomon, Elizabeth Stanley, Alan Stone, Sean Sweeney, Neera Tanden, Marcia Lee Taylor, Paul Tough, Tevi Troy, Anthony Weiner, Paul Weinstein, Barry Wellman, Darrell West, Alan Wolfe, Gordon Wood, Michael Woolcock, Robert Wuthnow, Harold Wylie, and Ethan Zuckerman. In particular, I thank Alan Ehrenhalt, Todd Gitlin, Nathan Glazer, Daniel Kurtz-Phelan, and Andy Rotherham for offering extensive notes and feedback.

After a more than a decade of living in New York and Washington, my wife and I decided during the summer of 2013 to move, almost on a whim, to Providence, Rhode Island. I'd like to thank Professors Marion Orr and Ross Cheit for welcoming me into the intellectually stimulating world housed within Brown University's

Taubman Center for Public Policy and American Institutions. I've benefited enormously from my perch there as a research Fellow, and I continue to be impressed by the vibrant and free-flowing exchange of ideas incubated within Taubman's walls.

My editor at W. W. Norton, Brendan Curry, has helped mold a series of disjointed and half-baked ideas into a book that expresses exactly what I hoped to say. Without question, I have him to thank for making me a better writer. His colleagues at Norton, including Nancy Green, Elizabeth Riley, and Mitchell Kohles, have helped polish and present the book. Rachael Brown helped me to ensure that the book was factually accurate—whatever oversights or errors that remain are entirely of my doing. And Elizabeth Shreve helped to ensure that the ideas got into the hands of those who would be most interested in my argument.

This project would not have gotten off the ground but for two other partners. Yuval Levin, the editor of *National Affairs*, agreed to publish a version of this book's thesis in the summer of 2011. Yuval is a conservative, and I'm a progressive, so his decision to offer my ideas a forum was evidence of what's too often lost in the nation's political discourse: opportunities for people with divergent points of view to discuss ideas. Many of the arguments presented in these pages are the product of his edits and suggestions.

I'm indebted to my literary agent, Bridget Wagner Matzie of the Zachary Shuster Harmsworth Agency. When she agreed to represent me, I'd never written a book, and there were few, if any, decision makers in the world of book publishing who had ever heard my name. Nevertheless, she held fast to an enduring belief in the value of my ideas. But for her investment in my career, this book would never have been published.

At the close of a project that's spanned roughly a quarter of my life, it would be an oversight not to thank those who put me in a position to toil away on this kind of journey. I was lucky enough to have excellent teachers throughout my young life in Cincinnati and

Buffalo, and stimulating professors, bosses, mentors, and colleagues during my years between New York and Washington. My in-laws, Pat and John Prael, provided indispensable support during the periods when I was wrapped up in the lonely process of research and writing. Most importantly, my parents and sister, Martha, David, and Anna Dunkelman, were instrumental in teaching me both how to think and how to write. They asked the right questions.

Lastly, the people who have suffered most through the long process of writing this book have been the members of my innermost ring. My wife, Kathryn, our daughters, Emilia and Helen (who avoided much of the sacrifice by virtue of their youth), and our dog, Artie, have endured long hours of my absence. Moreover, as Kathryn would likely testify, even when I was with the family in body, my mind was frequently stuck in the prose. Kathryn read and edited countless revisions of each chapter and cheerily participated in what must have been mind-numbing conversations about new bits of data I'd stumbled upon—many of which never made their way into final manuscript. That is evidence of intelligence and grit—but most powerfully of love. Back at you, babe.

Writing a book is a team effort, and this project was no exception. I'm enormously grateful for everyone who offered an idea, leveled a criticism, made a suggestion, or lent a hand. I hope what we've produced together makes a real contribution to our collective understanding of how American community has evolved. Regardless, I feel blessed to have been given the opportunity to try.

Notes

Introduction: From One Queen City to the Next

1   http://sugar-n-spice-restaurant.com/about/mort-kellers-beginnings/.

2   Robert Wuthnow, *Loose Connections* (Cambridge, Mass.: Harvard University Press, 1998), 85–87.

3   Pew Research Center, "Families Drawn Together by Communications Revolution," February 21, 2006.

4   Gordon S. Wood, *The Radicalism of the American Revolution* (New York: Vintage, 1995), 6–7, 347–48, 365.

5   *Downton Abbey*, it's worth noting, is set at the beginning of the twentieth century and *Little House on the Prairie* during the late nineteenth. Both significantly postdate the American Revolution. Nevertheless, they represent two separate sorts of social architecture, a crucial distinction.

6   Tocqueville wasn't the first to use the term, but he leaned heavily on the concept in *Democracy in America* (first published in two volumes in 1835 and 1840).

7   Thomas L. Friedman and Michael Mandelbaum, *That Used to Be Us* (New York: Farrar, Straus and Giroux, 2011), 3–5.

8   Fareed Zakaria. "Are America's Best Days Behind Us?" *Time*, March 3, 2011; Valerie Strauss. "Key PISA test results for U.S. Students" *Washington Post*, December 3, 2013; http://www.washingtonpost.com/blogs/answer-sheet/wp/2013/12/03/key-pisa-test-results-for-u-s-students/.

9   Committee on Prospering in the Global Economy of the 21st Century: An Agenda for American Science and Technology; Committee on Science, Engineering, and Public Policy (COSEPUP); Institute of Medicine (IOM);

Policy and Global Affairs (PGA); National Academy of Sciences; National Academy of Engineering, *Rising Above the Gathering Storm: Energizing and Employing America for a Brighter Economic Future*, (Washington, D.C.: The National Academies Press, 2007), 16.

10   Gallup Organization, "Final Topline," June 9–12, 2011.

11   Annie Lowery, "Rise in Household Debt May Be Sign of a Strengthening Recovery," *New York Times,* October 26, 2012; Joseph E. Stiglitz, *The Price of Inequality* (New York: W. W. Norton, 2012), 13.

12   http://www.urban.org/publications/412281.html, as cited in Jim Tankersley, "Who Destroyed the Economy? The Case Against the Baby Boomers," *The Atlantic*, October 2012.

13   "The Trillion Dollar Gap: Underfunded State Retirement Systems and the Roads to Reform," Pew Center on the States, February 2010, 1.

14   http://www.fiscalcommission.gov/sites/fiscalcommission.gov/files/docu ments/TheMomentofTruth12_1_2010.pdf.

15   http://www.bloomberg.com/news/2013-12-19/budget-deal-easing-63-bil lion-in-cuts-advances-in-senate.html.

16   Frank Newport, "Congressional Approval Falls to Record Low," *Gallup Politics,* November 12, 2013, http://www.gallup.com/poll/165809/congres sional-approval-sinks-record-low.aspx.

17   "Congress Less Popular than Cockroaches, Traffic Jams," Public Policy Polling, January 8, 2013, http://www.publicpolicypolling.com/main/2013/01/congress-less-popular-than-cockroaches-traffic-jams.html.

18   The reforms imposed in late 2013 to limit the filibuster's use applied only to certain presidential nominations—not to substantive legislation.

19   "Elbridge Gerry, 5th Vice President (1813–1814)," United States Senate Web site, http://www.senate.gov/artandhistory/history/common/generic/VP_Elbridge_Gerry.htm.

Chapter 1: The Warning

1   Address of President Woodrow Wilson before a joint session of Congress, April 2, 1917, http://www.ourdocuments.gov/doc.php?flash=true&doc=61.

2   For a clear portrayal, see the movie *Far From Heaven* (2002).

3   While set in the 1960s, the central tension in Mike Nichols's film is between those living within the social conventions epitomized by the 1950s and those striving, through the 1960s, to move beyond.

4   Sloan Wilson, *The Man in the Gray Flannel Suit* (New York: Pocket Books, 1964).

5   Alan Ehrenhalt, *The Lost City: The Forgotten Virtues of Community in America* (New York: Basic Books, 1995), 61–62.

6   William H. Whyte, *The Organization Man* (Philadelphia: University of Pennsylvania Press, 2002), 7.

7   "David Riesman, Sociologist Whose 'Lonely Crowd' Became a Best Seller, Dies at 92," *New York Times,* May 11, 2002.

8   Todd Gitlin, 2001 foreword to *The Lonely Crowd,* by David Riesman with Nathan Glazer and Reuel Denney (1950, reprint, New Haven: Yale Nota Bene, 2001), xiin3, citing Herbert J. Gans, "Best-Sellers by American Sociologists: An Exploratory Study," in *Required Reading: Sociology's Most Influential Books,* ed. Dan Clawson (Amherst: University of Massachusetts Press, 1998), 19–27.

9   Riesman, 1961 introduction to *The Lonely Crowd,* xlii.

10 Riesman, *The Lonely Crowd,* 24–25.

11 Charles McGrath, "Big Thinkster," *New York Times Magazine,* December 29, 2002.

12 "Interview with Malcolm Gladwell," *Charlie Rose,* December 3, 2013.

13 McGrath, "Big Thinkster."

14 Steven D. Levitt and Stephen J. Dubner, *Freakonomics: A Rogue Economist Explores the Hidden Side of Everything* (New York: William Morrow, 2005).

15 Chris Cillizza, "Best year in Washington: Nate Silver," *Washington Post,* December 28, 2012.

16 http://espn.go.com/nba/salaries/_/year/2011.

17 Walter Isaacson, *Steve Jobs* (New York: Simon & Schuster, 2011).

18 Daniel Kahneman, *Thinking Fast and Slow* (New York: Farrar, Straus and Giroux, 2011).

Chapter 2: The Third Wave

1   John B. Judis, "Newt's not-so-weird gurus," *New Republic,* October 9, 1995.

2   http://www.alvintoffler.net/?fa=biospartnership.

3   Nathan Gardels, "Lunch with the FT: He has seen the future," *Financial Times,* August 19, 2006.

4   Alvin Toffler, *The Third Wave* (New York: Bantam Books, 1981), 9–11.

5   http://www.presidency.ucsb.edu/ws/?pid=25958.

6   Judis, "Newt's not-so-weird gurus."

7   Toffler, *The Third Wave,* 4.

8   Toffler, *The Third Wave,* 14.

9   An argument made along similar lines can be found in Daniel Bell, *The Coming of Post-Industrial Society* (New York: Basic Books, 1999).

10   Marshall McLuhan and Bruce R. Powers, *The Global Village* (New York: Oxford University Press, 1970).

11   Thomas L. Friedman, *The World Is Flat: A Brief History of the Twenty-First Century* (New York: Farrar, Straus and Giroux, 2005).

12   Fareed Zakaria. *The Post-American World* (New York: W. W. Norton, 2009), 19–21.

13   Lee Rainie and Barry Wellman, *Networked: The New Social Operating System* (Cambridge, Mass.: MIT Press, 2012), Fig. 2.7, 28.

14   http://www.freedomhouse.org/sites/default/files/Country%20Status%20%26%20Ratings%20Overview%2C%201973-2012.pdf, accessed November 2, 2012.

15   Zakaria, *The Post-American World,* 3.

16   Rainie and Wellman, *Networked,* Figure 2.5, 26.

17   "Social Networking Site and Politics," Pew Internet & American Life Project, March 12, 2012; "Social Networking Popular Across Globe," Pew Research Center Global Attitudes Project, December 12, 2012.

18   "Social Networking Popular Across Globe."

19   Interview with Eric Schmidt, *Charlie Rose,* March 6, 2009.

20   Rainie and Wellman, *Networked,* Fig. 2.10, 31; Fig. 2.3, 24.

21   Matt Richtel, "Attached to Technology and Paying a Price," *New York Times,* June 6, 2010; Robert D. Putnam, *Bowling Alone: The Collapse and Revival of American Community* (New York: Simon & Schuster, 2000), 36. It is important to note, as Charles Murray did in *Coming Apart: The State of White America 1960–2010* (New York: Crown Forum, 2012), the way different socioeconomic groups have engaged with online communities in different ways. For example, as the Pew Center for Internet and American Life found, families making incomes of more than $75,000 are much more likely to connect through the Internet.

22   Patrick Lane, "A Sense of Place," *Economist,* October 27, 2012; Sanja Kelly, Sarah Cook, and Mai Truong, eds., "Freedom on the Net 2012: A Global Assessment of Internet and Digital Media," Freedom House, September 24, 2012.

23   Rainie and Wellman, *Networked,* Fig. 2.11, 32.

24   Between 1950 and 2001: Alan Ehrenhalt, *The Great Inversion and the Future of the American City* (New York: Knopf, 2012), 44; between 1960 and 2010: Murray, *Coming Apart,* 73.

25   Robert D. Putnam, *Bowling Alone,* 81–82; News Release, Bureau of Labor Statistics, January 23, 2012.

26   Adam Davidson, "Empire of the In-Between," *New York Times Magazine,* November 24, 2012.

27   Davidson, "Empire of the In-Between," MM26.

28   Joseph E. Stiglitz, *The Price of Inequality* (New York: W. W. Norton, 2012), 57.

29   Claude S. Fischer and Michael Hout, *Century of Difference: How America Changed in the Last One Hundred Years* (New York: Russell Sage Foundation: 2006), 128.

30   http://www.bis.org/publ/wgpapers/cgfs27broadbent3.pdf.

31   Bill Clinton, Address Before a Joint Session of the Congress on the State of the Union, January 23, 1996, http://www.presidency.ucsb.edu/ws/index .php?pid=53091#ixzz2ifeuu67a.

32   http://opinionator.blogs.nytimes.com/2013/09/29/the-glass-floor -problem/?_r=0.

33   Larry Bartels, *Unequal Democracy: The Political Economy of the New Gilded Age* (New York: Russell Sage Foundation and Princeton University Press, 2008), 6–13, 16.

34   Raghuram G. Rajan, *Fault Lines: How Hidden Fractures Still Threaten the World Economy* (Princeton, N.J.: Princeton University Press, 2010), 8.

35   "The rich and the rest," *Economist*, October 13, 2012.

36   Zanny Minton Beddoes, "For Richer, for Poorer," *Economist*, October 13, 2012.

37   Stiglitz, *The Price of Inequality*, 8.

38   Beddoes, "For Richer, for Poorer."

39   "The Lost Decades of the Middle Class: Fewer, Poorer, Gloomier," Pew Research Social & Demographic Trends, August 22, 2012.

40   "The Rich and the Rest."

41   Stephen S. Roach, "More Jobs, Worse Work," *New York Times*, July 22, 2004.

42   Interview with Joseph Stiglitz, quoted in Henry Blodget, "The 'American Dream' Is Now a Myth," *Business Insider,* June 10, 2012. More recent academic studies have cast doubt on this conclusion. David Leonhardt, "Upward Mobility Has Not Declined, Study Says," *New York Times*, January 23, 2014.

43   Angus Deaton, *The Great Escape: Health, Wealth, and the Origins of Inequality* (Princeton, N.J.: Princeton University Press, 2013).

44   Joseph Lowery, "Civil Rights Figure Rev. Joseph Lowery Reflects on a Movement," *Chicago Tribune*, January 19, 2009.

45   Rainie and Wellman, *Networked,* 22.

46   http://www.freakonomics.com/2011/10/10/where-have-all-the-hitchhik ers-gone-a-new-freakonomics-radio-podcast; Rainie and Wellman, *Networked,* 22.

47   Kenneth T. Jackson, *Crabgrass Frontier: The Suburbanization of the United*

States (New York: Oxford University Press, 1985); Putnam, *Bowling Alone,* 213; Wuthnow, *After the Baby Boomers,* 43; Claude S. Fischer, *Still Connected* (New York: Russell Sage Foundation, 2011), 7.

48   Fischer and Hout, *Century of Difference,* 163, 172–73; "Commuting in America: The Third National Report on Community Patterns and Trends," Transportation Research Board of the National Academies, Figure ES-1, xiv.

49   "Community in America," xiv.

50   Fischer and Hout, *Century of Difference,* 72–76.

51   Warren Buffett, "Warren Buffett at Fortune's Most Powerful Women Summit," CNNMoney.com, October 4, 2011, http://management.fortune.cnn .com/2011/10/04/warren-buffett-transcript/.

52   Gail Collins, *When Everything Changed: The Amazing Journey of American Women from 1960 to the Present* (New York: Back Bay, 2010).

53   Buffett, "Warren Buffett at Fortune's Most Powerful Women Summit"; Robert Wuthnow, *Loose Connections* (Cambridge, Mass.: Harvard University Press, 1998), 241; Fischer, *Still Connected,* 7.

54   Andrew J. Cherlin, *The Marriage-Go-Round: The State of Marriage and the Family in America Today* (New York: Vintage, 2009), 125.

55   Collins, *When Everything Changed.*

56   Putnam, *Bowling Alone.* 192, 197–201; Wuthnow, *After the Baby Boomers,* 28–29, 59.

57   Jacqueline Olds and Richard S. Schwartz, *The Lonely American: Drifting Apart in the Twenty-First Century* (Boston: Beacon Press, 2009), 15.

58   Robert Wuthnow, *After the Baby Boomers: How Twenty- and Thirty-Somethings Are Shaping the Future of American Religion* (Princeton, N.J. Princeton University Press, 2007), xvi.

59   Stiglitz, *The Price of Inequality,* 14.

60   Wuthnow, *After the Baby Boomers,* 62.

61   Fischer, *Still Connected,* 5; Wuthnow, *After the Baby Boomers,* 55–56

62   Olds and Schwartz. *The Lonely American,* 130.

63   Wuthnow, *After the Baby Boomers,* 144; Fischer, *Still Connected,* 6.

64   Putnam, *Bowling Alone,* 277.

65   Murray, *Coming Apart,* 150.

66   Cherlin, *The Marriage-Go-Round,* 156, 185–86.

67   Cherlin, *The Marriage-Go-Round,* 154–55.

68   Fischer and Hout, *Century of Difference,* 70.

69   Fischer and Hout. *Century of Difference,* 70; Tom Brokaw, *The Greatest Generation* (New York: Random House, 2005), 231.

70   James J. Heckman and Dimitriy V. Masterov. "The Productivity Argument for Investing in Young Children," *Review of Agricultural Economics* 29, no. 3: 462.

71   Jason DeParle, "Two Classes, Divided by 'I Do,' " *New York Times,* July 14, 2012.

72   Alan Ehrenhalt, *The Great Inversion and the Future of the American City* (New York: Knopf, 2012), 12.

73   Gardels, "Lunch with the FT."

74   Lewis Mumford,. "The Fourth Migration," *Survey Graphic,* May 1, 1925, 130–33.

75   Fischer and Hout, *Century of Difference,* ix.

Chapter 3: The Chinatown Bus Effect

1   Graham T. Beck, "The Buses Are Coming," *Next American City,* Summer 2010.

2   Charles Murray, *Coming Apart: The State of White America 1960–2010.* (New York: Crown Forum, 2012), 2.

3   Thomas E. Mann and Norman J. Ornstein, *It's Even Worse Than It Looks: How the American Constitutional System Collided with the New Politics of Extremism* (New York: Basic Books, 2012), 59.

4   Bill Carter, "Prime-Time Ratings Bring Speculation of a Shift in Habits," *New York Times,* April 23, 2012.

5   Eli Pariser, *The Filter Bubble: What the Internet Is Hiding from You* (New York: Penguin Press, 2011), 6–10.

6   Cramer, Ruby. "2 Charts That Explain What Your Food Says About Your Politics," Buzzfeed.com, October 31, 2012, http://www.buzzfeed.com/rubycramer/2-charts-that-explain-what-your-food-says-about-yo.

7   Natasha Singer, "Your Online Attention, Bought in an Instant," *New York Times,* November 17, 2012.

8   Kenneth T. Jackson, *Crabgrass Frontier: The Suburbanization of the United States* (New York: Oxford University Press, 1985).

9   Lizabeth Cohen, *A Consumer's Republic: The Politics of Mass Consumption in Postwar America* (New York: Vintage Books, 2003), 288–89, 292–344.

10   Chris Rock, *Saturday Night Live,* November 2, 1996.

11   Cohen, *A Consumer's Republic,* 258.

12   Douglas S. Massey, Jonathan Rothwell, and Thurston Domina, "The Changing Bases of Segregation in the United States," *The Annals of the American Academy of Political and Social Science* 1, no. 626 (2009): 74–90.

13   Claude S. Fischer and Greggor Mattson, "Is America Fragmenting?" *American Review of Sociology* 35 (2009): 445.

14   "Trends in American Values: 1987–2012: Partisan Polarization Surges in Bush, Obama Years," Pew Research Center for the People and the Press, June 4, 2012, 72–74.

15 "Changing Views of Gay Marriage: A Deeper Analysis," Pew Research Center for People and the Press, May 23, 2012, http://www.people-press .org/2012/05/23/changing-views-of-gay-marriage-a-deeper-analysis/.

16 "Inspire Hope Change," pamphlet published by the It Gets Better Project, accessed December 12, 2013.

17 Robert D. Mare, "Five Decades of Educational Assortative Mating," *American Sociological Review* 56, no. 1 (1991): 15–32, in Christine R. Schwartz and Robert D. Mare, "Trends in Educational Assortative Marriage from 1940 to 2003," California Center for Population Research, July 2005, 4.

18 Schwartz and Mare, "Trends in Educational Assortative Marriage From 1940 to 2003," 20, 23–24.

19 Theda Skocpol, *Diminished Democracy: From Membership to Management in American Civic Life* (Norman: University of Oklahoma Press, 2003), 163–71.

20 Skocpol, *Diminished Democracy,* 158.

21 Robert D. Putnam, *Bowling Alone: The Collapse and Revival of American Community* (New York: Simon & Schuster, 2000), 54–55.

22 Putnam, *Bowling Alone,* 49; Skocpol, *Diminished Democracy,* 127, 138–39, 153–57, 174.

23 Murray, *Coming Apart,* 74–75.

24 John Kelly III, "Attentive Structures: Mapping Communities of Interest in Weblogs" (PhD diss., Columbia University, 2010).

25 David Brooks, "People Like Us," *The Atlantic.* September 2003, http://www .theatlantic.com/magazine/archive/2003/09/people-like-us/302774/.

26 Bill Bishop with Robert G. Cushing, *The Big Sort: Why the Clustering of Like-Minded America is Tearing Us Apart* (New York: Houghton Mifflin, 2008), 45.

27 "Social Networking Sites and Politics," Pew Internet & American Life Project, March 12, 2012.

28 Alan Ehrenhalt, *The Lost City: The Forgotten Virtues of Community in America* (New York: Basic Books, 1995), 15, 255.

29 Ehrenhalt, *The Lost City,* 10–11, 22–23, 254.

Chapter 4: The Big Climb

1 Angus Deaton, *The Great Escape: Health, Wealth, and the Origins of Inequality* (Princeton, N.J.: Princeton University Press, 2013).

2 Bill Clinton, "A Remarkable Evening," New Albany Community Foundation, New Albany, Ohio, November 29, 2012.

3 John Kenneth Galbraith, *The Affluent Society* (New York: Mariner Book, 1998).

4   Nicholas Carr, *The Shallows: What the Internet Is Doing to Our Brains* (New York: W. W. Norton, 2010).

5   Robert Skidelsky and Edward Skidelsky, *How Much is Enough? Money and the Good Life* (New York: Other Press, 2012).

6   Robert Wuthnow, *After the Baby Boomers: How Twenty- and Thirty-Somethings Are Shaping the Future of American Religion* (Princeton, N.J.: Princeton University Press, 2007), 32.

7   Claude S. Fischer and Michael Hout, *Century of Difference: How America Changed in the Last One Hundred Years* (New York: Russell Sage Foundation: 2006), 152.

8   Charles Murray, *Coming Apart: The State of White America 1960–2010* (New York: Crown Forum, 2012), 8. "Poverty Status of People by Family Relationship, Race, and Hispanic Origin: 1959 to 2012" by the U.S. Census Bureau, accessed on December 13, 2013. It's worth noting that poverty rates *since* the Great Society have fluctuated—as Eduardo Porter pointed out (http://www.nytimes.com/2013/12/18/business/economy/in-the-war-on-poverty-a-dogged-adversary.html?ref=economicscene). But even during that period, the figure has fluctuated, falling by nearly a quarter during the Clinton years, then rising by more than 15 percent during George W. Bush's presidency, http://www.dlc.org/documents/TheLostDecade.pdf.

9   Lizabeth Cohen, *A Consumer's Republic: The Politics of Mass Consumption in Postwar America* (New York: Vintage Books, 2003), 123–24.

10   Fareed Zakaria, *The Post-American World* (New York: W. W. Norton, 2009), xvi.

11   Andrea Elliott, "Girl in the Shadows: Dasani's Homeless Life," *New York Times*, December 9, 2013.

12   David Leonhardt, "A Closer Look at Middle-Class Decline," *New York Times,* July 23, 2012, http://economix.blogs.nytimes.com/2012/07/23/a-closer-look-at-middle-class-decline/.

13   Joseph E. Stiglitz, *The Price of Inequality* (New York: W. W. Norton, 2012), 2–3.

14   Robert D. Putnam, *Bowling Alone: The Collapse and Revival of American Community* (New York: Simon & Schuster, 2000), 267, 270.

15   Robert J. Sampson, *Great American City: Chicago and the Enduring Neighborhood Effect* (Chicago: University of Chicago Press, 2012), 143.

16   Richard A. Oppel Jr., "Steady Decline in Major Crime Baffles Experts," *New York Times*, May 23, 2011.

17   Fischer and Hout. *Century of Difference,* 63–65.

18   http://www.cdc.gov/nchs/data/databriefs/db88.pdf; David Cutler, David and Grant Miller, "The Role of Public Health Improvements in Health

Advances: The 20th Century United States." National Bureau of Economic Research, Working Paper 10511, May 2004.

19   Cutler and Miller, "The Role of Public Health Improvements in Health Advances."

20   Fischer and Hout, *Century of Difference,* 63–65.

21   Jonathan E. Fielding, "Public Health in the Twentieth Century: Advances and Challenges," *Annual Review of Public Health* 20 (1999): xiii, xx.

22   "Ten Great Public Health Achievements—United States, 1900–1999," *MMWR Weekly,* April 2, 1999, 241–43.

23   Angela Greiling Keane, "U.S. Highway Deaths Decline for a Fifth Year, Longest Streak Since 1899," *Bloomberg News,* December 8, 2011.

24   "Ten Great Public Health Achievements."

25   Lawrence K. Altman, "So Many Advances in Medicine, So Many Yet to Come," *New York Times,* December 26, 2006.

26   Paul C. McCabe and Steven R. Shaw, *Genetic and Acquired Disorders: Current Topics and Interventions for Educators* (New York: Corwin, 2010), 3.

27   Altman, "So Many Advances in Medicine, So Many Yet to Come."

28   http://aids.gov/hiv-aids-basics/hiv-aids-101/statistics/.

29   Fischer and Hout, *Century of Difference,* 97.

30   Kelly Greene and Vipal Monga, "Workers Saving Too Little to Retire," *Wall Street Journal,* March 19, 2013.

31   Abraham H. Maslow, "A Theory of Human Motivation," *Psychological Review* 50 (1943): 370–96.

32   Abraham H. Maslow, *Motivation and Personality* (New York: Harper and Row, 1970).

33   Joel Berg, "Can We End Child Hunger by 2015?" Center for American Progress, March 31, 2010.

Chapter 5: Conformity Comes Full Circle

1   Jessica Grose, "The Reality TV Family Tree," *New Republic,* May 13, 2013.

2   Andrea Seigel, "The Life Lessons Hidden in Reality TV," *New York Times Magazine,* November 30, 2012.

3   David Riesman, 1961 introduction to *The Lonely Crowd,* by David Riesman with Nathan Glazer and Reuel Denney (1950, reprint, New Haven: Yale Nota Bene, 2001).

4   Andrew J. Cherlin, *The Marriage-Go-Round: The State of Marriage and the Family in America Today* (New York: Vintage, 2009), 23–30.

5   Alexis de Tocqueville, *Democracy in America* (1835, 1840, reprint, Chicago: University of Chicago Press, 2000).

6   Ronald Inglehart and Christian Welzel, *Modernization, Cultural Change, and Democracy* (New York: Cambridge University Press, 2005), 20.

7   Cherlin, *The Marriage-Go-Round,* 154, 176–78.

8   Lee Rainie and Barry Wellman, *Networked: The New Social Operating System* (Cambridge, Mass.: MIT Press, 2012), 33.

9   James Davison Hunter, *Culture Wars: The Struggle to Define America* (New York: Basic Books, 1991).

10 Inglehart and Welzel, *Modernization, Cultural Change, and Democracy,* 2–-3, 7–8, 20, 28, 98–99, 109.

11 Cherlin, *The Marriage-Go-Round,* 63.

12 Tom Brokaw, *The Greatest Generation* (New York: Random House, 2005), 232.

13 Cherlin, *The Marriage-Go-Round,* 31, 39, 88, 90, 130.

14 Cherlin, *The Marriage-Go-Round,* 88.

15 Cherlin, *The Marriage-Go-Round,* 140.

16 "U.S. Religious Landscape Survey," Pew Forum on Religion and Public Life, June 2008.

17 Cherlin, *The Marriage-Go-Round,* 106.

18 Rainie and Wellman, *Networked,* Table 2.1, 30.

19 Robert D. Putnam, *Bowling Alone: The Collapse and Revival of American Community* (New York: Simon & Schuster, 2000), 52.

20 Robert Wuthnow, *After the Baby Boomers: How Twenty- and Thirty-Somethings Are Shaping the Future of American Religion* (Princeton, N.J.: Princeton University Press, 2007), 98–99.

21 Inglehart and Welzel, *Modernization, Cultural Change, and Democracy,* 22, 31–32.

22 Joel Osteen, *Your Best Life Now: Seven Steps to Living to Your Full Potential* (Nashville: Warner Faith, 1994).

23 Inglehart and Welzel, *Modernization, Cultural Change, and Democracy,* 20.

24 Jacqueline Olds, and Richard S. Schwartz, *The Lonely American: Drifting Apart in the Twenty-First Century* (Boston: Beacon Press, 2009), 86.

25 Inglehart and Welzel, *Modernization, Cultural Change, and Democracy,* 94–114.

Chapter 6: A Brief History of American Community

1   Interview with Toni Morrison, Canadian Broadcast Corporation's *Writers and Company,* May 13, 2012.

2   Alexis de Tocqueville, *Democracy in America* (1835, 1840, reprint, Chicago: University of Chicago Press, 2000), 40–41, 57, 63–64.

3 Tocqueville, *Democracy in America,* 266.

4 Seymour Martin Lipset, *American Exceptionalism* (New York: W. W. Norton, 1996), 18.

5 Edmund Burke, *Reflections on the French Revolution,* The Harvard Classics, 1909–14, http://www.bartleby.com/24/3/4.html.

6 Marc Dunkelman, "The Transformation of American Community," *National Affairs,* no. 8 (Summer 2011).

7 Robert N. Bellah and Richard Madsen, William M. Sullivan, Ann Swidler, and Steven M. Tipton, *Habits of the Heart: Individualism and Commitment in American Life* (Berkeley: University of California Press: 1996), 168–69. The source of the phrase is Alexis de Tocqueville, *Democracy in America* (1835, 1840, reprint, Chicago: University of Chicago Press, 2000), 275.

8 Gordon S. Wood, *The Radicalism of the American Revolution* (New York: Vintage, 1995).

9 Thomas Bender, *Community and Social Change in America* (Baltimore: Johns Hopkins University Press, 1978), 65–71, 75, 81.

10 Lewis Mumford, "The Fourth Migration," *Survey Graphic,* May 1, 1925: 130–33.

11 Louis Wirth, "Urbanism as a Way of Life," *American Journal of Sociology* 44, no. 1 (July 1938).

12 Richard Florida, *The Rise of the Creative Class: And How It's Transforming Work, Leisure, Community and Everyday Life* (New York: Basic Books, 2002); Barry Wellman, "The Community Question: The Intimate Network of East Yorkers," *American Journal of Sociology* 84, no. 5 (March 1979): 1201–31.

13 Robert Park, "The City: Suggestions for the Investigation of Human Behavior in the Urban Environment," *The American Journal of Sociology* 20 (1915), in *Classic Essays on the Culture of Cities,* ed. Richard Sennett (New York: Appleton-Century-Crofts, 1969).

14 Daniel Okrent, *Last Call: The Rise and Fall of Prohibition* (New York: Scribner, 2010).

15 Thomas Bender, *Community and Social Change in America* (Baltimore: Johns Hopkins University Press, 1978), 131–33.

16 Hillary Rodham Clinton, *It Takes a Village: And Other Lessons Children Teach Us* (New York: Simon & Schuster, 1996).

17 Wellman, "The Community Question," 1201–31.

18 Martin Gansberg, "Lindsay, Recalling the Genovese Murder, Deplores Apathy," *New York Times,* October 13, 1965.

19 Jim Rasenberger, "Kitty, 40 Years Later," *New York Times,* February 8, 2004.

20 Robert Nisbet, *The Quest for Community* (Wilmington, Del.: ISI Books, 1990), 72.

21 Jane Jacobs, *The Death and Life of Great American Cities* (New York: Vintage, 1992), 121–40.

22 Jacobs, *The Death and Life of Great American Cities,* 150–51.

23 Claude S. Fischer, "Toward a Subcultural Theory of Urbanism," *American Journal of Sociology* 80, no. 6 (May 1975).

Chapter 7: Bands, Villages, and Tribes

1 Robin I. M. Dunbar, "The Social Brain Hypothesis," *Evolutionary Anthropology* 6 (1998): 178.

2 Dunbar, "The Social Brain Hypothesis," 178–90.

3 Michael Harre, "Social Network Size Linked to Brain Size," *Scientific American,* August 7, 2012.

4 R. I. M. Dunbar, "Coevolution of Neocortical Size, Group Size, and Language in Humans," *Behavioral and Brain Sciences* 16 (1993): 681–735.

5 Malcolm Gladwell, *The Tipping Point: How Little Things Can Make a Big Difference* (New York: Little, Brown and Company, 2000).

6 Dunbar, "Coevolution of Neocortical Size, Group Size, and Language in Humans," 683.

7 Dunbar, "Coevolution of Neocortical Size, Group Size, and Language in Humans," 685–86.

8 Dunbar, "Coevolution of Neocortical Size, Group Size, and Language in Humans," 684–85; http://www.businessweek.com/articles/2013-01-10/the-dunbar-number-from-the-guru-of-social-networks.

9 R. A. Hill and R. I. M. Dunbar, "Social Network Size in Humans," *Human Nature* 14, no. 1 (2003).

10 John Markoff and Somini Sengupta, "Separating You and Me? 4.74 Degrees," *New York Times,* November 21, 2011.

11 Claude S. Fischer, *To Dwell Among Friends: Personal Networks in Town and City* (Chicago: University of Chicago Press, 1982), 139–44.

12 Sam G. B. Roberts, Robin I. M. Dunbar, Thomas V. Pollet, and Toon Kuppens, "Exploring Variation in Active Network Size: Constraints and Ego Characteristics." *Social Networks* 31 (2009): 138.

13 Nicholas A. Christakis and James H. Fowler, *Connected: The Surprising Power of Our Social Networks and How They Shape Our Lives—How Your*

Friends' Friends' Friends Affect Everything You Feel, Think, and Do (New York: Back Bay Books, 2009), 18.

14   Barry Wellman and Bernie Hogan et al., "Connected Lives: The Project," chapter 8 in *Networked Neighbourhoods*, ed. Patrick Purcell (Berlin: Springer, 2005), 20.

15   Keith N. Hampton and Richard Ling, "Communication Displacement and Explaining Large-Scale Social Change in Core Networks: A cross-sectional comparison of why bigger is not better and less can mean more," February 14, 2012, 26, http://www.mysocialnetwork.net/downloads/offprint/Why%20Bigger%20is%20Not%20Better%20and%20Less%20Can%20Mean%20More.pdf.

16   Robin I. M. Dunbar, "The Social Brain Hypothesis," 187.

17   James Coleman, "Social Capital in the Creation of Human Capital," *American Journal of Sociology* 94, (supplement): S98.

18   Coleman, "Social Capital in the Creation of Human Capital," S98.

19   Robert D. Putnam, *Bowling Alone: The Collapse and Revival of American Community* (New York: Simon & Schuster, 2000).

20   Roberts, Dunbar, Pollet, and Kuppens, "Exploring Variation in Active Network Size: Constraints and Ego Characteristics," 143.

21   John F. Helliwell and Haifang Huang, "Comparing the Happiness Effects of Real and On-Line Friends," *National Bureau of Economic Research Working Paper 18690*, January 2013, 10.

22   Sam G. B. Roberts, "Constraints on Social Networks," 121–22.

Chapter 8: The Search for Affirmation

1   http://www.youtube.com/watch?v=fAT5UkTc-SQ.

2   http://findthatsong.net/dr-pepper-commercial-gotta/.

3   Hyo Kim, Gwang Jae Kim, Han Woo Park, and Ronald E. Rice, "Configurations of Relationships in Different Media," *Journal of Computer-Mediated Communication* 12, no. 4 (2007): 1183–1207.

4   Amazing stories today tell how mobile phones are changing the developing world, connecting farmers to markets and making crucial information accessible to individuals who would otherwise be off the grid. In the United States, however, the patterns of use are strikingly different.

5   Alan Ehrenhalt, *The Lost City: The Forgotten Virtues of Community in America* (New York: Basic Books, 1995), 258.

6   Between 1973 and 1994, the General Social Survey surveyed Americans, asking what they most preferred in a job: high income, no danger of being

fired, chances for advancement, short working hours, or a feeling of accomplishment. Among white people in their thirties and forties, the last option—a sense of fulfillment—consistently vanquished the alternatives, at an average of 58 percent. But when the same questions were asked in 2006, that response was down to 43 percent—while short working hours and no danger of being fired had doubled. Charles Murray, *Coming Apart: The State of White America 1960–2010* (New York: Crown Forum, 2012), 169.

7   Richard Sennett, *The Culture of the New Capitalism* (New Haven: Yale University Press, 2006), 36, 72–81, 129.

8   It's worth noting that divorce rates, in particular, have begun to fall among some demographics after reaching a high just a few years ago.

9   Claude S. Fischer, *Still Connected* (New York: Russell Sage Foundation, 2011), 56.

10   Miller McPherson, Lynn Smith-Lovin, and Matthew E. Brashears, "Social Isolation in America," *American Sociological Review* 71 (June 2006): 361.

11   Suzanne Bianchi, John P. Robinson, and Melissa A. Milkie, *Changing Rhythms of American Family Life* (New York: Russell Sage Foundation, 2006), 63.

12   Conversation with Claude S. Fischer, March 15, 2012.

13   Stephanie Armour, "'Helicopter' Parents Hover When Kids Job Hunt," *USA Today*, April 23, 2007; Jennifer Finney Boylan, "A Freshman All Over Again," *New York Times*, August 23, 2012.

14   Kim Parker, "The Boomerang Generation: Feeling OK about Living with Mom and Dad," *Pew Research Social & Demographic Trends*, March 15, 2012.

15   Parker, "The Boomerang Generation," 6–7.

16   "Families Drawn Together By Communication Revolution." Pew Research Center, February 21, 2006.

17   Phil Gardner, "Parent Involvement in the College Recruiting Process: To What Extent?" Collegiate Employment Research Institute, 2007.

18   Lee Rainie and Barry Wellman, *Networked: The New Social Operating System* (Cambridge, Mass.: MIT Press, 2012).

19   Dalton Conley, *Elsewhere, U.S.A.: How We Got from the Company Man, Family Dinners, and the Affluent Society to the Home Office, BlackBerry Moms, and Economic Anxiety* (New York: Vintage, 2010), 37.

20   Sherry Turkle, *Alone Together: Why We Expect More from Technology and Less from Each Other* (New York: Basic Books, 2011), 176–77.

Chapter 9: The Missing Rings

1   Robert D. Putnam, "Bowling Alone: America's Declining Social Capital," *Journal of Democracy* 6, no. 1 (January 1995); Putnam: *Bowling Alone: The Collapse and Revival of American Community* (New York: Simon & Schuster, 2000).

2   Margaret Talbot. "Who Wants to Be a Legionnaire?" *New York Times,* June 25, 2000.

3   James Davison Hunter, *Culture Wars: The Struggle to Define America* (New York: Basic Books, 1991).

4   Nicholas Lemann, "Kicking in Groups," *The Atlantic Monthly,* April 1996, http://xroads.virginia.edu/~HYPER/detoc/assoc/kicking.html.

5   Theda Skocpol, *Diminished Democracy: From Membership to Management in American Civic Life* (Norman: University of Oklahoma Press, 2003), 127–74; Robert Wuthnow, *Loose Connections* (Cambridge, Mass.: Harvard University Press, 1998), 10–11, 15.

6   Skocpol, *Diminished Democracy,* 108–9, 117

7   Miller McPherson, Lynn Smith-Lovin, and Matthew E. Brashears, "Social Isolation in America," *American Sociological Review* 71 (June 2006).

8   Henry Fountain. "The Lonely American Just Got a Bit Lonelier," *New York Times,* July 2, 2006.

9   McPherson, Smith-Lovin, and Brashears, "Social Isolation in America," Table 2, 359.

10 Claude S. Fischer, "The 2004 GSS Finding of Shrunken Social Networks: An Artifact?" *American Sociological Review* 74 (August 2009): 657–69.

11 Claude S. Fischer, *Still Connected* (New York: Russell Sage Foundation, 2011), 51.

12 Marc Morjé Howard, James L. Gibson, and Dietlind Stolle, "The U.S. Citizenship, Involvement, Democracy Survey," Center for Democracy and Civil Society (CDACS), Georgetown University, 2005: 7.

13 Avery M. Guest and Susan K. Wierzbicki, "Social Ties at the Neighborhood Level: Two Decades of GSS Evidence," *Urban Affairs Review* 35, no. 1 (September 1999): 92–111.

14 Keith Hampton, Lauren F. Sessions, and Eun Ja Her, "Core Networks, Social Isolation, and New Media," *Information, Communication and Society* 14, no. 1 (February 2011): 141.

15 Hampton, Sessions, and Her, "Core Networks, Social Isolation, and New Media," 149.

16 Hampton, Sessions, and Her, "Core Networks, Social Isolation, and New Media," 141.

17   Peter V. Marsden and Sameer B. Srivastava, "Trends in Informal Social Participation, 1974–2008," *Social Trends in the United States, 1972–2000s* (Princeton, N.J.: Princeton University Press, 2012).

18   Andrew J. Cherlin, *The Marriage-Go-Round: The State of Marriage and the Family in America Today* (New York: Vintage, 2009).

19   Interview with Chris DeWolfe and Tom Anderson, *Charlie Rose,* February 3, 2009.

20   http://www.ign.com/articles/2010/10/07/world-of-warcraft-reaches-12 -million-subscribers.

21   "Digital Nation," *Frontline,* PBS, February 2, 2010, http://video.pbs.org/video/1402987791/.

22   Sherry Turkle, *Alone Together: Why We Expect More from Technology and Less from Each Other* (New York: Basic Books, 2011).

23   Richard Ling, *New Tech, New Ties* (Cambridge, Mass.: MIT Press, 2008), 4.

24   Ling, *New Tech, New Ties,* 159.

25   http://www.amazon.com/The-Body-Stephen-King/dp/0143143921.

26   Barry Wellman and Bernie Hogan et al., "The Project," chapter 8 in *Networked Neighbourhoods,* ed. Patrick Purcell (London: Springer, 2005).

27   Keith N. Hampton, Chul-joo Lee, and Eun Ja Her. "How New Media Affords Network Diversity," *New Media and Society.* 13, no. 7: 1045. Other studies have found variant results: http://pewinternet.org/~/media//Files/Reports/2011/PIP%20-%20Social%20networking%20sites%20and%20our%20lives.pdf.

28   Norman H. Nie, D. Sunshine Hillygus, and Lutz Erbring, "Internet Use, Interpersonal Relations, and Sociability: A Time Diary Study," *The Internet in Everyday Life* (Malden, Mass.: Blackwell Publications, 2002), 216, 224.

29   Nie, Hillygus, and Erbring, "Internet Use, Interpersonal Relations, and Sociability," 236.

Chapter 10: Exit Tocqueville

1   Louis Wirth, "Urbanism as a Way of Life," *American Journal of Sociology* 44, no. 1 (July 1938).

2   Claude S. Fischer, *To Dwell Among Friends: Personal Networks in Town and City* (Chicago: University of Chicago Press, 1982), 85, 118–22.

3   Fischer, *To Dwell Among Friends,* 56–57, 59, 79–84, 94–95, 101–3, 158–78.

4   Kenneth T. Jackson, *Crabgrass Frontier: The Suburbanization of the United States* (New York: Oxford University Press, 1985).

5   "America's Suburbs: An Age of Transformation," *Economist,* May 29, 2008, http://www.economist.com/node/11449846.

6   Jacqueline Olds and Richard S. Schwartz, *The Lonely American: Drifting Apart in the Twenty-First Century* (Boston: Beacon Press, 2009), 21.

7   Robert Wuthnow, *Loose Connections* (Cambridge: Harvard University Press, 1998), 50–54.

8   Richard Sennett, *The Culture of the New Capitalism* (New Haven: Yale, 2006), 48.

9   Richard Florida, *The Rise of the Creative Class: And How It's Transforming Work, Leisure, Community and Everyday Life* (New York: Basic Books, 2002), 53–55.

10 http://www.foreignpolicy.com/posts/2009/12/07/social_science_and_the_public_sphere#sthash.Ok1NDHao.dpbs.

11 Wuthnow, *Loose Connections*, 66, cites Tom Peters' *Liberation Management*.

12 http://www.freakonomics.com/2011/10/10/where-have-all-the-hitchhikers-gone-a-new-freakonomics-radio-podcast/.

13 Robert D. Putnam, *Bowling Alone: The Collapse and Revival of American Community* (New York: Simon & Schuster, 2000), 139–41.

14 Isabel Wilkerson, *The Warmth of Other Suns: The Epic Story of America's Great Migration* (New York: Vintage, 2011).

15 Thomas Bender, *Community and Social Change in America* (Baltimore: Johns Hopkins University Press, 1978), 46.

16 William H. Whyte, *The Organization Man* (Philadelphia: University of Pennsylvania Press, 2002).

17 Samuel J. Abrams and Morris P. Fiorina, "'The Big Sort' That Wasn't: A Skeptical Reexamination," *PS: Political Science and Politics,* April 2012, 208.

18 Alan Ehrenhalt, *The Lost City: The Forgotten Virtues of Community in America* (New York: Basic Books, 1995), 28.

Chapter 11: And Now for Something Completely Different

1   Thomas L. Friedman, *The Lexus and the Olive Tree* (New York: Anchor Books, 2000).

2   Marshall McLuhan and Bruce R. Powers, *The Global Village* (New York: Oxford University Press, 1989).

3   Thomas L. Friedman and Michael Mandelbaum, *That Used to Be Us* (New York: Farrar, Straus and Giroux, 2011), 58, 62.

4   McLuhan is also famous for the phrase "the medium is the message."

5   Charles Murray, *Coming Apart: The State of White America 1960–2010* (New York: Crown Forum, 2012), 238.

6   Murray, *Coming Apart.*

7   Personal communication from Herbert Gans, July 26, 2012.

8   R. I. M. Dunbar, "Coevolution of Neocortical Size, Group Size, and Language in Humans," *Behavioral and Brain Sciences* 16 (1993).

9   Jenna Wortham, "WhatsApp Deal Bets on a Few Fewer 'Friends,' " *New York Times*, February 21, 2014.

10 Barry Wellman and Bernie Hogan et al., "Connected Lives: The Project," chapter 8 in *Networked Neighbourhoods,* ed. Patrick Purcell (London: Springer, 2005).

11 Norman D. Nie, D. Sunshine Hillygus, and Lutz Erbring, "Internet Use, Interpersonal Relations, and Sociability: A Time Diary Study," in *The Internet and Everyday Life,* ed. Barry Wellman and Caroline Haythornthwaite (Malden, Mass.: Blackwell Publishing, 2002).

12 Robin I. M. Dunbar, "The Social Brain Hypothesis," *Evolutionary Anthropology* 6 (1998).

13 Joseph Lowery, "Civil Rights Figure Rev. Joseph Lowery Reflects on a Movement," *Chicago Tribune*, January 19, 2009.

14 Claude Fischer, "Tolerating Americans," *Made in America* blog, March 26, 2012, http://madeinamericathebook.wordpress.com/2012/03/26/tolerating -americans/.

15 Frank Newport, "In U.S., 77% Identify as Christian," Gallup, December 24, 2012.

16 Bill Bishop with Robert G. Cushing, *The Big Sort: Why the Clustering of Like-Minded America Is Tearing Us Apart* (New York: Houghton Mifflin, 2008), 136–41.

17 Sharad Goel, Winter Mason, and Duncan J. Watts, "Real and Perceived Attitude Agreement in Social Networks," *Journal of Personality and Social Psychology* 99, no. 4 (2010).

18 George L. Kelling and James Q. Wilson, "Broken Windows: The Police and Neighborhood Safety," *The Atlantic*, March 1982.

19 Robert J. Sampson, *Great American City: Chicago and the Enduring Neighborhood Effect* (Chicago: University of Chicago Press, 2012), 180–82, 189–91, 195.

20 George Packer, *The Unwinding: An Inner History of the New America* (New York: Farrar, Straus and Giroux, 2013).

Chapter 12: Valuable Inefficiency

1   Stefan Riedel, "Edward Jenner and the History of Smallpox and Vaccination," *Baylor University Medical Center Proceedings* 18, no. 1 (January 2005).

2   Eventually, a more effective agent for vaccination was found using the germs for a disease other than cowpox.

3 The Pasteur story is from Riedel, "Edward Jenner," and Arthur Koestler, *The Act of Creation* (New York: Macmillan, 1964), 112–13.

4 Steven Johnson, *Where Good Ideas Come From: The Natural History of Innovation* (New York: Riverhead Books, 2010), 23–42.

5 Richard Ogle, *Smart World: Breakthrough Creativity and the New Science of Ideas* (Boston: Harvard Business School Press, 2007), 17–19, 55–57.

6 Koestler, *The Act of Creation*, 120.

7 Robert A. Bennett, "Whoever Dreamed That Up?" *New York Times*, December 29, 1985.

8 Ogle, *Smart World*, 69.

9 Koestler, *The Act of Creation*, 230.

10 Johnson, *Where Good Ideas Come From*, 152–53; Ogle, *Smart World*, 183–207.

11 Ogle, *Smart World*, 158.

12 Frans Johansson, *The Medici Effect: Breakthrough Insights at the Intersection of Ideas, Concepts, and Cultures* (Boston: Harvard Business School Press, 2004), 11–13.

13 Johnson, *Where Good Ideas Come From*.

14 Jon Gertner, "True Innovation," *New York Times*, February 25, 2012.

15 Walter Isaacson, *Steve Jobs* (New York: Simon & Schuster, 2011), 430–31.

16 Ronald S. Burt, "Social Origins of Good Ideas," January 2003, 3, http://www.upcomillas.es/personal/rgimeno/doctorado/SOGI.pdf.

17 Burt, "Social Origins of Good Ideas," January 2003, 5.

18 Richard Locke, *Remaking the Italian Economy* (Ithaca, N.Y.: Cornell University Press, 1995), xii.

19 Nicholas A. Christakis and James H. Fowler, *Connected: The Surprising Power of Our Social Networks and How They Shape Our Lives—How Your Friends' Friends' Friends Affect Everything You Feel, Think, and Do* (New York: Back Bay Books, 2009), 162–4; Brian Uzzi and Jarrett Spiro, "Collaboration and Creativity: The Small World Problem," *American Journal of Sociology* 111, no. 2 (September 2005): 447–504.

20 Jane Jacobs, *The Economy of Cities* (New York: Vintage: 1970), 85–93, 96–97, 181.

21 Jacobs, *The Economy of Cities*, 142.

22 Jacobs, *The Economy of Cities*, 55.

23 Mark S. Granovetter, "The Strength of Weak Ties," *American Journal of Sociology* 78, no. 6 (May 1973): 1360–80. Granovetter's paper predates Burt's work by decades; nevertheless, they were both focused on the same question.

24 Johnson, *Where Good Ideas Come From*, 61.

25 Sean Safford, *Why the Garden Club Couldn't Save Youngstown* (Cambridge, Mass.: Harvard University Press, 2009), 15–16.

26 Safford, *Why the Garden Club Couldn't Save Youngstown*, 22, 31–32, 63–68.

27 Safford, *Why the Garden Club Couldn't Save Youngstown*, 83, 92–95.

28 Locke, *Remaking the Italian Economy*, 134.

29 Michael Mandel, "The Failed Promise of Innovation in the U.S.," *Bloomberg Businessweek*, June 3, 2009.

30 Tyler Cowen, *The Great Stagnation* (New York: Dutton, 2011).

31 http://news.cnet.com/8301-31921_3-20096067-281/peter-thiel-thinks -tech-innovation-has-stalled/.

32 Edward Glaeser, *Triumph of the City: How Our Greatest Invention Makes Us Richer, Smarter, Greener, Healthier, and Happier* (New York: Penguin Press, 2011).

33 Richard Florida, *The Rise of the Creative Class: And How It's Transforming Work, Leisure, Community and Everyday Life* (New York: Basic Books, 2002).

34 Elsa Brenner, "In Westchester County, the Platinum Mile Is Reinvented, Again," *New York Times*, January 3, 2012.

35 Charles V. Bagli, "Regretting Move, Bank May Return to Manhattan," *New York Times*, June 8, 2011.

36 Eli Pariser, *The Filter Bubble: What the Internet Is Hiding from You* (New York: Penguin Press, 2011).

Chapter 13: The Roots of Deliberation

1 I do not mean to diminish the plight of those living in the favelas. There's nothing high-class about Brazilian poverty.

2 Peter Blair Henry and Conrad Miller, "Institutions versus Policies," Brookings Institution, January 2009.

3 "Social Contract," *This American Life*, NPR, June 18, 2010, http://www .thisamericanlife.org/radio-archives/episode/410/social-contract.

4 Courtney Blackman, *The Practice of Economic Management: A Caribbean Perspective* (Jamaica: Ian Randle Publishers, 2006).

5 http://www.gallup.com/poll/164393/fewer-americans-ever-trust-gov -handle-problems.aspx.

6 Thomas E. Mann and Norman J. Ornstein, *It's Even Worse Than it Looks: How the American Constitutional System Collided with the New Politics of Extremism* (New York: Basic Books, 2012).

7 Michael Tomasky, "The Specter Haunting the Senate," *New York Review of Books*, September 30, 2010.

8 http://www.pollingreport.com/right.htm

9 "Trends in American Values: 1987–2012: Partisan Polarization Surges in

Bush, Obama Years," Pew Research Center for the People and the Press, June 4, 2012, 17.

10   http://www.washingtonpost.com/blogs/the-fix/wp/2013/10/07/repub lican-disapproval-grows-in-budget-battle-post-abc-poll-finds/.

11   Thomas L. Friedman and Michael Mandelbaum, *That Used to Be Us* (New York: Farrar, Straus and Giroux, 2011), 261–62.

12   Ronald Brownstein, *The Second Civil War* (New York: Penguin Press, 2007).

13   Carl Hulse, "Senate Retains Money for Disputed Alaska Bridges and Other Pet Initiatives," *New York Times,* October 21, 2005.

14   Bruce Reed and Marc Dunkelman, "When Candidates Can't Lose," *Washington Post,* April 28,2008.

15   Bill Bishop with Robert G. Cushing, *The Big Sort: Why the Clustering of Like-Minded America is Tearing Us Apart* (New York: Houghton Mifflin, 2008).

16   Alan I. Abramowitz, *The Disappearing Center: Engaged Citizens, Polarization, and American Democracy* (New Haven: Yale University Press, 2010), 141.

17   Charles Mahtesian and Jim VandeHei, "It's Going to Get Worse," *Politico,* May 1, 2012.

18   David A. Lieb, "Powerful Supermajorities Elected to Statehouses," *Associated Press,* November 19, 2012.

19   Lieb, "Powerful Supermajorities Elected to Statehouses."

20   Tomasky, "The Specter Haunting the Senate."

21   Friedman and Mandelbaum, *That Used to Be Us,* 244.

22   Ezra Klein, "The Rise of the Filibuster: An Interview with Barbara Sinclair," *Washington Post,* December 26, 2009.

23   Don Wolfensberger, "Special Rules Providing for the Original Consideration of Legislation in the House 103rd-112th Congresses (1993–2012)," chart, Bipartisan Policy Center, http://bipartisanpolicy.org/sites/default/files/rule-table-112th-FINAL.pdf.

24   Jan Witold Baran, "Can I Lobby You?" *Washington Post,* January 8, 2006.

25   Robert A. Caro, *Master of the Senate: The Years of Lyndon Johnson* (New York: Vintage, 2003).

26   Daniel Okrent, *Last Call: The Rise and Fall of Prohibition* (New York: Scribner, 2010), 297.

27   http://ajrarchive.org/Article.asp?id=2429.

28   Tomasky, "The Specter Haunting the Senate."

29   Jason Grumet, "Keep the Rules—Change the Culture," *The Hill,* July 31, 2013, http://thehill.com/blogs/congress-blog/121-politics/314391-keep-the-ruleschange-the-culture.

30   Bishop and Cushing, *The Big Sort.*

31 Bishop and Cushing, *The Big Sort,* 37–40.

32 Charles Murray, *Coming Apart: The State of White America 1960–2010* (New York: Crown Forum, 2012), 100–101.

33 James S. Fishkin, *When the People Speak* (New York: Oxford University Press, 2009), 96–97.

34 "By The People: What's Next California?" MacNeil/Lehrer Productions, 2011.

35 Fishkin, *When the People Speak.*

36 Robert Nisbet, *The Quest for Community* (Wilmington, Del.: ISI Books, 1990).

37 Amy Mitchell, Jocelyn Kiley, Jeffrey Gottfried, and Emily Guskin, "The Role of News on Facebook," Pew Research Journalism Project, October 24, 2013. Eli Pariser, *The Filter Bubble: What the Internet Is Hiding from You* (New York: Penguin Press, 2011), 161, 164.

38 http://www.economist.com/news/special-report/21565006-internet-going-local-your-friendly-neighbourhood-app.

39 Alexis de Tocqueville, *Democracy in America* (1835, 1840, reprint, Chicago: University of Chicago Press, 2000), 222.

Chapter 14: The Giant Sucking Sound

1 Bob Drummond, "Private Jobs Increase More With Democrats in White House," *Bloomberg News,* May 8, 2012.

2 "The Unsustainable Cost of Health Care," Social Security Advisory Board, September 2009.

3 Fareed Zakaria, "Are America's Best Days Behind Us?" *Time,* March 3, 2011.

4 Alan Ehrenhalt, *The Great Inversion and the Future of the American City* (New York: Knopf, 2012), 12.

5 Jim Tankersley, "Who Destroyed the Economy? The Case Against the Baby Boomers," *The Atlantic,* October 2012.

6 Bill Clinton, *Back to Work: Why We Need Smart Government for a Strong Economy* (New York: Alfred A. Knopf, 2011).

7 Joseph E. Stiglitz, *The Price of Inequality* (New York: W. W. Norton, 2012), 14.

8 Jonathan Rauch, "The Hospital Is No Place for the Elderly, *The Atlantic,* December 2013.

9 http://www.nytimes.com/2013/04/04/health/dementia-care-costs-are-soaring-study-finds.html?hp&_r=0.

10 Hendrik Hartog, "Bargaining for a Child's Love," *New York Times,* January 14, 2012.

11   Theda Skocpol, *Diminished Democracy: From Membership to Management in American Civic Life* (Norman: University of Oklahoma Press, 2003), 59–60.

12   Lewis Mumford, "The Fourth Migration," *Survey Graphic,* May 1, 1925 130–33.

13   Lizabeth Cohen, *Making a New Deal: Industrial Workers in Chicago, 1919–1939* (New York: Cambridge University Press, 1991).

14   Bill Clinton, Address Before a Joint Session of the Congress on the State of the Union, January 23, 1996, http://www.presidency.ucsb.edu/ws/index .php?pid=53091#ixzz2ifeuu67a.

15   Robert Nisbet, *The Quest for Community* (Wilmington: ISI Books, 1990), 43, 52–54.

16   Lee Rainie and Barry Wellman, *Networked: The New Social Operating System* (Cambridge, Mass.: MIT Press, 2012), 33–34.

17   Todd Zywicki, "The Auto Bailout and the Rule of Law," *National Affairs,* Spring 2011.

18   Matt Krantz, "Many Have Little to No Savings as Retirement Looms," *USA Today,* December 4, 2011; Darrell J. Canby, "First Baby Boomers Turn 65, but Are They Ready to Retire?" *Metro West Daily News,* October 24, 2011.

19   Peter Orszag, "Pension Funding Scare Won't Frighten All States," *Bloomberg View,* October 23, 2012.

20   Binyamin Appelbaum and Robert Gebeloff, "Even Critics of Safety Net Increasingly Depend on It," *New York Times,* February 12, 2012.

21   Glenn Kessler, "Sarah Palin, 'Death Panels' and 'Obamacare,'" *Washington Post,* June 27, 2012.

22   Christine Montross, "The Woman Who Ate Cutlery," *New York Times,* August 3, 2013.

Chapter 15: The Marshmallow Test

1   Paul Tough, *How Children Succeed* (New York: Houghton Mifflin Harcourt, 2012), 62.

2   Walter Mischel, Yuichi Shoda, and Philip K. Peake, "The Nature of Adolescent Competencies Predicted by Preschool Delay of Gratification," *Journal of Personality and Social Psychology* 54, no. 4 (1988): 688–89.

3   Yuichi Shoda, Water Mischel, and Philip K. Peake, "Predicting Adolescent Cognitive and Self-Regulatory Competencies From Preschool Delay of Gratification: Identifying Diagnostic Conditions," *Developmental Psychology* 26, no. 6 (1990): 978–79.

4 Mischel, Shoda, and Peake, "The Nature of Adolescent Competencies Predicted by Preschool Delay of Gratification," 691.

5 Sarah Zielinski, "Marshmallows and a Successful Life," Smithsonian.com, August 11, 2009, http://blogs.smithsonianmag.com/science/2009/08/marshmallows-and-a-successful-life/.

6 Mischel, Shoda, and Peake, "The Nature of Adolescent Competencies Predicted by Preschool Delay of Gratification," 692.

7 Joachim de Posada, TED Talk, February 2009.

8 Daniel Goleman, *Emotional Intelligence* (New York: Bantam Books, 2006).

9 Terrie E. Moffit et al., "A Gradient of Childhood Self-Control Predicts Health, Wealth and Public Safety," *PNAS Early Edition* 108, no. 7 (February 15, 2011): 1.

10 Moffit et al., "A Gradient of Childhood Self-Control Predicts Health, Wealth and Public Safety," 2.

11 Moffit et al., "A Gradient of Childhood Self-control Predicts Health, Wealth and Public Safety," 5.

12 R. N. Wolfe and S. D. Johnson, "Personality as a predictor of college performance," *Educational and Psychological Measurement* 55 (1995): 177–85, in Angela L. Duckworth and Martin E. P. Seligman, "Self-Discipline Outdoes IQ in Predicting Academic Performance of Adolescents," *Psychological Science* 16, no. 12 (2005): 939.

13 Duckworth and Seligman, "Self-Discipline Outdoes IQ in Predicting Academic Performance of Adolescents," 941–42.

14 Tough, *How Children Succeed, xii,* xv.

15 Angela L. Duckworth, Christopher Peterson, Michael D. Matthews, and Dennis R. Kelly, "Grit: Perseverance and Passion for Long-Term Goals," *Journal of Personality and Social Psychology* 92, no. 6 (2007): 1087–1101.

16 Duckworth, Peterson, Matthews, and Kelly, "Grit: Perseverance and Passion for Long-Term Goals," 1093, 1098.

17 Duckworth, Peterson, Matthews, and Kelly, "Grit: Perseverance and Passion for Long-Term Goals," 1095–96.

18 *Field of Dreams* (1989).

19 Paul Tough, *Whatever It Takes: Geoffrey Canada's Quest to Change Harlem and America* (New York: Mariner Books, 2009), 40–52.

20 Tough, Paul. "What if the Secret to Success Is Failure?" *New York Times,* Sept. 14, 2011.

21 Tough, *Whatever It Takes.*

22 http://www.thisamericanlife.org/radio-archives/episode/474/back-to-school.

23 Tough, *How Children Succeed,* 27–30; Nicholas D. Kristof, "Cuddle Your

Kid!" *New York Times,* October 20, 2012; Moffit et al., "A gradient of child-hood self-control predicts health, wealth and public safety," 1.

24　James J. Heckman and Dimitriy V. Masterov, "The Productivity Argument for Investing in Young Children," *Review of Agricultural Economics* 29, no. 3 (2007): 478–79.

25　Heckman and Masterov, "The Productivity Argument for Investing in Young Children," 480.

Conclusion: The Crisis of American Exceptionalism

1　*Time*/Abt SRBI Poll, October 9–10, 2011, http://swampland.time.com/full-results-of-oct-9-10-2011-time-poll/#ixzz2AEZTz9Oz.

2　David Leonhardt, "Standard of Living Is in the Shadows as Election Issue," *New York Times,* October 23, 2012.

3　Scott Shane, "The Opiate of Exceptionalism," *New York Times,* October 19, 2012.

4　"The Lost Decade of the Middle Class: Fewer, Poorer, Gloomier," Pew Research Social & Demographic Trends, August 22, 2012, 13.

5　"The Lost Decade of the Middle Class," 58–62.

6　Jim Tankersley, "Who Destroyed the Economy? The Case Against the Baby Boomers," *The Atlantic,* October 2012.

7　David Brooks, "Another Fiscal Flop," *New York Times,* December 31, 2012.

8　Thomas L. Friedman and Michael Mandelbaum, *That Used To Be Us* (New York: Farrar, Straus and Giroux, 2011), 5; Nick Anderson, "College net price is rising," *Washington Post,* October 24, 2012

9　"The Lost Decade of the Middle Class," 30.

10　"The Lost Decade of the Middle Class," 48.

11　"Trends in American Values: 1987–2012: Partisan Polarization Surges in Bush, Obama Years," Pew Research Center for the People and the Press, June 4, 2012, 47.

12　Alexis de Tocqueville, *Democracy in America* (1835, 1840, reprint, Chicago: University of Chicago Press, 2000).

13　Tocqueville, *Democracy in America,* 576.

14　David Brooks, "Ryan's Biggest Mistake," *New York Times,* August 23, 2012.

15　Fareed Zakaria, *The Post-American World* (New York: W. W. Norton, 2009), 211–12.

16　Niall Ferguson, *Civilization: The West and the Rest* (New York: Penguin Press, 2011), 12.

17　Binyamin Appelbaum and Robert Gebeloff, "Even Critics of Safety Net Increasingly Depend on It," *New York Times,* February 12, 2012.

18 Martin Wolf, "How Austerity Has Failed," *New York Review of Books,* July 11, 2013.

19 Friedman and Mandelbaum, *That Used to Be Us.*

20 Paul Weinstein Jr., "Cut to Invest: Establish a 'Cut-to-Invest Commission' to Reduce Low-Priority Spending, Consolidate Duplicative Programs, and Increase High-Priority Investments," Brookings Institute, November 2012.

21 http://www.nytimes.com/2013/03/11/opinion/krugman-dwindling-deficit-disorder.html.

22 Francis Fukuyama, *The End of History and the Last Man* (New York: Free Press, 2006).

23 Seymour Martin Lipset, *American Exceptionalism* (New York: W. W. Norton, 1996).

24 Lipset, *American Exceptionalism,* 54, 81–83.

25 *The Daily Show with Jon Stewart,* November 15, 2012.

26 Emma Lazarus, "The New Colossus," http://www.libertystatepark.com/emma.htm.

27 Edmund Burke, *Reflections on the French Revolution* (Cambridge, Mass.: The Harvard Classics, 1909–14).

28 Thomas Bender, *Community and Social Change in America* (Baltimore: Johns Hopkins University Press, 1978).

29 Gordon S. Wood, *The Radicalism of the American Revolution* (New York: Vintage, 1995).

30 Monique Morrissey, "Private-Sector Pension Coverage Fell by Half over Two Decades," *The Economic Policy Institute Blog,* January 11, 2013, http://www.epi.org/blog/private-sector-pension-coverage-decline/.

31 Lee Rainie and Barry Wellman, *Networked: The New Social Operating System* (Cambridge, Mass.: MIT Press, 2012): 8–9.

32 Claude S. Fischer and Michael Hout, *Century of Difference: How America Changed in the Last One Hundred Years* (New York: Russell Sage Foundation: 2006).

33 Martin Luther King Jr., *A Testament of Hope: The Essential Writings and Speeches of Martin Luther King Jr.* (New York: HarperCollins, 1990), 479.

34 Bill Bishop with Robert G. Cushing, *The Big Sort: Why the Clustering of Like-Minded America is Tearing Us Apart* (New York: Houghton Mifflin, 2008), 173.

35 Robert Wuthnow, *Loose Connections* (Cambridge, Mass.: Harvard University Press, 1998), 16–18, 28.

36 Theda Skocpol, *Diminished Democracy: From Membership to Management in American Civic Life* (Norman: University of Oklahoma Press, 2003).

37   Michael J. Karter Jr. and Gary P. Stein, "U.S. Fire Department Profile Through 2011," National Fire Protection Association, October 2012.

38   Wuthnow, *Loose Connections*, 17.

39   Friedman and Mandelbaum, *That Used to Be Us*, xiii.

Index